The
DEAD SEA
SCROLLS

ILENE COOPER

illustrated by

JOHN THOMPSON

MORROW JUNIOR BOOKS
New York

Printed in the United States of America.

1   2   3   4   5   6   7   8   9   10

Library of Congress Cataloging-in-Publication Data
Cooper, Ilene.
The Dead Sea scrolls/Ilene Cooper; illustrated by John Thompson.
p.   cm.
Includes index.
Summary: Details the important archaeological discovery of
the ancient manuscripts known as the Dead Sea Scrolls, and
discusses efforts to translate them, the battle over their possession,
and the people who have figured in their history.
ISBN 0-688-14300-8
1. Dead Sea scrolls—Juvenile literature.   [1. Dead Sea scrolls.]
I. Thompson, John, ill.   II. Title.
BM487.C59 1997   296.1'55—dc 20   96-21983   CIP AC

For Meredith, fellow time traveler, with thanks

CONTENTS

FROM THE SHORES OF THE DEAD SEA...

Tune in to one of today's popular talk radio stations, and you will hear people discussing all sorts of topics that interest or upset them: politics, crime, gun control, health care. If talk radio had been around two thousand or so years ago in the land we now call Israel, people would have been discussing how their country was in a state of unrest, what was to become of the Jewish religion, and whether or not the end of the world was near, as some prophets claimed.

Up until the discovery of the Dead Sea Scrolls, listening in on that long-ago era could only be done secondhand. Although there were historical documents concerning the period, they were written later or they were copies of older documents that have disappeared. Scholars assumed that the original texts—written on leather or papyrus more than two millennia ago—were too old to be still in existence. At least, that's what they thought until a young Bedouin shepherd and his goat proved them wrong.

What are the Dead Sea Scrolls? They are manuscripts found in eleven caves near the northwest shore of the Dead Sea. Both original writings and copies of biblical books have been found, some in pottery jars, and they've been dated from between 250 B.C.E. to 68 C.E. Many scholars believe that a group of monklike Jews who lived near the Dead Sea were responsible for the writings, but there is still intense debate about the scrolls' authorship and how they came to be in the caves.

Although we call them scrolls, only a very few of them were found intact and rolled up the way we picture scrolls to be. They were that way once, but almost all the scrolls had disintegrated into pieces and fragments, some no bigger than the tip of your pinkie.

Scholars believe that originally there were more than eight hundred intact scrolls, now crumbled into thousands, perhaps hundreds of thousands, of fragments. It was like finding the world's biggest jigsaw puzzle, and part of this story is how the scrolls were discovered and put together. But this is also a story about politics, religion, rivalries, and treasure that spans more than two thousand years. It has its roots in the era when Judaism was changing and Christianity was being born, and the scrolls hold tantalizing clues to the development of both. It is a complicated tale, for which this book can serve only as an introduction.

Imagine that we are going to tune in to one particular radio station from that long-ago time. Broadcasting from a remote and desolate area along the shore of the Dead Sea, this station will give us a firsthand impression of the practices and politics that were swirling around Israel, the cradle of Western religious beliefs. The Dead Sea Scrolls let us listen to voices unheard for two millennia. That's why they've been called the greatest archaeological discovery of the twentieth century.

A DISCOVERY IN PALESTINE

ONE DAY IN 1947, when winter was warming into spring, a young Bedouin shepherd watched his goats nimbly pick their way along barren limestone cliffs. The stark landscape overlooked the northwest shore of the Dead Sea, in a country then called Palestine. This was the same fierce area where the biblical David, who was also a shepherd, had once watched his own flock searching for food.

Suddenly Jum'a Muhammed noticed that one of his goats was climbing too high. As he scaled the rocks after it, something caught his eye: a small opening in the face of one of the cliffs that looked like an entrance to a cave. Curious, Jum'a Muhammed stopped and looked in. The opening was too small to enter, so he picked up a stone and threw it inside. Then he heard something—the sound of pottery shattering. Treasure!

The Bedouin shepherd was right. The cave was filled with treasure, but not the gold or jewels he hoped to see. Inside the cave were crumbling scrolls, stuffed into pottery jars. For decades after their discovery people schemed to possess them and argued about their meaning.

In 1947 the territory known both as Palestine and eretz Yisrael (the land of Israel) was a place of terror and tension. Two peoples who dwelled there, the Arabs and the Jews, each claimed it for their own.

Although in some places Muslim Arabs and Jews (along with Christians) lived side by side, many areas were comprised of one group or the other. The Arabs were angry at talk of dividing this territory into separate states, one Arab, one Jewish. The Jews, who had suffered under Nazi terrorism during World War II, wanted their ancient homeland back so they could have the security of their own state.

While the fate of the land was being debated at the United Nations in New York, the British were in charge of keeping order in Palestine. This was not an easy job. Both sides had grudges—against the British and of course against each other. Day or night gunfire might erupt, and both the Arabs and the Jews were capable of setting off bombs, which they did with regularity.

It was in the middle of this near anarchy that the Dead Sea Scrolls saw their first light in almost two thousand years. Of course, no one dreamed how old they were when they surfaced. Certainly Jum'a Muhammed didn't.

The entrance to the cave was too small for him to fit through, so he returned with two friends. One of them was slim enough to crawl into—and, more important, out of—the opening. The teenager, who was nicknamed the Wolf, lowered himself into the cave. Littering the floor of the cave was nothing but broken pottery. However, lined up along the wall were a number of large jars, some with their lids still on. Eagerly he looked inside them. Some were empty, but when he reached into one of the jars, he found a dirty leather bundle covered in a tattered cloth and smelling bad. Reaching further, he discovered several more odd, odorous bundles. On further inspection each seemed to be a sort of scroll.

The young men brought their finds, along with some pottery pieces, to the elders of their Ta'amireh tribe, who puzzled over them. Sometimes in their nomadic wanderings the Bedouin did find ancient artifacts, such as jewelry or coins, but they'd seen nothing like these scrolls of brittle leather, green with age.

In the following days, Jum'a, along with several of his fellow tribesmen, went back to the caves and extracted more scrolls, seven altogether. But what were they to do with them? These sorts of finds were supposed to be turned over to the Palestine Department of Antiquities. But the Bedouin usually took them to Bethlehem, a market town where the Ta'amireh tribe sold the goat cheese they produced from their flock. They knew people in Bethlehem who would purchase the artifacts and sell them to collectors. These filthy old scrolls didn't seem valuable, but maybe they could be sold as well.

It was April when a group of tribesmen took their find to the shop of a shoemaker, Khalil Iskander Shahin, nicknamed Kando, who also traded in antiquities. After looking over the scrolls and bits of pottery from the cave, Kando was not certain if the find was of any special importance, but he thought he might have a buyer for them anyway. He kept one of the scrolls and took it to Athanasius Yeshue Samuel, who was an archbishop (called a metropolitan) of the Syrian Orthodox Church. Metropolitan Samuel was in charge of St. Mark's Monastery in Jerusalem, which had a large library. Surely he would know what the scrolls were, and perhaps he'd want to add them to the library's collection.

Metropolitan Samuel could hardly contain his excitement when

Kando brought him the scroll and told him the story of how it was found. First, he pressed a fragment, and it crumbled to dust. Then, to Kando's amazement, the metropolitan pinched off another tiny piece of the scroll and lit it with a match. The scroll gave off the distinctive odor of leather. Finally, he unrolled it and studied the writing. He recognized it as Hebrew, the ancient language of the Jews.

Metropolitan Samuel could not read Hebrew, but he was certain the scrolls were old, and their discovery in long-hidden caves, in an area that had not been inhabited for a thousand years, made him suspect they were very old indeed. When Kando told Samuel that he knew of more scrolls, the metropolitan insisted on seeing them. Kando said he would try to arrange a meeting with the members of the Ta'amireh. Then he left, taking the scroll with him. There would be much haggling back and forth before a price could be decided upon.

With all the tumult in the region, it took awhile for Kando to set up a meeting between the metropolitan and the nomadic tribesmen. On the day the Bedouin were to bring the new scrolls, a Saturday in July, Metropolitan Samuel waited impatiently at St. Mark's for their arrival. When they did not appear at the appointed time, the metropolitan was certain that they weren't coming. Greatly disappointed, he went to lunch, where he heard one of the monks telling his companions about a group of ragtag Bedouin who had shown up at the gate with some smelly old manuscripts. The monk had turned them away.

Metropolitan Samuel despaired, even more so after he talked to Kando. The dealer told him that the Bedouin had been so insulted by their treatment at St. Mark's that they might just sell the scrolls to another buyer. A month later, however, the tribesmen returned to the monastery with four scrolls. Although the metropolitan had very little money for the purchase, only about $100, the Bedouin agreed to sell him the manuscripts.

Now four scrolls were in Metropolitan Samuel's possession. What he was going to do with them, he hadn't decided.

ACROSS THE BARRICADES

LATER IN 1947 three more scrolls from the same limestone cave were to consume the imagination of another man. Dr. E. L. Sukenik was a distinguished professor of archaeology at Hebrew University in Jerusalem. One day in November the professor was in his office when he received a call from an old friend named Faidi Salahi, who, like Kando, was an antiquities dealer. Salahi told Sukenik he must see him immediately. There was one problem: With tensions at an all-time high, it was not easy to get together easily or safely.

Finally, the two men, the Jewish professor and the Armenian dealer, met across one of the barbed-wire barricades that the British had erected to keep warring factions apart. Salahi thrust a piece of old leather through the wire. Scrolls had been found by Bedouin in a cave near the Dead Sea, the dealer told Sukenik, and this was a piece of one of them. Was it genuine? Was it old?

Professor Sukenik examined the scrap. The writing was Hebrew, a very old script used around the time of Jesus. It must be a forgery, Sukenik thought. As he examined the fragment more closely, however, he saw that the writing resembled a script he had seen on ancient tombs dating from the time of the Roman sacking of Jerusalem, around 70 C.E. Though he had seen such letters scratched or painted on stone, he had never seen this kind of lettering written with ink on leather. Sukenik's heart began to beat faster. What if this *wasn't* a forgery? Like the metropolitan, Sukenik knew he must see more of this find.

Later that week, carrying a pass that allowed him through the Jerusalem barricades, Sukenik went to see Salahi. After examining a few more scroll pieces, Professor Sukenik was even more convinced they were genuine. He knew that if he was right, these fragments could be part of an astounding discovery—manuscripts thousands of years old that had been preserved by the desert climate. Salahi told Sukenik that if he wished to purchase the scrolls, he had to go to Bethlehem, where the scrolls were being held in the shop of yet another antiquities dealer. Apparently the Bedouin had decided to split their bounty between these dealers and Kando, though it is not clear if the men knew of each other.

The trip could not have come at a worse time. The very next day the United Nations was scheduled to vote on whether to divide Palestine into two states, one Arab, one Jewish. No matter what the outcome of the vote was, it was sure to mean the start of a new round of violence. How could a Jewish professor set off to the Arab city of Bethlehem at such a time?

One person who knew the dangers of such a trip very well was Sukenik's son Yigael Yadin. Yadin, an officer in the Jewish defense forces, had come home to await his orders while the UN debated his country's fate. Yadin, who was also an archaeologist like his father, shared in the excitement over news of the scrolls. But he was torn when Sukenik asked whether it was safe to travel to Bethlehem. Sukenik's wife had already begged her husband not to go. Yadin later wrote, "As a military man, I answered that he ought not to make the journey; as an archaeologist, that he ought to go; as his son—that my opinion had to be reserved."

Back and forth they discussed the risks of the trip, stopping only when Yadin had to return to his command post in Tel Aviv. Sukenik continued to listen to radio reports of what was happening at the United Nations.

Suddenly the UN decided to postpone the vote. This meant there would be a short window of opportunity for Professor Sukenik to go to Bethlehem and examine the scrolls before the inevitable violence that would follow the UN's decision. The next morning, Sukenik and Salahi took a bumpy, nail-biting bus ride to Bethlehem. At the dealer's shop they heard the whole story of the young herder, his lost goat, and the discovery in the cave.

Sukenik was shown two of the pottery jars in which the scrolls were found. They were of an unfamiliar shape. He picked up one of three scrolls presented to him. With trembling hands Professor Sukenik unrolled it. It looked like a prayer of thanksgiving to God. Sukenik knew his Bible almost by heart. This prayer had words and ideas in it that were new and different from anything he had ever read in the Bible. It was like reading a personal note or poem in the biblical language.

To Sukenik, this was proof that the scrolls were legitimate. Any forger, he reasoned, might try to copy a part of the Bible and pass it off as an authentic ancient document. That would be the logical way to make money. But how many would have the skill to compose an original prayer and write it down in an ancient script only a few could recognize? No, Sukenik thought, this was the real thing.

The dealer agreed to let Sukenik take the scrolls home with him. If, after looking them over, he wanted to buy them for Hebrew University, the price would be about $4,000. Either this dealer was shrewder than Kando, who had sold his scrolls to the metropolitan for only $100, or he had a stronger belief they were valuable.

With the documents in his possession, the journey home was even more nerve-racking for Sukenik than the bus trip to Bethlehem. As soon as he was safely back in his study, the professor gently unrolled one of the scrolls. He spent the next hours full of wonder as he examined the scroll writings. Somehow he had to raise the money to buy this amazing find for Hebrew University.

As he ran his finger across the texts, still incredibly legible after two thousand years, he heard a shout from the next room. His youngest son rushed into the study. The United Nations had voted to partition Palestine, creating two states. One of them would be the Jewish state, the state of Israel.

Outside Sukenik's window the streets began filling with shouting, dancing people. Watching the tumultuous celebration, the professor could hardly believe that he was part of two such momentous events. On the very day the Jewish people were at last able to claim a homeland, a precious part of their past had found its way home.

BUYERS AND SELLERS

SEVEN INTACT SCROLLS were now divided between Metropolitan Samuel and Dr. Sukenik, though neither man was as yet aware of the other.

Of the metropolitan's four scrolls, one was a copy of the Old Testament book of the teachings of the prophet Isaiah. Interestingly, the text is almost exactly the same as the Book of Isaiah you would read in your Bible today. This scroll was in very good condition, neatly written in Hebrew on pieces of stitched-together leather. The original, closely related, languages of ancient Israel were Hebrew and Aramaic. The metropolitan's Isaiah Scroll and the other Dead Sea discoveries would turn out to be some of the oldest biblical texts written in these languages. Before this the oldest-known copies of the Bible were Greek translations now belonging to the Vatican.

Another of the metropolitan's scrolls records the teachings of an Old Testament prophet named Habakkuk. But unlike the Isaiah Scroll, this is more than just a copy. The writer quotes verses from the Book of Habakkuk and then adds his own explanations of what they meant. The commentary tells a fascinating story of a Wicked Priest, the enemy of the Teacher of Righteousness, who seems to have been the leader of a Jewish settlement very near where the scrolls were found. Some people have suggested that the Teacher of Righteousness was John the Baptist, or even Jesus, but today most scholars disagree.

The metropolitan's third scroll was a version of Genesis, the first book of the Bible. But unlike the familiar biblical story, this one is written as though Abraham—founder of the Hebrew people—were recalling it.

The fourth scroll was not a biblical text at all. It is a book of rules that came to be called *The Manual of Discipline,* and it proved to be one of the most important finds of all.

Professor Sukenik, too, had a mix of biblical and nonbiblical texts. He had his own copy of Isaiah, one less complete than the metropolitan's and deteriorating. He also had the Thanksgiving Scroll, the book of original psalms that he first saw in Bethlehem.

But Professor Sukenik was most excited about the War Scroll. The War Scroll tells the story of the War of the Sons of Light and the Sons of Darkness. This is not the history of a real war but a prophetic tale, and it contains elaborate descriptions of a final battle at the end of time waged with angels fighting one another. The scroll predicts that the Sons of Light will win the war when God weighs in on their side.

Professor Sukenik had managed to raise the money to pay for his scrolls in part by taking out a mortgage on his house. Sukenik didn't mind; he thought this was a small inconvenience for the privilege of being able to donate such an important piece of Jewish heritage to Hebrew University. When he learned of the existence of the metropolitan's scrolls, he was startled but eager to buy them as well.

The news of the metropolitan's scrolls came to Dr. Sukenik in a surprisingly casual way. Not long after he had purchased his scrolls, Sukenik, thrilled by his acquisition, was telling all his colleagues about them. How odd, said one university librarian. Some months before, he and another staff member had been called to St. Mark's Monastery to look at four manuscripts that were also supposed to be ancient documents found in a Dead Sea cave. They were owned by Metropolitan Samuel, who wanted to know their age and their contents. The two librarians hadn't been much help. After looking over the documents, they had told the metropolitan that in their opinion, the scrolls were probably forgeries.

Sukenik was astounded. More scrolls had been discovered in a cave near the Dead Sea? Surely the metropolitan's scrolls must be part of the same collection as his own. The professor desperately wanted to see them, but he couldn't. St. Mark's was in Arab-held Jerusalem, and since the UN vote, traveling there would be even more dangerous than his trip to Bethlehem had been.

In the winter of 1948 Professor Sukenik got a letter from a Syrian man named Anton Kiraz, on whose property Sukenik had once done some archaeological excavations. Kiraz, a parishioner at St. Mark's, had been asked by Metropolitan Samuel to help find a buyer for the four scrolls in his possession. Despite his great interest in the scrolls, the metropolitan realized that if he sold them, the profits could be used to help the poor of his church. He was also worried that his scrolls might be confiscated by the Jordanian Department of Antiquities. Arab Palestine had become a part of Jordan, which was now overseeing archaeological finds in the region. Better to sell the scrolls now, the metropolitan reasoned, than to have them taken away later.

Sukenik made immediate arrangements to view the scrolls. Eagerly he made his way to the YMCA in Jerusalem, a relatively safe spot, where Kiraz was waiting for him. As Dr. Sukenik unrolled the long Isaiah Scroll, it was plain that it was of the same age as the one in his possession. He looked over the other scrolls. Even though he still didn't know how he would pay for them, Sukenik immediately said he would buy all four. He asked if he might take one home to look over more carefully. Kiraz agreed he could take a scroll for one week. Sukenik took the Isaiah Scroll back to the university with him. The other scrolls stayed in a drawer at the Y.

The next week was a roller-coaster ride for Sukenik. The excitement of knowing there were more scrolls in existence had him elated. But trying to organize their purchase seemed a near-impossible task. The interim government for the state of Israel had been moved from Jerusalem to Tel Aviv. Sukenik thought he could persuade officials to buy the scrolls, but, because of the chaotic conditions, no one could be reached by phone or even by mail. Sukenik tried to raise money from other sources, but when the deadline arrived, he simply didn't have enough to offer the metropolitan. With a heavy heart Dr. Sukenik returned the Isaiah Scroll. He wrote in his diary, "The Jewish people have lost a priceless heritage."

By the early 1950s the Dead Sea Scrolls had made news around the world. But because the ownership of the scrolls was in question (though never in Metropolitan Samuel's mind), and because some biblical scholars continued to insist they were a hoax, the metropolitan was unable to sell them.

Disgusted that his reputation was under attack and that, as he'd feared, the Jordanian government persisted in declaring that it owned the scrolls, Samuel decided to find a buyer for the scrolls any way he could. The metropolitan was now living in the United States, and, desperate, he ended up putting an advertisement on the back page of the *Wall Street Journal.* It appeared on June 1, 1954.

MISCELLANEOUS FOR SALE

THE FOUR DEAD SEA SCROLLS

Biblical manuscripts dating back to at least 200 B.C. are for sale. This would be an ideal gift to an educational or religious institution by an individual or group. Box F 206 *Wall Street Journal.*

Dr. Sukenik had died in 1952, but his son Yigael Yadin, now an Israeli war hero, was out of the army and once again immersed in the work of archaeology. Knowing of his father's passion for the Dead Sea Scrolls, Yadin always hoped he could fulfill his father's dream of bringing together all seven scrolls.

What happened next seems almost as incredible as the discovery of the scrolls. In 1954, Professor Yadin was on a speaking tour of the

United States. A friend showed him Samuel's advertisement in the *Wall Street Journal*. Yadin couldn't believe his eyes. These must be the four original scrolls belonging to the metropolitan. He had been trying to locate them, and here they were being sold in the newspaper next to ads for used cars and apartments to rent.

Yadin of course wanted to buy the scrolls, but he wasn't sure that Metropolitan Samuel would sell them to the state of Israel. Besides, Israel was a fledgling country, still struggling for survival. The price of the scrolls had gone up considerably since Samuel had purchased them. Finally, a figure was agreed on: $250,000. But with its military obligations would the Israeli government be willing to pay so much? Yadin was relieved that the answer was yes. The scrolls were part of the new country's heritage.

After secret, exhaustive negotiations using a stand-in buyer, Yadin at last secured the scrolls. The Israeli government built a special building at Jerusalem's Israel Museum to house both the metropolitan's scrolls and the ones Yadin's father, Professor Sukenik, had acquired. Called the Shrine of the Book, it is a very interesting and unusual structure with special temperature and lighting controls to preserve the ancient documents. It is built in the shape of a covered jar, patterned after the pottery jars in which the scrolls were found.

When Metropolitan Samuel learned that the buyer of the scrolls was the state of Israel, he was surprised. Later he wrote that he was pleased the scrolls were in such a beautiful place, all together once more.

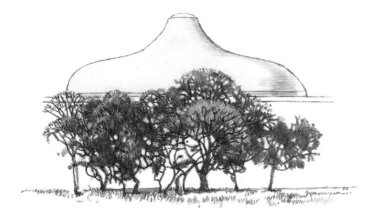

THE MYSTERY OF QUMRAN

IT IS REMARKABLE that the Dead Sea Scrolls were ever found. To realize just how remarkable, it's important to understand the desolate area that sheltered them.

Above the Judean desert a vast honeycomb of limestone caves sits near the northwest shore of the Dead Sea. Not a sea at all, this body of water is really a lake that is so salty nothing can live in it, so salty that a swimmer cannot sink. It is the lowest place on the surface of the earth, more than twelve hundred feet below sea level. Though only about ten miles from bustling Jerusalem, the locale is a wasteland. It's all rock and rubble, cut by an occasional ravine known locally as a wadi. Boiling hot in the summer and with almost no rainfall except for short torrents in the winter, the desert helped "mummify" the scrolls, and its inhospitable terrain kept people away.

Of course, two thousand years is still a very long time. The first seven scrolls that were found had been preserved in miraculously good shape. In part this was because the scrolls had been protected by their clay jars, some several feet tall. The jars were cylindrical, with flat bottoms, and were fitted with tight covers. Some of the jars were broken, but others were intact.

Eventually scrolls were found in eleven caves in the area. These scrolls had not fared as well. Time, humidity, insects, and small animals all had taken their toll. Most of these scrolls had broken into small fragments; some had disintegrated into dust.

For about a year after the discovery of the first seven scrolls, only the Bedouin knew the exact location of the cave where they had been found. They continued to explore the area, hoping to find more scrolls, which they now realized could bring them money. Many scroll fragments were removed from the Dead Sea caves before the proper authorities even knew the caves existed. When those officials did learn about the caves and their scroll treasure, they were furious.

An Englishman named G. Lankester Harding was the head of the Jordanian Department of Antiquities. With all the chaos and fighting still going on, no one at that agency had heard about the scrolls. One day Harding was flipping through a several-month-old copy of an archaeological magazine that had just arrived in the mail. He stopped in shock at an article about the discovery of the Dead Sea Scrolls.

Why hadn't he been told? Harding fumed. The Dead Sea area was under Jordan's control. As important relics, the scrolls should have been turned over to his department. Just as frustrating was the thought that the Bedouin were probably right at that moment finding other scrolls in other caves and that more historical treasure was being lost. As soon as he could, Harding called upon a colleague and prominent archaeologist, Father Roland de Vaux. They had to find the cave site, and there wasn't a moment to lose.

Like Harding, Father de Vaux had recently learned about the scrolls, and he immediately agreed to help locate the place where they had been found. But things progressed much more slowly than the duo would have liked. Besides the turmoil that came with their being in a war-torn land, no one wanted to give them any information. The Bedouin did not want to reveal the whereabouts of the caves, nor did the antiquities dealers they questioned. Eventually it was a monk at St. Mark's, Metropolitan

Samuel's monastery, who accidentally gave the location away.

By the early 1950s, Harding, de Vaux, and their team were excavating the cave site and the surrounding area. Under brutal conditions, in the broiling summer sun and during the intense winter rains, the work of digging in and around the caves continued.

But the archaeologists wanted to do more than just find more relics. They also wanted to know who actually wrote these texts and who put the scrolls in the caves in the first place.

Very near the caves, between the shore of the Dead Sea and the rocky cliffs, were ruins of a site known locally as Qumran. The remains of a stone wall and a cemetery had been excavated before, but it was thought they belonged to a Roman fortress—not especially interesting and so promptly forgotten. Now Harding and de Vaux wondered if there was more there than met the eye. Although the spot itself is bleak, there is an oasis nearby called Ein Feshka, or the spring of Feshka, that could have provided water and an agricultural base for a settlement. Harding and de Vaux were anxious to learn more about Qumran. Two questions in particular needed answers. Had it been an actual community at one time? And if so, had the people who lived there been responsible for the scrolls?

The first clue came from the cemetery. It was clear from the burial habits that these were bodies of Jews rather than Romans or Arabs, so the location was not just an old Roman fort. At one time Jews had lived there. As they explored further, the archaeologists found that almost a thousand male bodies were buried in the cemetery but that there were only a few remains of women or children. This made de Vaux and Harding wonder whether the site had been some sort of Jewish monastery-like settlement before the Romans took it over.

The visible ruins, however, didn't seem to indicate a structure that could hold so many people. The archaeologists then came up with the idea of having the Jordanian government take aerial shots of Qumran. When Harding and de Vaux looked at the pictures, they began to understand the scope of the place. The photos from the sky made it clear that markings extended far beyond the area of the Roman fort; at one time a much larger group of structures had stood there.

With renewed vigor the excavations continued, going on for a number of years. Eventually the site at Qumran began to take on definite shape. Walls were revealed. One central triangle about forty yards long and thirty yards wide was divided into what seemed to be small rooms. A watchtower was uncovered in the northwest corner of the site. The excavators discovered another room that some archaeologists called a scriptorium (a place where scribes wrote and copied manuscripts). The room housed a low table, seventeen feet in length, long enough for scrolls to be stretched out and sewn together. A desktop was also discovered, with holes that were presumed to be inkwells. To many scholars and archaeologists, this scriptorium was proof that the scrolls had been written at Qumran, but others remained unconvinced.

While the excavations at Qumran were continuing, new caves, each numbered in order of its discovery, were also being located. They contained thousands of scroll fragments, other artifacts, and a particularly exciting find—a scroll made of copper. All these were eventually taken to the Palestine Archaeological Museum in Jordan-controlled East Jerusalem, where a team of international experts had been assembled. These men were faced with the arduous task of sorting all the finds, putting together the scroll fragments, and deciphering them.

This team did not, of course, have the seven scrolls that had been purchased by Dr. Sukenik and Metropolitan Samuel. But as the years went on, de Vaux and the others, along with the rest of the world, learned what was in those seven through published translations. These translations helped the team immensely as they tried to draw conclusions about Qumran and their own cave discoveries.

New scientific techniques helped as well. Carbon 14 dating is a method of determining the age of organic materials—materials of plant or animal origins. Some of the scrolls had been wrapped in linen, which

is spun from a plant called flax. When pieces of linen were burned and then measured for carbon 14, the linen was dated at between 168 B.C.E. and 100 C.E. with a two-hundred-year margin of error.

Archaeologists are also able to date manuscripts by paleography, the study of ancient writing styles. Because Dr. Sukenik had studied paleography, he immediately realized that the formation of the scrolls' Hebrew letters was the kind used by scribes about two thousand years ago.

Other evidence that helped date the Qumran site were the artifacts, including arrowheads, coins, utensils, and pieces of pottery. Today we know that the manuscripts found in the caves around Qumran come from three different periods of history. A small group of the scrolls are from a period that dates from 250 to 150 B.C.E. The largest group of manuscripts were written between 150 and 30 B.C.E. The rest of the scrolls are dated between 30 B.C.E. and 70 C.E. It was in 70 C.E. that the Roman occupiers of Israel, after years of fighting, destroyed the country and dispersed its citizens. There is archaeological evidence that a fire destroyed the settlement at Qumran about 68 C.E.

In 1956 Harding resigned his post at the Jordanian Department of Antiquities. What he and Father de Vaux had accomplished in five years was impressive. They had completed their excavations and what was once thought to be a plateau with an insignificant piece of wall and a cemetery was now revealed to be a large settlement with rooms, workshops, kitchens, and a tower. They and their team had collected from the caves an enormous amount of artifacts and scroll fragments that were now in safekeeping.

As the evidence was collected and analyzed, the theory evolved that Qumran was occupied by a Jewish settlement during the period the scrolls were being produced. Most archaeologists, including Harding and de Vaux, believed that the people who occupied the settlement at Qumran were the same people who wrote the scrolls. This was the accepted theory for almost forty years, but as we shall see, it is a theory that is now being questioned.

VOICES FROM AN ANCIENT TIME

WHO WROTE THE DEAD SEA SCROLLS? That's a question people started asking almost as soon as news of the scrolls leaked out. After Professor Harding and Father de Vaux's excavations at Qumran, the answer seemed to be that the group that lived in the settlement was responsible. If so, who were they, and what had compelled them to come to such a desolate spot in the first place?

To begin to answer that question, we must pull back from Qumran and look at what was happening throughout the country then known as Judea—in its cities, such as Jerusalem, where Jewish rulers and Roman invaders plotted and fought, and in its villages, where ordinary folk worried and whispered and tried to survive in an uncertain world.

The origins of much of this trouble began in 167 B.C.E. Judea had come under the rule of a dynasty (or powerful family) of Syrian Greeks. These Greek rulers, the Seleucids, were very cruel, and they forced the Jews into many hateful religious practices. A Jewish clan, the Maccabees, rebelled against the Seleucids in a guerrilla war that lasted for three years (from 167 to 164 B.C.E.). Finally the oppressors were pushed out of power, and the Maccabees became the leaders of the Jews.

At first the Maccabees (later called the Hasmoneans) were popular among the people. But over a period of almost two hundred years they became proud and cruel toward those they had once protected and served. To stay in control, they invited Rome, a growing world power, into Judea to help resolve a problem among Jewish leaders. The Hasmoneans thought the Romans would help them stay in power. Instead they became puppet kings, and the Romans were able to conquer Judea without any bloodshed.

In the midst of turmoil and uprisings and against the background of civil war in Rome, the citizenry of Judea broke into four major factions: the Pharisees, the Sadducees, the Zealots, and the Essenes. All were Jews, but they were very different in their beliefs.

The Pharisees were against the Roman rulers and were the most popular group with the common people. They introduced the idea of rabbis. These were lay teachers, which means that they were not priests. The Pharisees believed that the Torah (the first five books of the Bible) was a way of life. They loved teaching and interpreting the Torah by telling midrashim, or stories and tales.

The Sadducees were aligned with the Hasmoneans. They did not like popular methods of interpreting and teaching the Torah. They were the party of the priests who served in the Temple. The priesthood was a position of authority like a kingship that is passed from father to son within only certain select families. The Sadducees were not popular with the everyday Jewish people.

The Zealots were true rebels. Fewer in number than the Sadducees and Pharisees, they wanted to overthrow the government, and later, in the first century C.E., they led revolts against their Roman conquerors.

The smallest group was the Essenes. Up until the discovery of the Dead Sea Scrolls, everything we knew about the Essenes came from three first-century C.E. historians: Pliny, who was Roman, and Josephus and Philo, Jews who became Roman citizens. Their writings certainly seem to link the Essenes with the sect living at Qumran.

Pliny, for example, said the Essenes lived in the wilderness near the

shore of the Dead Sea, near the town of "En Gedi" and with "only the palm trees for company." This almost exactly describes the location at Qumran.

Josephus and Philo described the Essenes as a group of extremely pious Jews, all men, who believed that they alone were worthy to uphold the Law of Moses. Some of the Essenes lived in cities and towns, but others separated themselves from the rest of their country-men to lead lives of sharing and stringent religious beliefs.

That description tallies very well with what scholars have learned about the Qumran group from *The Manual of Discipline,* one of the scrolls originally owned by Metropolitan Samuel. This manual, also known as the Community Rule, is exactly what it sounds like—a rule book that lists all the regulations the Qumran members had to obey, as well as the punishments that would befall them if they failed to live up to the rules. Fragments from at least eight copies of this handbook were eventually found in the caves.

The Manual of Discipline was one of the first scrolls to be translated, and as soon as it was published, biblical scholars all over the world began studying it, trying to get a picture of the unusual group that lived by it. Among the things they learned: A newcomer who wanted to join the community was on probation for a year and then was voted in by the members; all property was held in common; the order was only for men; and unlike the Temple in Jerusalem, animal sacrifice was not allowed. Living in righteousness was considered a fitting offering to God. The group also believed that there is a predetermined plan for everything that happens in the world.

All these rules from *The Manual of Discipline* are believed to have guided the community at Qumran. Many of the same rules of behav-ior were also mentioned by the ancient historians Josephus, Philo, and Pliny in their writings about the Essenes. There were even similar rules about spitting! Josephus wrote that the Essenes were "careful not to spit in company or to the right," while *The Manual of Discipline* states,

"Whoever has spat in an Assembly of the Congregation shall do penance for 30 days."

As one longtime scholar of the scrolls has said, those who don't believe that the Essenes were the founders of the community at Qumran place themselves in an "astonishing" position. They ask people to believe that there were two communal groups living in the same part of the desert near the Dead Sea at the same time, performing almost identical rituals and ceremonies, but that somehow they were not the same.

Still, there *are* scholars who disagree. They point out that the word *Essene* doesn't appear in any of the scrolls, and they question whether some of the ideas raised in certain manuscripts sound more like the thoughts of Sadducees than Essenes. Others want to wait until all the material from the scrolls has been published and studied before deciding definitely on the identity of the Qumran sect.

Whatever its identity, did the Qumran community write (or, in the case of the biblical scrolls, copy) all the material that was found in the caves? For some people that is the only answer that makes sense. An ultra-

religious group like the Qumran sect would have copies of the Bible in its library, and in fact, fragments of every book of the Bible except the Book of Esther have been found in the caves. Other scrolls like *The Manual of Discipline* and the War Scroll seem to have been written by people who considered themselves the true believers and upholders of Jewish tradition and Mosaic law.

There are also compelling arguments against believing the scrolls were produced at Qumran. For instance, they seem to have been written in letter-perfect Hebrew by professional scribes, perhaps hundreds of them, far too many to have been living at Qumran. Some of the scrolls predate the time Qumran was inhabited and others seem to represent ideas that do not fit in with Essene philosophy at all. It is possible that the scrolls represent a major library originally housed in Jerusalem that was removed from that city during the Roman wars and moved for safekeeping to the caves of Qumran. If this theory is true, the Dead Sea Scrolls represent not just the ideas of a tiny group, but the spectrum of Jewish ideas of the time.

Will we ever know the exact origin of the scrolls or their authors? New theories that raise new questions are continually being set forth. For instance, digs at Qumran in 1993 suggest to some scholars that the site may have been a Hasmonean fortress and not a monastery at all. If true, this finding would set Dead Sea scholarship on its ear. The scholarly arguments, it seems, will go on for a long, long time.

OF TEMPLE AND TREASURE

BY THE MID-1950s the imaginations of archaeologists and ordinary citizens alike were sparked by the thought of uncovering the secrets of the scrolls. Movies like the Indiana Jones series make archaeology seem exciting, even glamorous. It can certainly be exciting, less often glamorous, but mostly it is tedious, exacting, difficult work. Imagine lifting spadeful after spadeful of earth under a brutal sun, or using tiny brushes to clean sand out of the cracks of ancient walls, or spending hours putting together a collage of pottery pieces. Then, you must summon up every bit of intelligence you have to figure out what it all means.

That was what life was like for Harding, de Vaux, and their team. It was a small crew that did the digging. Harding and de Vaux felt it would be impossible for just the two of them to supervise a large group. Things moved slowly with so few workers and because of the intensity of the weather. The archaeologists were worried. Always in the back of their minds was the fear that important artifacts were being removed from the caves by those who would sell them on the black market.

For the most part, though, the Bedouin were cooperating with Harding and de Vaux. The archaeologists had agreed to pay about

$5.60 per square inch of scroll fragment. Thousands of fragments were brought to them—though not always handled carefully.

Once de Vaux was called to the garden of the monastery in Jerusalem where he lived. A dozen or so Bedouin were waiting there to see him, holding boxes. When de Vaux arrived, the tribesmen began dumping the contents of their boxes on a conveniently placed table. De Vaux watched in astonishment as scroll fragments fell out of the boxes like snow. In a short time the whole table was covered with a drift of fragments about a foot high. Father de Vaux didn't know whether to laugh or cry. On one hand, he was delighted to have the scroll fragments; on the other, he wondered how much they had been damaged by such a casual method of delivery. It seemed unlikely that there would be another find as well preserved as the seven scrolls from Cave 1.

However, in 1952 another incredible discovery was made. An assistant of Father de Vaux's was searching Cave 3. It seemed to hold only fragments of pottery and a few pieces of leather scrolls. Then at the back of the cave he saw two large scrolls. When he examined them, the young archaeologist found that they were made of copper.

The scrolls seemed impossible to unwind. Aging had turned them hard and brittle, and de Vaux feared they would crumble and break if they were disturbed. It was decided to bring them back to the Palestine Archaeological Museum. Soon the archaeologists realized the scrolls were actually two pieces of one long scroll. They could see that there was writing on the copper because the letters were visible from the outside. With difficulty, they made out what the scroll was about, and they were astounded. The scroll described the hiding places of massive amounts of silver and gold! Maybe there was treasure in the caves, as the young Bedouin men had dreamed, after all.

But how to open the scroll? The discussion went on for several years. Finally, in 1955, it was decided to send the smaller half of the scroll to Manchester College of Technology in England. A special tool was designed at the school for this delicate task.

John Allegro was one of the young archaeologists piecing scroll fragments together. He had been instrumental in choosing Manchester College, his alma mater, for the project. When the scroll was sent there, Allegro went along. He couldn't wait to see the instrument that would unroll the scroll. For a job this exacting, he expected that all the latest technology must have been used to design it.

Imagine Allegro's surprise when he saw the contraption that the Department of Mechanical Engineering had rigged up. Made of pieces of metal, wood, and string, it was basically a pulley with a small, movable circular saw on the end that would be used to cut through the copper. Allegro was skeptical, but he was assured it would work.

The process for cutting the scroll was both complicated and nerve-racking. The scroll was first coated with plastic and baked. This procedure gave the metal a "skin" that might prevent the scroll from breaking while it was being cut. Then, carefully, a spindle was inserted through the center of the scroll, and each end of the spindle was laid on uprights. Picture a leg of lamb being roasted on a spit, and you'll have the general idea.

A magnifying glass hung on the end of the special tool, and another hung around the head of the professor who was going to do the cutting. Using the tiny circular saw, he cut narrow strips lengthwise from the outermost layer; the scroll was rotated after each cut. Despite its homemade appearance, the instrument worked beautifully. Once the strips were cut away, they were cleaned of centuries and centuries' worth of dust and then photographed.

Allegro began studying the strips of scroll immediately. He found that they listed in a businesslike manner sixty-four locations of hidden treasure. The amounts of gold and silver were so large that after the information in the scroll was made public, many scholars were convinced that the treasure was only imaginary. Others believed that the treasure had to be real. Otherwise why would anyone bother to prepare such a list, on the finest copper no less, some of which seemed to be in code?

But who would have such a vast amount of treasure? Certainly not the community that lived near Qumran. The members, as they said in their own *Manual of Discipline,* lived a communal life and disdained money. Even all their shared wealth could hardly add up to such a vast amount.

Some scholars thought the Copper Scroll was proof of the theory that the Dead Sea Scrolls were part of an extensive library that had been brought from Jerusalem to the caves for safekeeping during the turbulent period in the first century C.E. when the Jews were fighting the Romans. They believed this unrest might hold the secret to the Copper Scroll.

Around 70 C.E., the fighting in Jerusalem grew so intense that the Temple, the holiest site in Israel, was destroyed by the Romans. It is known that in times of peace the priests had collected contributions, called tithes, that grew into a great treasure. When the Temple was threatened, the priests may have buried the treasure in and around Jerusalem. In fact, at that time stories existed that treasures from the Temple *were* hidden. Then, some guess, the Copper Scroll was written, so that future generations would be able to dig it up. How the scroll got to Cave 3 remains a mystery.

Of course, the originators of the scroll did not think it would lie undiscovered for two thousand years. Many of the sites mentioned in the Copper Scroll are now gone, but that hasn't stopped people from trying to find the silver and gold. John Allegro was one of them. He got financial backing and, with the permission of the Jordanian government, went on a treasure hunt, but he never found so much as a piece of silver. So far neither has anyone else, but people still wonder if a magnificent horde of riches isn't hidden in the barren desert waiting for a real-life Indiana Jones to find it. Today the Copper Scroll is on display at the Archaeological Museum of Jordan, in Amman.

ONE MORE SCROLL caused an international sensation. Like the Copper Scroll, it was difficult to unroll, and there were many questions about who wrote it and why. Its long journey home involved a man who, as we've seen, was no stranger to the Dead Sea Scrolls.

By 1961 Yigael Yadin was considered one of the foremost archaeologists in the world. On a visit to London he received news of another scroll that had been taken from the caves near the Dead Sea. It was an intact scroll an extraordinary twenty-seven feet long. The original negotiations were secretive, with Yadin's being sent a scroll fragment wrapped in the foil of a cigarette package. From his previous work with the scrolls he knew immediately that this piece was authentic.

As it turned out, the scroll was owned by none other than Kando, the antiquities dealer, who was still living in Bethlehem. As with the other scrolls Yadin had obtained, the haggling turned out to be long, drawn-out, and, in this case, unsuccessful. Yadin was disappointed but went on with his own archaeological work. He was excavating Masada, a first-century desert fortress where a group of rebellious Jews, the Zealots, made their last stand against the Roman army.

Then something else came along to take up even more of Yadin's time and concern. In June 1967 a bloody and intense war broke out between Israel and its Arab neighbors. Within six days the Israelis had defeated the rival armies. The war became known as the Six-Day War, and in that time the map of Israel changed.

Israel's victory meant that its borders grew, on the east all the way to the Jordan River and Dead Sea. Before 1967 Qumran and part of Jerusalem had been under Jordan's control. Now they were under the control of Israel.

Yadin spent the war as a military adviser to the prime minister. When Israeli troops captured the new territory, Bethlehem, too, was included. Yadin thought again of Kando. Did he still have that very long scroll?

Sure enough, it was there, buried in a shoe box beneath some floor tiles in Kando's home. The Israeli government confiscated the scroll, although Kando was paid for it. The conditions in which he kept the

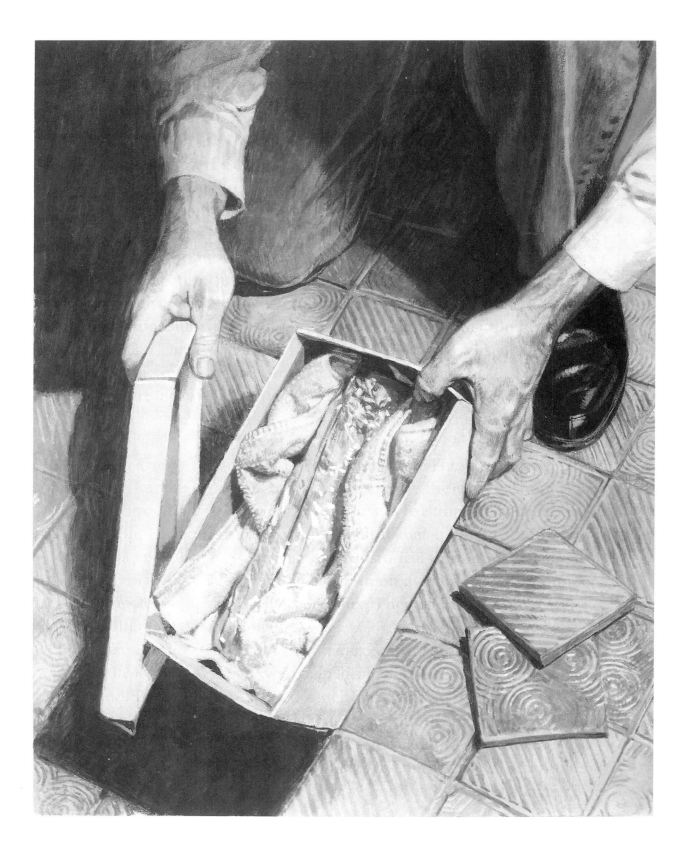

scroll had caused damage, but it was still readable. Readable, that is, once Yadin and the other Israeli archaeologists figured out how to unroll it.

The unrolling, done at the Israel Museum, was frustrating and at times impossible. As Yadin wrote, "The first part of the scroll we unrolled was a separate wad...which had been wrapped in cellophane inside the shoe box.... Letters and even words had peeled off some of the columns of script and attached themselves, in mirror image, on the backs of preceding columns." Another wad he described as a "black, macerated mass" that could be neither separated nor deciphered.

Although the process was hardly uncomplicated, archaeologists managed to unroll most of the scroll, softening the outer roll by humidifying it (treating it with warm steam), so it would be less brittle. Sometimes the scroll would be refrigerated immediately after it had been humidified so the leather would contract—or shrink—and be easier to pry apart. When this process proved to be too damaging, the archaeologists had to be content to leave the pieces stuck together and try to photograph them from back and front. Once in a while, Yadin wrote, "we were compelled to cut the columns lengthwise, a kind of plastic surgery, and then to rejoin them after their separation."

The scroll turned out to be a treasure trove of information for the archaeologists. Yadin called it the Temple Scroll because so much of it dealt with instructions for building a Jewish temple in Jerusalem. Of course, there was a real temple in Jerusalem at the time the scroll was written, but the strict Qumran sect did not recognize the already standing temple because they regarded it as impure.

The temple described in the scroll consists of an inner court, a middle court, and an outer court, as well as other connected buildings. But whoever wrote the Temple Scroll was not a very good architect. If that temple had actually been built, it would have been gigantic. Some experts estimate that the temple and its compound would have been almost exactly the size of the walled city of Jerusalem in the second century B.C.E. Yet the instructions are so detailed it seems someone thought the temple would be built, size notwithstanding.

About half the scroll gives these instructions for the temple construction. The other half is a book of laws. Unlike the Bible, this book is written in the first person, as if God were speaking. For instance, one line reads: "When a woman vows a vow to me..."

Yadin thought this book of laws was a holy book of the Essenes that might even have been written by their Teacher of Righteousness. Yadin died in 1984, and some later scholars disagreed with his assessment of the Temple Scroll, arguing that if it were so important to the Qumran sect, there would have been more copies found in the caves.

In any case, the scroll is full of information about Jewish festivals and holy days not mentioned in the Bible. It also sheds some light on sayings and parables found in the New Testament. One story that Jesus tells in Mark 8:14–21 had always puzzled biblical scholars because they didn't know to whom Jesus is referring when he speaks about the Herodians, nor was anything known about their seven-day festival in which bread played an important role. But when the Temple Scroll described a seven-day festival that involved seven baskets of bread, it became possible to imagine that *Herodians* was another name for the Essenes, and the parable began to make sense.

Despite all the mishandling and mistakes, trials and tribulations that surrounded the first seven scrolls and the Temple and Copper scrolls, in some ways they were still the easiest to work with and decipher. The rest of the scrolls were in fragments, and trying to make sense of them became not only an intellectual exercise but the cause of an international fight.

CONFLICT AND COMPUTERS

THE DEAD SEA SCROLLS contain information about the quarrels and problems between various religious sects that lived two thousand years ago. After their discovery they also caused quarrels and problems between the many scholars and researchers who wanted access to the scrolls and the information that they contained.

There was trouble right from the very first. Archaeologists G. Lankester Harding and Father Roland de Vaux had been displeased when they learned about the scrolls only after the first seven had been sold to Metropolitan Samuel and Dr. Sukenik. But at least the scrolls that came into Israel's possession were translated and published promptly so that other scholars around the world could read and debate the scroll material for themselves.

Although scroll fragments were found in all eleven caves, the bulk of them—approximately fifteen thousand fragments that represented about five hundred manuscripts—were found in Cave 4. To finance the excavation and subsequent work on the texts, money was solicited from several European and American archaeological and biblical studies schools in Jerusalem. The Vatican provided some money as well. The schools decided that once the fragments had been ordered into documents and published, they would divide the scrolls among them.

Harding and de Vaux gathered an international team of seven young scholars (none older than thirty-two) to be in charge of the texts. Each agreed to be a member of the team until the project was completed, and by May 1953 they had begun their work at the Palestine Archaeological Museum (now called the Rockefeller Museum) in East Jerusalem. It was their job to take the scroll fragments and assemble them into documents.

How did they do this? Like anyone who's ever put together a jigsaw puzzle, they looked for clues. When the fragments were copies of biblical texts, they looked to the original text as a guide, as if it were the completed picture on the puzzle box. It was harder to put the fragments into documents when the writings were unknown originals. Then the scholars looked at the physical characteristics of the fragment: whether it was written on parchment or leather, and what kind of animal the leather came from; the handwriting of the scribe and other physical characteristics; and the subject of the fragment.

Although we can use a jigsaw puzzle analogy, putting together the fragments wasn't like joining precut parts of a puzzle. Many of the fragments joined together in one or two spots, but not in a third. Did this mean that a piece of the puzzle was missing or that this was the wrong piece? Remember, there were thousands of pieces. If archaeologists had been in charge of clearing all the caves, they would have taken special care to keep piles of fragments together, logically assuming that these would be from the same scroll. Then each fragment would have been labeled. The Bedouin had simply swept out each cave and placed the fragments together in cigarette boxes or bags.

When the international team first arrived at the museum, they faced an almost insurmountable task. Most of the fragments were held in cabinet drawers identified only by the number of the cave where they'd been found. Each tiny piece of scroll had to be identified, labeled, and cleaned, even the tiniest bits of dust brushed away. Eventually they all would be put under pieces of glass, but first many of the fragments had to be softened by humidifying techniques. Otherwise they were so brittle they would simply break. Just preparing the fragments so they could be deciphered took countless hours.

The fragments were grouped together into manuscripts. These were preliminary groupings that could well change. Then infrared photographs were taken. The infrared technique helped make more visible writing that was almost too faint to read.

The conditions at the Palestine Archaeological Museum, where the young scholars worked, were hardly helpful to the scrolls' preservation either: Windows were open, allowing in damaging dirt and harsh sunlight. The men even smoked cigarettes while poring over the scrolls.

Their colleagues around the world, who also would have liked access to the scrolls, could have sympathized with the team about the difficulty of their task, but they soon became angered by the young scholars' selfishness in not sharing the material. The team divided among themselves hundreds of manuscripts, clearly more than they could translate and publish in their lifetime.

There is an unwritten rule among scholars that when they are assigned a text, they have complete control over it. They can take as long as they like to publish it and can refuse to show it to anyone they don't want to see it. They can even "will" it to an assistant in the case of death.

The Dead Sea Scrolls team took full advantage of this unwritten rule. During the next thirty years the team published fewer than one hundred of their texts. All around the world scholars who wanted to see the Dead Sea material were getting more and more furious. One Oxford professor called the closely held scroll material the "academic scandal of the twentieth century."

The team tried to speed up its work, but without much success. In 1988 it finally decided to publish a concordance (or index of important words) that had been prepared in the 1950s. It had been stored in the basement of the museum since then. The concordance listed each found word in many of the texts, as well as the words around it, and stated which document the word was in and where in the document it was located.

Once the concordance was published, two scholars took things into their own hands. Professor Ben Zion Wacholder of the Hebrew Union College in Cincinnati, Ohio, a man in his sixties and nearly blind, teamed up with Martin Abegg, a graduate student and computer whiz. Combining the professor's knowledge of the scrolls and the student's knowledge of computers, the duo was able to use the concordance to reconstruct various texts. In 1991 they published the texts, and the news made the front page of the *New York Times*. The *Times* applauded the computer-generated texts, saying, "[The official editorial team], with its obsessive secrecy and cloak-and-dagger scholarship, long ago exhausted its credibility with scholars and laymen alike."

A further surprise came from the Huntington Library in San Marino, California. Unbeknownst to almost everyone, the library had in its possession a set of photographic negatives of the scroll fragments from Cave 4 that had been taken decades back for security purposes. A

recently appointed director of the library decided in the name of intellectual freedom to release the negatives. The official team was outraged, but there was nothing the scholars could do. They were even angrier when later that year the Biblical Archaeology Society published a two-volume edition of the photographs of the scroll fragments for everyone to see. The monopoly over the Dead Sea Scrolls had ended.

Now the scrolls were out in the world for anyone to decipher, study, and debate. One of the biggest questions surrounding the scrolls was what light, if any, they could shed on early Christianity. The accusation had been made that one reason the scrolls hadn't been published was that there was some secret information about Christianity that the original team, all Christians, did not want the world to know.

As more scrolls are being published, that allegation appears not to be true. What can be said is that both the early Christians and the Qumran group were breakaway Jewish sects that shared the same territory and some of the same ideas.

How were the Qumran sect and the earliest Christians alike? All of Jesus' earliest followers were Jewish, just like the community at Qumran. It would take years before the early Christians were recognized as something other than a Jewish sect. Both groups were unhappy with organized Judaism.

Most Jews of that period were concerned about the Temple and its daily operations. They were worried about the possible corruption of the priests who were so closely aligned with the Romans. The early Christians and those in the Qumran sect were even more ready for change. They both dreamed of the day when God would intercede in the world and right its wrongs. A special emphasis was put on prayer, and interestingly, both groups used some similar terms, such as "the Sons of Light." Eventually Jesus and some of his followers and most, perhaps all, of the Qumran sect were killed by the Roman occupiers of their country, as were many other Jews.

Look at the practices of the early Christians and the Qumran sect, and you'll see some noteworthy similarities. Both groups held property in common, valued a simple lifestyle, and shared sacred meals emphasizing bread and wine.

But there were major differences as well. Those in the Qumran sect were much more rigid in their beliefs than were Jesus and his followers. For one thing, they said that only their own Teacher of Righteousness understood the Scriptures. For another, they hated people who were not as strict in their religious beliefs and practices as they were. Jesus, through both word and action, tried to include people in God's message. Another difference was in their expectations about the Messiah who was to save Israel. The early Christians believed that Jesus was the Messiah. But the Qumran sect saw the possibility of two messiahs, one priestly and peaceful, the other a warrior, and neither appeared while the sect was in existence.

John the Baptist, who is remembered for baptising Jesus, was known to have roamed and preached in the area. The New Testament describes this biblical figure as a man who disdained any kind of worldly wealth. He wore a camel skin and ate locusts and honey, and the Book of Luke even says that John grew up in the wilderness. Some have speculated that John at some time in his life was an Essene, and it is known from historians that the Essenes took in young boys and raised them in their ways. John claimed that his baptisms washed away sins. We know from their own writings that the Qumran sect, too, put a great emphasis on washing and cleansing for purification.

If John had once belonged to a wilderness community, whether we call them Essenes or the Qumran sect, he must have kept some of their practices while developing his own particular philosophy, some of which Jesus incorporated into his preaching.

One reason the Dead Sea Scrolls have so excited the imagination of the ordinary person on the street is that they may hold clues to the beginnings of Christianity. Even though no references to Jesus himself or his followers have been found, the scrolls have certainly tuned us in to the world from which Christianity emerged and given us tantalizing clues to the connection between that fledgling religion and Judaism, from which it sprang.

As WE HAVE SEEN, the Dead Sea Scrolls raise as many questions as they answer, maybe more. Perhaps for that very reason the scrolls continue to fascinate us. There is nothing quite so intriguing as a mystery.

It is also interesting to note that these ancient documents continue to be inextricably linked with modern technology. Newspaper articles keep appearing about how computer technology is helping scholars decipher the scrolls. Recently there has been an advance in the restoration of ancient texts, a method of electronically rejoining and reading tiny fragile fragments of the scrolls without the risk of damaging them. This digital imaging technology also allows the script from other parts of a particular scroll to be analyzed; researchers can then use this information to reproduce missing scroll pieces, making it possible to rebuild the document.

Regardless of what scholars conclude about the scrolls and their meaning, the very existence of these ancient artifacts will continue to fascinate new generations. Jum'a Muhammed, throwing that rock inside that cave, was curious, just as we are when we explore in the woods, dig in the sand, or reach for the stars. The scrolls show us that there were people alive thousands of years ago who had hopes and fears like us, who wondered about their futures and contemplated the role that God played in their lives. The fact of the scrolls—and the story of their discovery—establishes a lifeline between us and our ancestors. Who's to say that two thousand years from now some young man or woman may not find our own messages to the future?

AUTHOR'S NOTE

STUDENTS ARE TAUGHT that fiction is a book that is "not true," while nonfiction is "true." The story of the Dead Sea Scrolls is most assuredly true, but as with many works of history, it is not always easy to pin down exactly the way things happened. Take, for instance, the discovery of the scrolls themselves in a cave near the Dead Sea. One source claims they were found in October or November 1946, others place the event in the early months of 1947, while still another has it later in the spring of that year. When confronted with pieces of information that seemingly contradict one another, an author is forced to dig even more deeply to see if he or she can find out what really occurred or, lacking that, can bring the information into some harmony. In the case of the scrolls' discovery, most sources put the event in the very late winter of 1946–47, and this is the date I have used. One problem solved. But throughout the book, I have had to make those sorts of decisions as well as try to reconcile both events of two thousand years ago and scholarly disputes that continue today. As my court of final authority, I have used the book *Understanding the Dead Sea Scrolls,* edited by Hershel Shanks, because of both the depth and breadth of its coverage and its distinguished contributors. I would also like to thank Dr. Henry Schriebman, Dead Sea Scrolls scholar, for his examination of the manuscript and his suggestion of the talk-radio metaphor.

TIME LINE

Historical Events (many dates are approximate)

1800–1500 B.C.E. The Israelites begin settling in the land of Canaan.

1010–965 B.C.E. King David reigns.

965–922 B.C.E. King Solomon reigns and the first Temple is built.

722 B.C.E. Israel is conquered by the Assyrians.

586 B.C.E. Babylonians conquer Jerusalem and destroy Solomon's Temple; the Jews are exiled and deported to Babylonia.

539 B.C.E. Persians defeat Babylonia; King Cyrus of Persia allows the Jews to begin returning home.

516 B.C.E. Persians oversee the building of the Second Temple in Jerusalem.

333 B.C.E. Alexander the Great launches an attack on the Persian Empire. By the time of his death ten years later, Syria, Egypt, and Judea have been added to his empire.

198 B.C.E. Syrian Greeks take control of Judea.

168 B.C.E. Syrian Greek King Antiochus IV bans Judaism in Jerusalem and desecrates the Temple.

167 B.C.E. Led by Judah Maccabee, the Jews revolt and recapture the Temple. Eventually the Maccabee family, later known as the Hasmonean dynasty, wins Judean independence from Syria.

Approximately 140 B.C.E. The Qumran sect, angry that the Hasmoneans have usurped the powers of the priests at the Temple, withdraws to the wilderness, where it builds a community and considers itself "the true Israel."

63 B.C.E. The Roman general Pompey enters Jerusalem, and Judea is occupied by Rome.

39 B.C.E. Herod, named king of the Jews by the Romans, expands the Temple.

6 B.C.E. Jesus is born.

30 C.E. Jesus is crucified.

66 C.E. The Jewish revolt begins.

68 C.E. The settlement at Qumran is burned by the Romans.

70 C.E. Rome conquers Jerusalem, destroying the city and the Temple.

1870s C.E. After almost 2,000 years of limited Jewish settlement in the land of Israel, Jews begin returning in larger numbers.

The Discovery of the Dead Sea Scrolls

1946–1947. Bedouin shepherds of the Ta'amireh tribe find Cave 1, containing seven scrolls.

April 1947. The tribesmen bring their scrolls to an antiquities dealer named Kando, in Bethlehem.

Spring 1947. Kando shows one scroll to Metropolitan Samuel of the Syrian Orthodox Church.

July 1947. Members of the Ta'amireh tribe are turned away from St. Mark's, where the metropolitan lives, but later in the summer return with four scrolls, which Samuel purchases sometime in the late summer or early fall.

November–December 1947. Professor E. L. Sukenik of Hebrew University hears about scrolls found near the Dead Sea from a friend who is an antiquities dealer.

November 1947. The United Nations votes to partition Palestine into two states, one Jewish, one Arab.

November 1947. Professor Sukenik purchases three scrolls.

Winter 1948. Professor Sukenik has an opportunity to buy the metropolitan's scrolls, but the deal falls through for lack of funds.

1949. G. Lankester Harding, head of the Jordanian Department of Antiquities, learns of the Dead Sea Scrolls.

1951. Harding, along with Father Roland de Vaux, begins excavating the Qumran site and searching for other caves.

1952. The Copper Scroll is found.

May 1953. An international team of scholars begins trying to piece together the thousands of scroll fragments found in eleven caves along the shore of the Dead Sea.

June 1954. Metropolitan Samuel, now living in New York, places an advertisement in the *Wall Street Journal* in an effort to sell his four scrolls.

Summer 1954. After secret negotiations the metropolitan's scrolls are sold to Professor Sukenik's son Yigael Yadin, for the state of Israel.

1955. The Copper Scroll is sent to Manchester, England, to be unrolled.

1956. G. Lankester Harding resigns his post at the Jordanian Department of Antiquities and ends five successful years of excavations.

1961. Yigael Yadin learns of the Temple Scroll but fails in his attempt to obtain it for Israel.

June 1967. The Six-Day War brings new land, including Bethlehem and East Jerusalem, into the hands of the Israelis.

Summer 1967. Yigael Yadin finds the Temple Scroll buried in a shoe box in Kando's house in Bethlehem.

1988. The concordance to the Dead Sea Scrolls is published.

1991. A computer-generated re-creation of the Dead Sea texts is published.

1991. The Huntington Library in California frees its photographic copies of the Dead Sea Scroll fragments from Cave 4, allowing scholars all over the world access to the scrolls.

GLOSSARY

ANTIQUITIES. Monuments or relics (such as coins, jewelry, or pottery) relating to ancient times. Ancient times are considered to be those before the Middle Ages.

ARAMAIC. Aramaic is a Semitic language known since the ninth century B.C.E. It was once used widely throughout the Near and Middle East and it was the language used by the Jewish people after their Babylonian exile (see time line). No longer a spoken language, it is still used in Jewish prayer and Talmudic text.

ARCHAEOLOGY. Archaeology is the science concerned with the material remains of past human environments. It seeks to reconstruct and understand the culture of ancient peoples. To do this, archaeologists recover and study such remains as utensils, weapons, pottery, ruins of settlements, and other objects.

Biblical archaeologists study those artifacts of the past that contribute to a better understanding of the Bible and biblical times. They try to fill in the background settings for events depicted in the Bible. Written and other materials are investigated in biblical archaeology. Among the ancient writing materials are papyri, inscriptions, leather scrolls, cuneiform tablets, and coins.

An excavation begins with the survey of a site based on surface examination and a study of historical records. A small flat hill, or *tell*, developed by the accumulation of stone, soil, and debris through many centuries, often marks the remains of an ancient city. After careful digging, archaeologists usually uncover the ruins of ancient buildings. They remove layer after layer of buildings and artifacts. All the remains are recorded and photographed for later study.

B.C.E./C.E. These are recent terms that are used in place of B.C. and A.D. B.C.E. stands for "before the common era." Many non-Christians prefer it to B.C., which stands for "before Christ." C.E. stands for "common era." The common era is also referred to as A.D., the abbreviation for *anno domini*, which is Latin for "In the year of our Lord." The B.C./A.D. system of dating was worked out in 532 C.E. by a monk who dated events from the year he believed Jesus was born. As it turns out, the monk miscounted. Jesus was probably born about six years earlier than the monk thought.

When counting years B.C.E. or B.C., count backward from 1. The higher the number, the earlier the event. For instance, something that happened in 500 B.C.E. took place one hundred years earlier than something that happened in 400 B.C.E. The opposite is true when counting forward from C.E. The scrolls were found in 1947 C.E., 1,947 years after the monk's dating of the birth of Jesus.

BIBLE. The Bible contains the sacred writings of the Jewish and Christian religions. The Hebrew Bible, also known as the Old Testament, is considered the first part of the Christian Bible, which adds the New Testament. Traditionally the Hebrew Bible is said to have been given by God to Moses, but modern scholars believe the Bible began as an oral tradition and was written down much later. The first book of the Bible, Genesis, was probably not transcribed, or recorded, until the fifth century B.C.E. The books of the New Testament were written down in the century after Jesus' death, probably in Greek, although some may have been written first in Aramaic and then translated.

The list of books that a religion has adopted as Scripture (and therefore sacred) is known as a canon. The canons of the Old and New Testament developed gradually. The canon of Jewish scripture is arranged in three groups: The Torah is comprised of the first five books of the Bible; the Prophets consists of books of history and prophecy; and the Holy Writings are a collection of narratives, poems, and prayers. The Old Testament as we know it was set around 250 B.C.E.

CARBON 14 DATING, also known as **RADIOCARBON DATING.** Carbon 14 is a radioactive isotope of carbon. All living things contain radiocarbon in predictable amounts. Radiocarbon dating is a process used to determine the age of an organic object by measuring its radiocarbon content. Radiocarbon atoms decay at a uniform rate. Half the radiocarbon disappears after about 5,700 years. After about 11,400 years, a fourth of the original amount of radiocarbon is left. This steady rate of decay is the reason scientists can determine an object's age by measuring the amount of radiocarbon that is left.

CHRISTIANITY. Christianity is the religion of those who follow the teachings of Jesus of Nazareth. Jesus, a Jew, was a preacher who taught that the kingdom of God was at hand. He asked his followers to repent of their sins to be ready for this kingdom, in which God would make himself known in a new way. Reportedly he performed miracles, and his popularity caused problems for the Jewish establishment and the Roman occupiers of Palestine. Jesus was crucified by the Romans around 30 C.E. His followers spread the gospel (good news) of his teachings through the Roman Empire.

After Jesus' death Christianity was considered a Jewish sect, but eventually it was seen as a separate religion. After the fall of Jerusalem in 70 C.E., the Roman emperors persecuted the Christians for about 250 years. In 313 C.E. the Roman emperor Constantine gave Christians the right to worship freely. By 393 Christianity had become the official religion of the Roman Empire.

Christians believe in the one God taught by the Jewish religion and that he sent his Son, Jesus, into the world as his chosen servant to help people fulfill their religious duties. They also believe that Jesus is God incarnate, a divine being who took on the appearance and characteristics of a man. They believe he is the Savior who died for humankind's sins.

HEBREW. This Semitic language originated in the general area now partly occupied by the land of Israel. For more than three thousand years Hebrew has been the language of the religious, and often the everyday, life of the Jewish people. An ancient form of Hebrew is believed to have been in use during the period that saw the migration of the patriarchs, such as Abraham, into Israel. Hebrew is also the language of modern-day Israel.

ISLAM. A world religion founded by the Prophet Muhammad in the seventh century. The word *Islam* is used repeatedly in the Koran, the Islamic Scripture, to mean "surrender to the will of Allah (God)." Muslims, followers of Islam, regard the Koran as the word of God as revealed through the Prophet Muhammad, the last and most perfect of a series of messengers from God to humankind.

JUDAISM. Judaism is the religion of the Jewish people. The basic laws and teachings of Judaism come from the Torah, the first five books of the Hebrew Bible, especially the belief that there is one God and that there is a covenant (or special relationship) between God and the Jewish people.

Jews believe God made this covenant with Abraham, the ancestor of the Jewish people. According to the Bible, God promised to bless Abraham and his descendants if they worshiped and remained faithful to him. Later God gave Moses the Ten Commandments and other laws to help them do that.

Jews traditionally believe that God will send a messiah who will end evil in the world and defeat their enemies. The word *messiah* comes from the Hebrew word for "anointed one." Christians believe that Jesus was the Messiah, but many Jews still are waiting for a messiah. Other Jews expect a messianic age of peace and justice that will come through the cooperation of all people with the help of God.

PALESTINE/ISRAEL. The land we now know as Israel has had many names. When the Semitic people first entered the area about 2000 B.C.E., it was known as Canaan. Around 1800 B.C.E. a Semitic tribe called the Hebrews left Mesopotamia and began settling in Canaan, where they were also known as the Israelites.

Eventually the Israelites formed twelve tribes. Some left Canaan and went to Egypt, where they stayed for about three hundred years. Moses led them out of Egypt in the twelfth century B.C.E., and they returned to their homeland, which was also called Philistia after the Israelites' strongest enemies in the area, the Philistines. About 1000 B.C.E. King David unified the twelve tribes of Israel into one nation and established his capital in Jerusalem. His son, Solomon, built the first Temple there. After Solomon's death the northern tribes of Israel split from the tribes in the south. The northern part of the country continued to be called Israel, while the southern section was called Judah.

Beginning in the early 700s B.C.E., there were many upheavals in the form of foreign occupation, war, exile, and revolts (see time line). In 142 B.C.E. the Jews established the kingdom of Judea—but not for long. Rome, the most powerful nation in the world, invaded Judea in 63 B.C.E. The Romans triumphed over Jewish revolts in the first century C.E. The area was renamed Palaestina, recalling the ancient name Philistia.

Palestine remained the name of the region through Arab rule from the sixth to the twentieth century C.E. In 1920 the League of Nations authorized Britain to be in charge of Palestine. In 1947 the UN General Assembly divided Palestine into an Arab state and a Jewish state. On May 14, 1948, the Jews proclaimed the independent state of Israel.

PROPHECY. The inspired utterance of a prophet, a human channel for God's words. In Hebrew the term means "one called by God." Prophets and prophecy have a place in many religions, especially those that emphasize a personal god, such as Judaism, Christianity, and Islam. Prophets often appear when large numbers of people feel cultural or economic strain. In ancient Israel the eighth to the sixth century B.C.E. was a time when the country was in turmoil. Prophets, such as Isaiah and Jeremiah, warned the people to obey the Lord strictly.

THE TEMPLE IN JERUSALEM. King Solomon built the first Temple in Jerusalem to house the Ark, or chest holding the sacred tablets given to Moses by God. The site Solomon selected was Mount Moriah, where his father, King David, had offered sacrifices. The most important place in the Temple was the Holy of Holies, a windowless cubical holding the Ark. The Court of the Priests surrounded the Holy of Holies. Outside was a Great Court that consisted of a complex of buildings, including the royal palace.

Only the high priest could enter the Holy of Holies. Worshipers might bring their offerings into the Court of the Priests, but usually they remained in the Great Court.

The Temple was destroyed in 587 C.E. by Nebuchadnezzar of Babylonia. It was later rebuilt and then destroyed again in 70 C.E. (except for a portion of the Western Wall) by the Romans. Even though the Temple was gone, Jews throughout history have remembered it and the special place it had in the lives of their ancestors.

WORKS CONSULTED

Armstrong, Karen. *Jerusalem: Three Cities One Faith.* New York: Knopf, 1996.
This examination of Judaism, Christianity, and Islam, set against the background of a city holy to all three, pays particular attention to the role of the Temple in the Jewish religion.

Comay, Joan. *The Temple of Jerusalem.* New York: Holt, Rinehart and Winston, 1977.
The history of the Temple and its importance in Jewish life are described in this informative book. Many photographs and historical engravings amplify the text.

Connolly, Peter. *Jews in the Time of Jesus: A History.* New York: Oxford University Press, 1995.
This very readable, profusely illustrated book for young people does an excellent job of explaining what was happening in Palestine in a period that roughly parallels the writing of the Dead Sea Scrolls. The scrolls are not the book's focus, but many of the events surrounding their writing and the establishment of the Qumran sect are covered here. Among them are the coming of Rome, the reign of Herod, the early Christian movement, and the importance of the Temple in Jerusalem.

Editors of Time-Life Books, *The Holy Land.* Alexandria, VA: Time-Life Books, 1992.
Heavily illustrated with color photographs, this historical overview is part of the Lost Civilizations series. Focusing on ancient history and archaeology, the text is easily understandable and features an excellent time line.

Gaster, Theodor, ed. *The Dead Sea Scriptures: In English Translation,* rev. ed. New York: Doubleday/Anchor, 1976.
For those who wish to read for themselves translations of the scrolls, this book contains, among other works, *The Manual of Discipline,* the War Scroll, and the Thanksgiving Scroll.

Golb, Norman. *Who Wrote the Dead Sea Scrolls?: The Search for the Secret of Qumran.* New York: Scribner's, 1995.
Dr. Golb, a longtime scrolls researcher, sets forth the theory that the scrolls were not written by the Essenes or by any one sect; rather they constituted a library that was smuggled out of Jerusalem before the city was sacked by Rome.

Noble, Iris. *Treasure of the Caves: The Story of the Dead Sea Scrolls.* New York: Macmillan, 1971.
In this book for young people Noble focuses on the discovery of the scrolls as well as the scientific know-how that went into their preservation and preparation so that they could be studied. The book does an especially good job of relating the story of the Copper Scroll and describing how it was unrolled at the university in Manchester, England.

Although there are no notes, the flap copy states that Noble interviewed some of the archaeologists and scholars who originally worked on the scrolls. Many fine black-and-white photographs amplify the text.

Schiffman, Lawrence. *Reclaiming the Dead Sea Scrolls.* New York: Jewish Publication Society, 1994.
Schiffman, one of the new generation of Dead Sea scholars, makes a case for the Sadducean origins of the Qumran sect.

Shanks, Hershel, ed. *Understanding the Dead Sea Scrolls: A Reader from the Biblical Archaeology Review.* New York: Random House, 1992.
Shanks, the editor of the magazine *Biblical Archaeology Review,* was instrumental in breaking the choke hold that the original scholars' team had on the scroll material. This book is a compilation of articles by leading scholars that have appeared in his magazine. The articles are grouped by topic. Among the subjects are the origins and identity of the Qumran sect, the Dead Sea Scrolls and the Bible, the Dead Sea Scrolls and Christianity, and the controversy over scholars who were perceived to be holding the scrolls hostage.

Swisher, Clarice. *The Ancient Near East.* San Diego: Lucent Books, 1995.
An easy-to-read book for young people in the World History series that encompasses the history of the ancient Near East. The time frame predates the Dead Sea Scrolls era. However, this book does an excellent job of providing a historical context. A reader-friendly layout and many black-and-white photographs make this very accessible.

VanderKam, James. *The Dead Sea Scrolls Today.* Grand Rapids, MI: Eeardmans, 1994.
VanderKam, one of the original scroll editors, provides readers with a complete overview of the scrolls' history, including their discovery, the excavations of the caves and Qumran, and the methods of dating the discoveries.

Wilson, Edmund. *The Scrolls from the Dead Sea.* New York: Oxford University Press, 1955.
Wilson, an important novelist, playwright, and critic, was the first author to write about the scrolls for a general audience. Although he is of course writing nonfiction, his personal writing style gives the material a novelistic flow. This is one of the earliest books about the scrolls, and much more has been learned about them since it was written.

Wise, Michael, Martin Abegg, Jr., and Edward Cook. *The Dead Sea Scrolls: A New Translation.* San Francisco: Harper, 1996.
The most up-to-date translations of the scrolls, prefaced by an informative introduction.

Yadin, Yigael. *The Message of the Scrolls.* London: Oxford University Press, 1957.
Yadin has a very accessible writing style that will engage young people who want to read the archaeologist's own story of his involvement with the Dead Sea Scrolls.

Pamphlets

The Dead Sea Scrolls. Jerusalem: The Israel Antiquities Authority and the Israel Museum, 1994.
Based on the exhibition catalog from the Library of Congress exhibit "Scrolls from the Dead Sea," this twenty-page brochure, illustrated with photographs, will entice readers of every age-group as it briefly describes the history and importance of the scrolls and other cave artifacts.

Articles

"The Bible's Last Secrets." *U.S. News & World Report.* (October 15, 1993), p. 64.
This article about the Dead Sea Scrolls can serve as a good overview for anyone who wants to know more about the subject. It was written at the time the scrolls were being released to scholars around the world and to the interested public.

"Dead Sea Scrolls Go Public." *Chicago Tribune,* April 29, 1993, Sec. 5, p. 1.
A discussion of the scholars' symposium that took place at the Library of Congress in conjunction with its Dead Sea Scrolls exhibit.

"Digitized Fragments Helping Decipher the Dead Sea Scrolls." *New York Times,* April 2, 1996, p. B7.
The latest digital technology and electronic imaging are helping decipher the scrolls and put fragments in their proper places in the manuscript.

"Scrolls from the Dead Sea: An Introduction to a Major Library Exhibition." *LC Information Bulletin* (March 22, 1993), p. 115.
In 1993, twelve of the Dead Sea Scrolls, along with artifacts from Qumran and the cave sites, were exhibited at the Library of Congress. This article gives a brief history of the scrolls and sums up some of the controversies surrounding them.

Website

Dead Sea Scrolls Exhibit
http://sunsite.unc.edu/expo/deadsea.scrolls.exhibit/intro.html
This website features selections from the Library of Congress exhibit, including twelve scroll fragments and twenty-nine other objects loaned by the Israel Antiquities Authority.

INDEX

egg-shaped

diamond-shaped

grasslike

spoon-shaped

canoe-shaped

heart-shaped

oblong

oval

arrowhead-shaped

lance-shaped

lance-shaped

swordlike

oblong

elliptical

arrowhead-shaped

egg-shaped

grasslike

Wildflowers

HOW TO IDENTIFY FLOWERS IN THE WILD
AND HOW TO GROW THEM IN YOUR GARDEN

Wildflowers

HOW TO IDENTIFY FLOWERS IN THE WILD
AND HOW TO GROW THEM IN YOUR GARDEN

◆ RICK IMES ◆

Foreword by Chy and Ray Allen

Rodale Press, Emmaus, Pennsylvania

A QUARTO BOOK

Copyright © 1992 Quarto Publishing plc
All rights reserved. No part of this publication
may be reproduced or transmitted in any form
or by any means, electronic or mechanical,
including photocopy, recording, or any other
information storage and retrieval system,
without the written permission of the
publisher.

Published in 1992 in the United States of
America by Rodale Press, Inc.

If you have any questions or comments
concerning this book, please write:
Rodale Press
Book Readers' Service
33 East Minor Street
Emmaus, PA 18098

This book was designed and produced by
Quarto Publishing plc
The Old Brewery
6 Blundell Street
London N7

Senior Editor: Sally MacEachern
Copy Editor: Catherine Bradley
Editorial Assistant: Katie Preston
Artists: Wayne Ford, Christine Wilson,
Rob Shone
Designers: Penny Dawes, Allan Mole
Assistant Art Director: Chloë Alexander
Picture Research Manager: Sarah Risley

Art Director: Moira Clinch
Publishing Director: Janet Slingsby

**Library of Congress Cataloging-in-Publication
Data**

Imes, Rick.
    Wildflowers: how to identify flowers in the wild
and how to grow them in your garden/Rick Imes:
foreword by Chy and Ray Allen.
        p.   cm.
    Includes bibliographical references and index.
    ISBN 0-87596-118-5 hardcover
1. Wild flower gardening. 2. Wild flowers –
Identification. 3. Wild flowers – Geographical
distribution. 4. Wild flowers – Pictorial works.
5. Wild flower gardening – North America. 6. Wild
flowers – North America – Identification. 7. Wild
flowers – North America – Geographical
distribution. 8. Wild flowers – North America –
Pictorial works. I. Title.
SB49.148 1992
635.9'876—dc20   92–327
                                  CIP

Distributed in the book trade by St. Martin's Press
Typeset by The Brightside Partnership, London
Manufactured in Hong Kong by Regent
Publishing Services, Ltd
Printed by Lee Fung Asco Printers Ltd,
China

    4 6 8 10 9 7 5 3   hardcover

Dedication
To my grandmother, Carrie
Dreibelbis, who appreciated nature
long before it became fashionable.

CONTENTS

FOREWORD

Since we began spending our summer vacations identifying wildflowers and started our first wild garden about 30 years ago, we've seen a stampede of others join us. Today, interest in native plants makes up one of the fastest growing segments of America's fastest growing hobby — gardening.

When we decided to turn our hobby into a family business over 10 years ago, most friends thought we were crazy. "A Wildflower Farm?" they all asked. Some laughed out loud. Others humored us with half-hearted interest. "Who will come?" they all wondered. And of course, we wondered too.

But we needn't have worried. Today, with 35,000 visitors every summer when our fields and woodland gardens are open to the public, and a couple of hundred thousand more reached through our winter catalog, we are now in contact with about 300,000 wildflower enthusiasts every year.

And why? Many for the same reasons we became interested decades ago. Observing and cultivating wildflowers is one of the least expensive and most fascinating hobbies nature offers. Certainly there is no less expensive and less labor-intensive landscaping scheme. And of course today, our growing environmental consciousness adds deep meaning and new pleasure to caring for and about native plants.

When you create a wild garden, you have

really created an ecosystem right at home, where the fascinating and beautiful life cycles of the plants proceed at close range for endless personal pleasure. And each wild garden comes with an environmental and personal bonus — the birds, bees, butterflies, and small wildlife that will surely enjoy your wild garden along with you. Because with wildflowers, rather than trying to keep insects and wildlife *out* of your garden, you'll be welcoming them in. After all, they are the pollinators of your flowers, and no wild garden is complete without them.

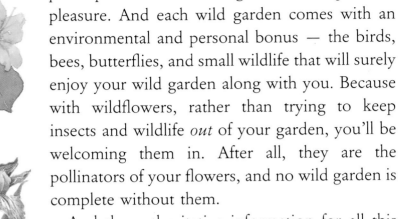

And the authoritative information for all this interest? After a long scarcity, good useful books finally are becoming available that go beyond the classic identification guides and the latest coffee-table compendium of mouth-watering flower photos.

This is one of those books. Here, you'll find clear concise information coupled with lovely but well-defined identification artwork. And this book is unique, to our knowledge, in combining identification and gardening information in one volume and in such an up-to-date organized fashion.

Welcome to the world of wildflowers. Whether you remain a casual observer, or end up nurturing hundreds of wildflower species on your own property, you've opened the door to a lifetime of fascination and pleasure.

Chy and Ray Allen

CHY AND RAY ALLEN, FOUNDERS/OWNERS
THE VERMONT WILDFLOWER FARM

INTRODUCTION

Growing wildflowers
will enable you to create
a beautiful garden, as
well as to contribute
toward the preservation
of America's natural
heritage.

Wildflowers: attractive and practical.

Wildflowers and You

The word wildflowers usually conjures up images of grassy meadows dappled with color. However, they grow virtually everywhere, from the darkest boreal forests to the high alpine tundra. Wetlands can flower profusely, while North American deserts literally explode into bloom after seasonal rains. In eastern deciduous forests, spring is heralded by the wildflowers that carpet the forest floor in their annual race to gather sunlight before the forest canopy leafs out and plunges them into shade. Even a freshly turned garden will host certain wildflowers, commonly known as "weeds."

As they bestow their beauty upon the world, what else do wildflowers contribute? They are green plants; that is, organisms that harness solar energy to make their own food and, in so doing, feed everything else and make all other life on Earth possible. Green plants constitute the most important part of any food web, a model of relationships within an ecosystem, likened by ecologists to a spider's web for its complexity and interconnectedness.

"So what?" you say, "I don't eat wildflowers." Perhaps not, although many are edible. However, most of the plants we and our livestock eat have been cultivated from wild, flowering plants. Wildflowers also feed many other animals, all of which are important in their own way and contribute to the healthy and diverse environment upon which our survival depends. Wildflowers attract many different insects, such as butterflies,

ABOVE *In addition to beautifying the landscape, wildflowers are also at least partially responsible for producing oxygen, humus, and food for many organisms, such as this black swallowtail.*

moths, bees, flies, leafhoppers, and others, some of which are the very insects responsible for pollinating many of our crops. These, in turn, draw predatory insects, and together they lure a variety of insect eaters, especially bats and birds such as flycatchers, swallows, warblers, orioles, and tanagers. The voracious appetites of a large assortment of insectivores assure that insect numbers are kept under control. The fruits of wildflowers provide food for still more birds and small mammals, which, in turn, feed small predators such as weasels, foxes, and hawks. This simplified example demonstrates the enormous ecological value of wildflowers.

Wildflower Anatomy

Wildflowers may be defined as flowering herbaceous or shrubby plants that propagate themselves and have not been selectively bred by humans to exhibit particular traits. Though they may vary greatly from one species to another, each plant can generally be divided into four distinct parts: roots, stems, leaves, and flowers. Each of these has different primary functions.

ROOTS

Roots anchor both the plant and the soil upon which they depend, and from the soil they extract water and nutrients, transporting them upward to the stems. There are three major types of true root systems: fibrous roots, taproots, and adventitious roots. Fibrous root systems are composed of masses of fine, branching rootlets growing in the nutrient-rich topsoil, where they collect precipitation before it sinks deeper into the ground. Taproots, in contrast, are large and fleshy, usually reach deep into the subsoil, and often store food. Adventitious roots usually grow perpendicularly from the axis of the stem and are typical of plants with climbing or creeping stems. They also occur on plants with

9

modified underground stems. Monocots (monocotyledons, which are plants having only one seed leaf) usually have fibrous roots, while dicots (dicotyledons, which are plants having two seed leaves) most often produce taproots. Some plants use a combination of these root systems.

STEMS

Stems support leaves and flowers in positions where they are best able to fulfill their respective purpose. They also house a vascular system of xylem and phloem, through which materials are transported from one part of the plant to another. Xylem only moves water and dissolved materials upward from the roots, while phloem moves substances either up or down. Phloem takes photosynthesized organic compounds, like carbohydrates and amino acids, either to the stem or the roots for storage or to the growing portions of the plant for immediate use. Stems may also be modified in some species to form underground food storage organs, such as bulbs, corms, rhizomes, or tubers.

· · · · · · · · ·

ROOTS *There are three major types of root systems: fibrous roots, which grow in threadlike masses; taproots, in which a fleshy or woody root with lateral branching rootlets reaches deep into the soil; and adventitious roots, which grow perpendicularly from creeping or climbing stems.*

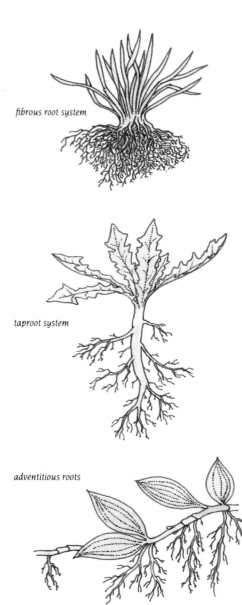

fibrous root system

taproot system

adventitious roots

· · · · · · · · ·

MODIFIED STEMS

Bulbs, corms, tubers, and rhizomes may be mistaken for roots but are actually underground portions of the stem modified for food storage. The division of rootstock, which includes both these structures and true root systems, is one of the fastest and most reliable methods of propagating perennials.

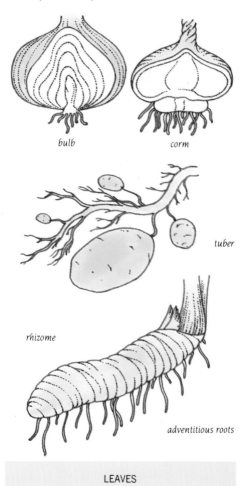

bulb   *corm*

tuber

rhizome

adventitious roots

LEAVES

Leaves are both solar collectors harnessing the energy of sunlight and factories producing most of the plant's food and molecular building blocks through photosynthesis. Leaves usually grow in a broad, flat shape, the blade, which may or may not be connected to the stem by a stalk, or petiole.

Leaves occur in an enormous variety of shapes and sizes. They may be simple (undivided) or compound (divided into a few or

palmate

pinnate

LEAF TYPE

Leaves may be palmate,

with leaflets radiating

from a single point, or

pinnate, with leaflets

opposite each other

and a terminal

leaflet at the tip.

entire

toothed

lobed

LEAF MARGINS

Margins may be entire

(smooth), toothed, or

lobed, or both toothed

and lobed. Teeth may be

fine or coarse. Margins

with shallow, uniform

lobes are said to be

scalloped.

alternate

opposite

whorl

LEAF
ARRANGEMENT

Alternate leaves occur

singly on alternate sides

of the stem. Opposite

leaves are located in

pairs opposite each

other. Three or more

leaves arising from a

single node form a

whorl.

many leaflets). Compound leaves may have either pinnate (leaflets extending from either side of the petiole) or palmate (leaflets radiating from one point at the tip of the petiole) configurations. Their edges may be entire (smooth), toothed, or lobed (which may also be characterized as pinnate or palmate).

Leaf arrangement is uniform within a given species. Alternate leaves originate from the stem with only one leaf per node, or point of attachment, but on alternate sides of the stem. Opposite leaves originate on the stem with two leaves per node, but opposite each other. Whorled leaves originate three or more leaves per node and radiate outward from the stem. Combined with previously mentioned characteristics, leaf arrangement is an important clue to the identity of any plant.

FLOWERS

Flowers are strictly reproductive structures, composed of modified shoots and leaves, whose sole function is to produce fertile seeds and ensure that as many of each individual's genes as possible are passed on to future generations. A flower begins at the tip of its stalk, or peduncle, and swells to form the receptacle, to which all other flower parts are attached. Though they vary greatly, most flowers include two or more petals, collectively known as the corolla, leaflike or petal-like sepals, which together form the calyx, one or more pistils, and few to numerous stamens. A typical pistil is composed of the ovary, which houses the eggs, a stigma, which receives pollen, and a style between the two. Each stamen consists of an anther, which produces pollen, perched atop a filament.

Flower shape is an important clue to species identity. Flowers may be either radially symmetrical (regular) or bilaterally symmetrical (irregular). An irregular flower, such as a violet, can be divided into two identical parts by only one plane, while a regular flower, like a buttercup, can be divided into two identical parts by more than one plane. The petals of regular flowers can be likened to the spokes of a wagon wheel.

Most wildflowers incorporate colors that have proven to be most effective at attracting pollinators, since this, in turn, results in more seeds passing on that color trait. Random mutations, a normal occurrence in every species, may result in occasional variations in color. Those colors more effective in drawing pollinators, or that lure a more efficient pollinator, will result in more

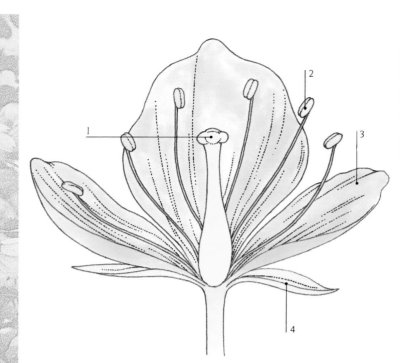

PARTS OF A
FLOWER A *typical
simple flower, with one
or more pistils (1), a few
to many stamens (2),
petals (3), and sepals (4).*

ABOVE *and* BELOW
LEFT *Many
pollinators, like
honeybees and
hummingbirds, visit
flowers in search of
nectar, a rich liquid food
source.*

individuals of that color in future generations, until the new color completely displaces the old. If the new color is less effective than the original, plants carrying that mutation will not compete for pollinators as well as "normal" individuals, and the trait will quickly disappear. What has been described here is an example of the process of natural selection, the driving force of evolution.

Which colors attact pollinators? One of the most effective, ultraviolet, is completely invisible to humans because it is above the highest end of our visible spectrum. To many insects, however, ultraviolet is a vivid and enticing color. Other colors frequently exhibited among wildflowers are various shades of purple, blue, yellow, orange, and white. There is a distinct scarcity, though not a total lack, of red wildflowers, and with good reason: Red is invisible to most insects and appears black to them. Most red wildflowers rely either on their fragrance to attract pollinators or on hummingbirds, which display a distinct preference for that color. Some reddish wildflowers also produce a fetid odor, which, in combination with their color, mimics rotting meat and draws various types of flies.

Wildflowers also use fragrance to attract potential pollinators. The vast majority of pollinators are insects, which have highly developed senses of smell, taste, and touch.

Wildflower Life Cycles

Not all wildflowers simply sprout from a seed, grow, flower, produce more seeds, and die. While this is true of annuals, many wildflowers are biennials or perennials (see diagram).

After flowering, the next step in seed production is pollination, the transfer of pollen from the anthers to the stigma, usually by a mechanism ensuring cross-pollination between different individuals of the same species. This promotes a random mixing of genes in the gene pool of that species and encourages diversity, which makes for a healthier, more adaptable population. Some species produce plants of separate sexes, while others delay maturation of the pistil until the stamens have

RIGHT

A hummingbird moth.

LIFE CYCLES

Annuals (1) bloom, produce seed, and die in one growing season, while biennials (2) require two. Perennials (3) persist over several seasons.

shed all of their pollen. Still others position the stigma so that incoming, pollen-laden insects encounter it before becoming contaminated with the plant's own pollen.

Most plants are either wind-pollinated or insect-pollinated. Wind-pollinated plants produce copious quantities of light, buoyant pollen grains that saturate the air currents, their sheer astronomical number ensuring that enough reaches other flowers of the same species. Insect-pollinated flowers produce heavy, sticky pollen grains that adhere to insects attracted to the flower, who then obligingly transfer the pollen to other flowers.

Once a pollen grain reaches the stigma on a flower of the correct species, it produces a fine pollen tube that conducts sperm through the style to the ovary, where fertilization of the eggs occurs. Afterward, the rest of the flower parts wither while the ovary swells with developing seeds.

Once the seeds mature, there remains the formidable task of dispersing them to suitable sites for germination in the next growing season. Seed dispersal is the primary means by which species colonize new areas; this is particularly important in the case of perennials so that the young plants do not have to compete with the established parent for sunlight, water, and nutrients.

The seeds of some wildflowers take to the air, using downy "parachutes" to ride wind currents, sometimes for many miles. Others employ Velcro-like hooks to hitchhike on the fur, feathers, or clothing of a passerby until they are dislodged some distance away. Many flowering plants produce fruit containing seeds which, after being eaten, pass through an animal's digestive tract to emerge elsewhere in a pile of fertilizer. The seeds of many wetland plants float away to their destiny.

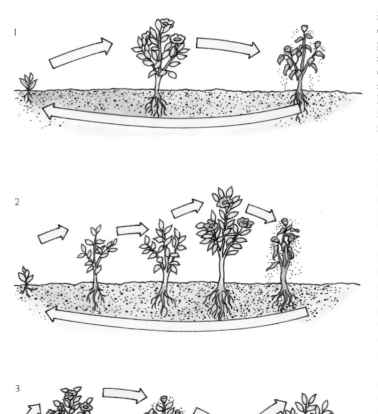

Wildflower Classification and Names

Taxonomy is the scientific discipline that puts order into an immensely diverse world and allows scientists around the globe to discuss any organism with the certainty that they are talking about the same species.

Scientists worldwide categorize organisms by means of a classification hierarchy, a system of groupings arranged in order from general to specific relationships. They are, in order of increasing specificity: kingdom, division (or phylum, in the animal kingdom), class, order, family, genus, and species. Each of these is a collective unit composed of one or more groups from the next more specific category. In other words, a genus is a related group of species and a family is a set of related genera.

Classification has always been a fairly simple affair, but not so naming or nomenclature. Normally, common names are used in everyday conversation, but by themselves they do not positively identify a particular species. Many plants and animals are known by different common names in different regions, and the same common name may refer to two or more distinct species. Adding to the potential for confusion, many species have more than one common name. Clearly, some sort of universal system is also needed.

By the early eighteenth century, Latin was commonly used in schools and universities, and it was customary to use descriptive Latin phrases to name plants and animals. Later, as books were printed in other languages, Latin descriptions and the names of organisms were retained. Since all organisms were grouped into genera, the descriptive phrase began with the name of the genus to which the organism belonged. For example, all mints known at the time belonged to the genus *Mentha*. The complete name for peppermint was *Mentha floribus capitatus, foliis lanceolatis serratis sub-*

RIGHT Plantago major is a prime example of the confusion that can be wrought by common names. Frequently known as broad-leaved plantain in English, this species is also reported to have at least 45 other English names, 106 German names, 75 Dutch names, 11 French names, and perhaps several hundred names in other languages. Like all other known plant species, however, it has only one recognized botanical name.

petiolatis, or "Mint with flowers in a head; leaves lance-shaped, saw-toothed, and with very short petioles," while the closely related spearmint was named *Mentha floribus spicatis, foliis oblongis serratis,* which meant "Mint with flowers in a spike; leaves oblong and saw-toothed." Though quite specific, this system was much too cumbersome.

In 1753, Swedish naturalist Carolus Linnaeus introduced a two-word system for naming organisms, the Binomial System of Nomenclature, which quickly replaced the older, clumsier method. This system easily identifies individual species by linking the generic name with another word, frequently an adjective. Occasionally, two or more subspecies are created out of what had been considered a single species; in this case, the subspecies name is tacked on after the genus and species. All scientific names are Latin, although some have descriptive Greek roots. The first name, or genus, is always capitalized, and both genus and species are either italicized or underlined. When more than one member of the same genus is being discussed, the first name may be abbreviated after it is first mentioned, as in *T. grandiflorum* for *Trillium grandiflorum.*

Classification of wild columbine.

KINGDOM	PLANTAE
Division	Magnoliophyta
Class	Magnoliopsida
Subclass	Magnoliidae
Order	Ranunculales
Family	Ranunculaceae
Genus	*Aquilegia*
Species	*canadensis*

Wildflower Conservation

Rare and endangered animals have received a great deal of attention in the last few decades. Most of us are aware of the plight of whales, California condors, whooping cranes, and other wildlife, but far fewer understand that many plants are also threatened. The common threat to both animals and plants is habitat loss. Monumental changes in the United States within the last century have accelerated habitat loss to crisis proportions. Foremost among these have been the settling of the West, the rapid expansion of agricultural land made possible by mechanization, and the spread of urban and suburban areas.

ABOVE "*Garden in the Woods,*" *Mass.*

THE PROBLEM

Habitat is a place or region that meets all of an organism's needs for survival. Every house, road, shopping mall, or factory built takes away habitat from the plants and animals native to that area. Current development practices, usually following no ecologically sound plan, carve up the landscape, creating "habitat islands" just as surely as if they were surrounded by water. The more isolated these habitat islands become, the more difficult it becomes for native species to move from one to another and balance their naturally fluctuating populations. Overpopulated species in isolated areas often suffer rapid population declines, brought on by disease, starvation, or both, while critically low populations may not recover because the chances of compatible individuals encountering each other to reproduce become too remote.

The marvelous diversity of life on Earth must be preserved for the sake of all its inhabitants. Genetic diversity promotes the mixing of genes to form new combinations, the key to adaptability and survival of all life. Once a species becomes extinct, it is gone forever, as are its genes and any future contribution that it might have made. Many of the so-called miracle drugs that have vastly improved our quality of life have been derived from plants. Who is to say that the showy lady's slipper, for instance, does not hold a cure for cancer, AIDS, or other diseases? One of the tragedies of extinction is that we can never know exactly what we've lost.

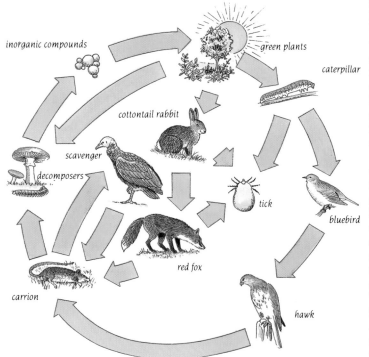

WEB OF LIFE All species on Earth are linked to one another in subtle interdependent relationships more complex than anyone yet understands. These intricate ties constitute what ecologists call the Web of Life, a very simplified model of which is shown above. As with a spider's web, if enough strands are disrupted, the Web of Life will collapse.

THE SOLUTION

Wildflower conservation is necessary to preserve the populations of uncommon species and to ensure that common species remain so. Wildflower preserves and botanical gardens may slow the rate of plant extinction, but their capacity in this respect is limited. While they are wonderful places to visit, they are but arks in a sea of human development. Once a rare species is relegated to refuges such as this, it is as good as gone.

There are courses of action that you can take to conserve wildflowers. First, become politically active in your local community. Advocate environmentally sound development policies, such as cluster development, in which homes and businesses are concentrated in a small area, while the larger surrounding region is left undeveloped and in its natural state. Question the need for all development, and actively oppose any that is unnecessary or ecologically unsound. Promote the creation of new parks and refuges and the expansion of those already established, and lobby government officials to keep them in their natural states. Support organizations like The Nature Conservancy, which buys unique and endangered habitats to preserve them.

The other course you can take is to start wildflower gardening. This can be as simple as replacing some of your cultivated varieties with native wildflowers, or as involved as landscaping your property with native species, re-creating one or more of the natural habitats in your region.

The remainder of this book is devoted to helping you identify, select, and grow wildflowers successfully.

Why Wildflower Gardening?

There are other reasons for wildflower gardening besides the noble cause of conserving wildflowers. Properly planned, a wild garden is attractive, *and* it requires much less time and money to maintain than a manicured lawn and shrubbery. Who can argue with that? Also, native plants are much more likely to thrive with less care than their cultivated counterparts.

FIELD NOTEBOOK

The most useful wildflower gardening tool is a well-kept field notebook. In it you should take notes about the wildflowers found in the natural habitats of your area, including information such as the common and scientific names, a description of the immediate area around the plant, blooming period, plant height, flower color, soil type, soil moisture, exposure to sun, nearby companion plants, and other relevant data. Such information, often not readily available elsewhere, will help you determine if that species is a good candidate for your landscape. Assign each entry a code number, which can be used to correlate your notes with a map of the area, photographs taken, or seeds collected. Also record the details of your wildflower gardening activities to help you keep track of your successes and failures and learn from them.

FIELD GUIDES

Before you can make the best use of your observations of a particular plant, you must first know what it is. There are many good field guides on the market that can help. One of the best by far is *Newcomb's Wildflower Guide*, written by Lawrence Newcomb and published by Little, Brown & Company. An easy-to-use key guides you to the pages on which the wildflower in question is described and illustrated. While *Newcomb's Wildflower Guide* lacks the flashy color photographs or artwork of other guides, its pen-and-ink illustrations are clear and detailed, showing all the identifying features of each species. Its sole drawback is that it only covers the northeastern corner of North America, roughly from North Carolina northward and from the Mississippi River eastward. Also very useful are *The Audubon Society Field Guides to North American Wildflowers*, whose descriptions are quite detailed.

OTHER TOOLS

There are a few basic items that wildflower gardeners will find useful. All are readily available and affordable.

● A good-quality glass hand lens, available from biological supply companies. Eight- to ten-power magnification is optimal; some models have several glass elements that can be used in different combinations to vary their magnifying power. Photographic loupes, sold in photography shops, will also serve well.

● Small paper envelopes or plastic bags in which to collect seeds. Always remember to label them immediately.

● A small tape measure. This is handy for determining plant heights and leaf or flower

dimensions to aid in identification. Also, when transplanting, there are often recommended intervals for spacing plants to avoid crowding.

● A sharp penknife is useful for pruning herbaceous plants and taking stem and root cuttings. However, if you are going to buy a knife, it might as well be a genuine Swiss army knife, which has a reputation of high quality and durability. In addition it has useful gadgets.

● A garden trowel for transplanting small plants, and also for separating root clumps during propagation.

● A spade, the blade of which should be kept sharp with a file. In addition to digging larger holes than can be managed easily with a garden trowel, a spade is useful for loosening compacted soil, amending topsoil with various additives like sand, compost, or peat moss, and mixing larger quantities of potting soil or rooting medium.

● A sharp pair of clippers to take cuttings for propagation.

· · · · · · · · ·

TOOLS *As with all other endeavors, the right tools can make a big difference in wildflower gardening. You will need: a field notebook, a good field guide, a trowel, spade, penknife, clippers, tape measure, hand lens, and paper envelopes or plastic bags.*

Site Evaluation

Your first step in wild gardening should be to identify what you already have. After taking a long, hard look at your property, you may be surprised at the number of wildflower species you'd previously dismissed as "weeds" as they clung tenaciously to their existence in your garden. If part of your property is wooded, wetland, or otherwise "unimproved," it's likely that you've already got a wealth of wildflowers as tenants. Note all trees, shrubs, and clumps of small plants, listing the species name, if known, as well as a general description. Since many species are rather fastidious in their requirements for growth, the plants already present can be a major clue as to what else will thrive there with little care.

A LANDSCAPE MAP

In addition to a wildflower survey, another preliminary step should be to map your property to show all fixed features, such as a house, garage, trees, utility poles, shed, pool, and so on. Using a large sheet of graph paper, let each small square represent 1 square foot, 1 square yard, or whatever unit will allow you to represent the entire property on one sheet. First, plot the boundaries of your property, the dimensions of which should be fairly easy to obtain. Now you have at least three known points from which to calculate the position of everything else. Using a method called triangulation, plot the location of your house, garage, and all features of your property that you plan to keep, including trees, shrubs, clusters of small plants, and established gardens. Once this has been done, the empty areas of your map will represent the "expendable" parts of your landscape that you have to work with.

EXPOSURE TO SUNLIGHT

The amount of sunlight that each site receives is one of the major factors in determining what will grow there. From the winter solstice, approximately December 21, until about June 21, the summer solstice, the sun traces a slightly higher arc in the sky each day. Over the next six months, the pattern reverses. Therefore, the date, combined with the location and the size of obstructions, such as buildings and trees, determines when a given portion of your property receives direct sunlight and how much.

It's easy to figure out which areas are sunlit at any given time. The direction of the sun at noon or 1:00 P.M. daylight savings time is due south. The height of the sun above the horizon at this time on the vernal and autumnal equinoxes (first days of spring and fall, respectively) is equal to 90 degrees minus your latitude (which can be obtained from any good atlas). The sun at this same time on the summer solstice would be 23.5 degrees, or roughly one-quarter the distance from the horizon to the zenith, higher. The winter solstice will find the noontime sun 23.5 degrees lower. Thus, the sun climbs about 1

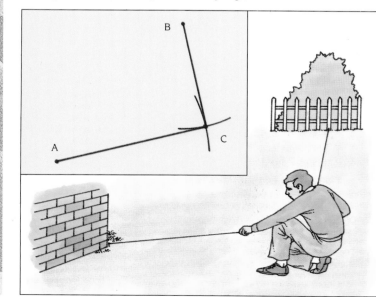

MAPPING BY TRIANGULATION

Suppose you wish to locate the exact position of a tree in your backyard. Using a tape measure, determine the distance to the tree from each of two known points, A and B, such as the two nearest corners of your property. Based on the scale of your map, set a compass at an interval representative of the distance from point A to the tree. (For example, if the distance from point A to the tree is 20 feet and ¼ inch on your map represents 1 foot, set your compass at 5 inches.) Place the point of the compass on point A and scribe an arc in the general vicinity on the map where the tree ought to be. Repeat this procedure for point B. The point where the two arcs intersect will closely approximate the location of the tree.

PLOTTING COMPASS DIRECTIONS ON YOUR LANDSCAPE MAP

Plotting compass directions on your map with the aid of a directional compass will help you envision which areas will be shaded at given times of the day and year. If you are able to read a directional compass and can find the bearing along one wall of your house or along a property boundary, simple mathematics will enable you to determine the angle between that line and magnetic north. (For our purposes, the difference between magnetic north and true north is negligible, so we will assume that they are one and the same.) Suppose, for example, that you found the bearing along one wall to be 315 degrees. Knowing that magnetic north lies at exactly 360 degrees, subtract 315 from 360, and you will find that the angle between that wall and magnetic north is 45 degrees. It is now a simple matter to plot compass directions on your landscape map with the aid of a protractor.

. . . .

SUN ARC Before planting so much as a dandelion, take time to become familiar with your site. Think like a wildflower: where is it sunny, shady, wet, dry, warm, cool, windy, sheltered? Draw a sun arc with your site's major features to help you envision which areas will receive sun or shade at certain times of the day and year.

degree higher every four days from December 21 until June 21, then declines at the same rate from June 21 until December 21.

To envision the sun arc using this bit of information, you must next determine the points on the horizon where the sun rises and sets. On the first days of spring (March 21) and fall (September 21), the sun rises exactly in the east, or 90 degrees on the compass, and sets due west, or 270 degrees. On the first day of summer, the sun rises at a compass bearing equivalent to 90 degrees minus your latitude and sets at 270 degrees plus your latitude. The opposite holds true on December 21, when the sun rises at 90 degrees plus your latitude and sets at 270 degrees minus your latitude.

Finally, we know that the sun appears to move across the sky at a rate of 15 degrees per hour (based on 180 degrees over a 12-hour period during the equinoxes). A 15 degree arc may be estimated by dividing the distance from the horizon to the zenith in half and then dividing that distance into thirds. Given this information, you can closely estimate the sun's position at any given time of the year. These

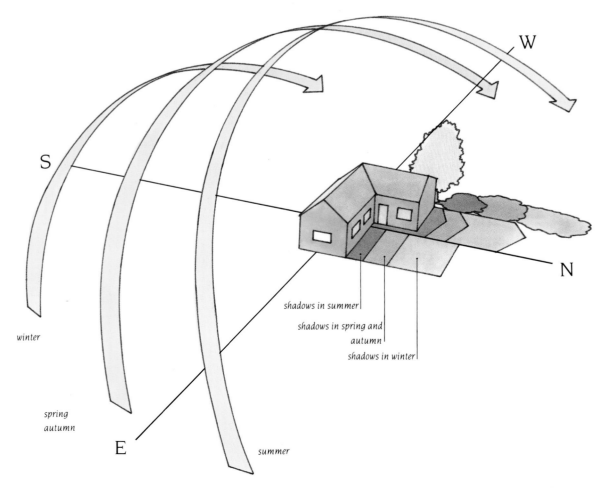

winter

spring
autumn

E

summer

S

W

N

shadows in summer
shadows in spring and autumn
shadows in winter

ZONE RANGE

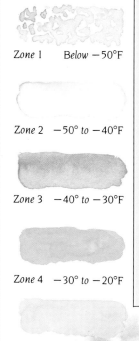

Zone 1 Below −50°F

Zone 2 −50° to −40°F

Zone 3 −40° to −30°F

Zone 4 −30° to −20°F

Zone 5 −20° to −10°F

Zone 6 −10° to −0°F

Zone 7 0° to 10°F

Zone 8 10° to 20°F

Zone 9 20° to 30°F

Zone 10 30° to 40°F

MAKING A SEXTANT

With only a protractor, drinking straw, string, and a nut or other small weight, you can make a simple version of this old-fashioned instrument of navigation to determine angular measurements above the horizon.

Secure the drinking straw along the protractor's base with cellophane tape. Next, suspend a nut, fishing sinker, or other small weight on a 6-inch piece of string, and attach the other end of the string to the exact middle of the protractor's base. With the protractor underneath, suspend the straw between two stacks of books that are exactly the same height so that it is perfectly level. You may check with a carpenter's level to be sure. The string should hang exactly over the 90 degree mark.

To measure a vertical angle, sight the object in question through the straw with the protractor underneath and the weight hanging freely. After the weight steadies itself, gently secure the string against the protractor by pinching the two between the thumb and forefinger of your free hand, and take the sextant from your eye to check the angle. Since the protractor is upside down, the result will be the angle from your target to the zenith. To find the target-horizon angle, simply subtract this figure from 90.

By aiming the sextant at the top of a potential shade-producing object, you can use your knowledge of the sun's apparent movement, taking into consideration compass bearing and time of day, to estimate whether the spot on which you're standing will be shaded at a given time of the year. The closer you are to ground level when taking a reading, the more accurate your estimate will be. Be aware that your sextant will only measure vertical angles.

USDA PLANT HARDINESS ZONES

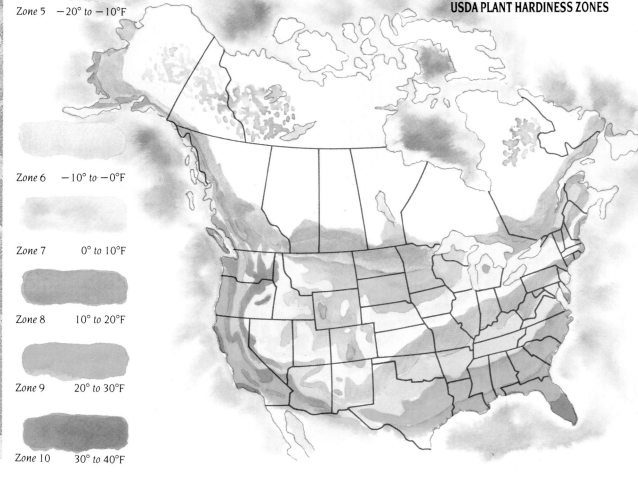

. . . .

HARDINESS ZONES

The native range of a perennial or biennial wildflower species, as well as where it will flourish in a garden, is determined by several factors, one of which is temperature. A single night of temperatures below its threshold can kill a plant. The United States Department of Agriculture has compiled a map of North America showing hardiness zones, which range in ten-degree increments from Zone 1, with an average annual minimum temperature below −50°F, to Zone 11, where the average minimum temperature falls between 40° and 50°F.

specific rules apply only to the Northern Hemisphere north of the Tropic of Cancer, but fortunately, that includes all of the continental United States and Canada.

TEMPERATURE

Various organizations keep numerous temperature statistics for the different regions of the country. These include the annual frost-free period, growing degree days, and hardiness zones. Average temperatures for a geographic region are largely determined by its sun arc, which is a function of latitude, and the USDA hardiness zones reflect this. However, temperature can also be influenced by other factors, such as elevation, where an increase results in relatively lower temperatures, and proximity to a large lake or the ocean, where closeness means relatively higher temperatures during winter.

CLIMATE AND MICROCLIMATES

Climate is the sum of a number of variables: sunny or cloudy, hot or cool, wet or dry, regular or seasonal precipitation, long or short growing season, high or low humidity, windy or calm, mild or severe winters. Every different combination of these variables will promote a different plant community whose members are adapted to those particular conditions.

Within an area defined as having a particular climate, there can be many different microclimates, small areas where physical or biological features cause conditions to differ from the average of that region.

Your property's orientation may create a microclimate. A given area on a north-facing hillside gets less energy from the sun than the same area on a south-facing hillside at the same latitude. This means that the soil of a north-facing slope gets colder in winter, takes longer to warm up through the spring, stays cooler in summer, and cools faster in the fall than that of a nearby south-facing slope. Level ground and east- or west-facing slopes, of course, fall somewhere in between these extremes. All of this contributes to a longer growing season on the south-facing slopes of a particular latitude than on slopes with different orientations.

Shade can produce cooler microclimates. Also, features cast longer shadows on north-facing slopes than they do elsewhere. This must be taken into consideration on sites with more than a slight pitch, when estimating the effect of the sun arc and the resulting micro-

climate. On the other hand, obstructions that shelter an area from the prevailing winds can create a warmer microclimate.

Water absorbs heat more slowly but holds it longer than either air or land. Therefore, proximity to a large body of water results in a more moderate microclimate than that of surrounding areas. However, if you live in a depression, such as a basin formed by mountain ranges, your microclimate will tend to be cooler than the surrounding area.

It's clear, then, that the microclimate of your site can largely determine what plants can be grown there. You may find a sheltered site with southern exposure that will support plants whose normal range is much farther south, or vice versa.

PRECIPITATION

As with all of the other factors we've discussed so far, there is tremendous variation in both the amount and pattern of annual precipitation within the United States and Canada. The water requirements of plants fluctuate with temperature, increasing greatly as temperatures rise and declining when they fall.

It is important to choose plants that can subsist on the natural precipitation in your area, a practice called xeriscaping. Perhaps the greatest offense routinely committed by gardeners is that of planting species that require more water than the normal precipitation patterns in that area will provide. Supplemental watering costs money, unnecessarily occupies the gardener's time, and depletes precious fresh water sources that may already be severely taxed.

Soil

There are basically two categories of soil: topsoil, the darker layer first encountered as one digs downward; and subsoil, usually a much thicker layer that underlies the topsoil. Soil is formed by the weathering of bedrock, as it is acted upon by both physical and chemical forces in nature. As this occurs, the rock is broken into smaller and smaller fragments, until it is reduced to its constituent particles. The size of the particles is determined by the type of bedrock from which they came. The largest of these particles is sand, and the finest is clay. Silt particles lie in between. The soil at any particular site may be original, or it may have been deposited there years earlier by floods, glaciers, or volcanic eruptions. However, gardeners should be aware of the possibility that the character of their soil may have been altered by past human activities on the site and their by-products, such as rubbish and toxins from construction or manufacturing.

SOIL COMPOSITION

Soil is typically composed of four components: sand, silt, clay, and organic matter. The proportions of these ingredients largely determine the character of the soil. Sand and silt are the chief sources of minerals required by plants, such as potassium, calcium, phosphorus, magnesium, copper, manganese, sulfur, zinc, copper, iron, and others. Silt particles are smaller than sand and have a relatively greater surface area exposed to chemical weathering, so they yield their minerals more readily than sand particles. Soils with a high proportion of silt are generally more fertile than those with less.

Organic matter, or humus, is decomposing plant or animal material deposited in soil. Organic matter is responsible for the soil's capacity to produce nitrogen, supports the community of soil microorganisms crucial to plant life, and retains bacterial by-products such as water, carbon dioxide, and other compounds. It also creates a moist environment critical for the transfer of minerals from soil particles to plants.

Clay particles are the finest component of soil. Soil with a high clay content has insufficient porosity, meaning that the pore space between soil particles is too small for water, air, and plant roots to penetrate effectively.

Porosity is an important factor determining the character of soil. Forty to 60 percent of

SOIL Soil texture is a function of the size of the constituent particles in the mineral soil. Sand particles are the largest, clay particles are the smallest, and silt particles fall in between. Ironically, the lightest soils are those containing the highest percentage of sand, because the volume of the resulting air spaces between the particles is correspondingly great. Sandy soil cannot be compacted nearly as much as clay soil, nor is it nearly as cohesive. As a general rule, medium soils, those with high percentages of both sand and silt and little clay, are the most hospitable to plants. They remain loose enough for air, water, and plant rootlets to penetrate readily, while draining and releasing minerals at a moderate rate.

		SAND	SILT	CLAY
LIGHT		70 Sandy	20	10
		60 Loamy sand	30	10
		50 Sandy loam	30	20
MEDIUM		40 Loam	40	20
		40 Clay loam	30	30
		30 Loamy clay	30	40
HEAVY		30 Sandy clay	20	50
		20 Clay	20	60

the volume of good soil is space between soil particles that is filled with air or water.

TOPSOIL

You will need to discover the character of your topsoil. The easiest way to obtain this information is to send a soil sample to the Cooperative Extension Service of your state's land grant university and request a comprehensive soil test. Such a test is also available from numerous commercial laboratories, although at a slightly higher fee than the very reasonable amount charged by an extension service. Most labs will send you a kit with detailed instructions for obtaining and mailing your soil samples. The test report should be received a few weeks after you mail the sample and will usually include soil texture, fertility, organic content, micronutrients, acidity, toxins, and recommendations for correcting significant abnormalities.

Soil types may well vary even within a relatively small area, so look out for indicators of this, such as a cluster of plants whose needs are known to differ from those of nearby vegetation, variations in topography, different bedrock, if exposed, and so on. If you suspect that there is more than one soil type on your site, have each questionable soil analyzed separately.

SOIL TEXTURE

Soil texture is the result of the proportions of different particle sizes within it, which in turn determines many other soil properties such as fertility, porosity, and water retention.

BELOW Plant or animal remains that fall to the ground, such as these maple leaves, are decomposed by bacteria, fungi, and insects and are eventually incorporated into the topsoil as a very important component called humus. Aside from enriching topsoil, humus also retains water and encourages a moist, slightly acidic environment that is ideal for the absorption of nutrients by plant roots.

USING COHESIVENESS TO JUDGE SOIL COMPOSITION

(1). Squeeze a handful of soil into a lump, or cast. (2). Roll the cast between your hands to form a cylinder, also called a thread. If you cannot form a cylinder, the sand content is high. (3). Pinch the thread into a ribbon. The longer, thinner, and more flexible the ribbon, the higher the clay content. Loam will lose cohesiveness somewhere between a thread and a ribbon.

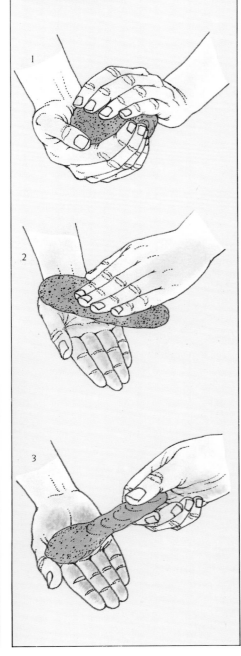

BELOW *The bulk of nutrients returned to the forest floor each year comes from fallen leaves. Invertebrate decomposers, such as insects and earthworms, mix humus into the topsoil, and their burrows enable air and water to reach plant roots.*

Clay soil is about 60 percent clay, 20 percent silt, and 20 percent sand. The fine particles compact, forming a heavy soil nearly impervious to plant roots and the oxygen and water required by them. Its gardening potential can be enhanced by mixing in large amounts of sand and organic matter. Adobe soil, a type of clay soil found in the hot, arid regions of North America, is baked hard and is quite difficult to manage.

Sandy soil typically contains about 10 percent clay, 20 percent silt, and 70 percent sand. The spacious gaps between these relatively large particles promote the rapid drainage of water laden with the soil's nutrients. This often results in a dry, infertile soil. Improve such soil by adding large quantities of organic matter.

Loam, characteristically composed of roughly 20 percent clay, 40 percent silt, and 40 percent sand, is the ideal gardening soil for many plants. Its composition encourages the retention of nutrients and water without saturation, and its texture makes it easy to work.

ORGANIC CONTENT OF SOIL

Humus, or decaying organic matter, is one of the most important components of topsoil. A healthy organic content, 3 to 5 percent, improves the water retention, aeration, fertility, and mi-

cronutrient level of topsoil, while encouraging the slightly acidic pH that is best for most plants. It creates a moist medium that facilitates the transfer of minerals from the inorganic soil constituents to plant roots. Humus could be anything that was once alive, but herbaceous plant debris generally breaks down more easily than animal remains. Some of the more readily available organic materials include cow or horse manure, peat moss, grass clippings, and leaves. Composting such material ensures that it will be in optimum condition to work into the soil.

SOIL FERTILITY

Generally, the darker the soil, the greater its fertility. Very fertile topsoil can be almost black, while poorer soils are usually lighter shades of reddish brown, yellowish brown, or tan. Waste soil, if it can be called soil, is the material found in places like railroad beds and road shoulders.

MAJOR NUTRIENTS

A soil's fertility is usually defined by its content of the major plant nutrients nitrogen, phosphorus, and potassium, often listed by their chemical symbols N, P, and K, respectively. Chemical fertilizers are available with these elements in various proportions. To fertilize soil naturally, first spade the soil to a shovel's depth, top it with about 6 inches of finished compost or manure, and work the organic matter into the soil. When you add fresh manure to soil, it must be left for about eight weeks while being kept constantly moist before it can be planted. After the initial application, a yearly addition of finished compost to the soil surface should be enough to maintain fertility indefinitely.

MICRONUTRIENTS

Like animals, plants need certain elements in minute quantities in order to grow and remain healthy. These include magnesium, manganese, calcium, zinc, copper, iron, sulfur, cobalt, sodium, boron, and iodine. Too much, on the other hand, will usually prove toxic to plants. The safest method of correcting micronutrient deficiencies is a healthy application of composted organic matter, since these trace elements were undoubtedly present in the living plants from which the compost was made.

SOIL ACIDITY OR ALKALINITY

Acidity and alkalinity are measured in terms of pH on a scale from 1 to 14, where 7 is neutral,

. . . .

ABOVE Fungi are

breaking down this tree

stump and will

eventually produce a

rich, moist, natural

seedbed. Gaps left by its

decomposed roots

conduct water and air

into the lower soil strata,

benefiting nearby

plants. Rotting logs

create the same effect.

numbers lower than 7 are increasingly acidic, and numbers higher than 7 are increasingly alkaline. Each whole number difference on the scale represents a tenfold difference in pH. For instance, a pH of 4 is 10 times more acidic than a pH of 5, 100 times more acidic than a pH of 6, and so on. Soil pH normally falls between 4 and 8.

The pH of soil affects the availability of nutrients necessary for plant growth. Magnesium, phosphorus, calcium, and potassium are most soluble when the pH is between 6 and 7; therefore, most plants prefer soil in this range. The pH of soil can be raised by adding calcium-rich (calcitic) or magnesium-rich (dolomitic) lime, depending upon which of these micronutrients is less abundant in the soil. It takes roughly 2 to 6 pounds of lime to raise the pH of 100 square feet of soil one unit on the scale, with clay soils requiring more than sandy soils. Add small amounts and mix it evenly into the upper 6 to 12 inches of soil, moisten the soil, and check the pH

again a day or two later. Repeat until it falls within the desired range. Acidity can be monitored with test kits, available through most garden-supply companies.

Mixing organic material, such as compost, peat moss, conifer needles, or oak leaves, into the soil will make it more acidic. Soil pH can also be lowered one unit by turning 2½ to 7 pounds of gypsum or ½ to 2 pounds of sulfur into 100 square feet, with sandy soils again requiring less than clay soils. Lowering soil pH via organic matter is preferable, however, because the change is more gradual and therefore easier to control and because the addition of organic matter yields other benefits as well.

TOXINS

Soil toxins are a difficult problem to cope with. Those you are the most likely to encounter are aluminum, lead, arsenic, and cadmium, all of which may be the result of previous activities on the site. While only aluminum is toxic to plants, the others are detrimental to humans, and so growing fruits, herbs, and vegetables is to be avoided in soils so contaminated. Your local Cooperative Extension Service can recommend ways to deal with moderate soil contamination.

Neither laboratory personnel nor the tests themselves are infallible, so if your soil test yields extreme results, it's better to repeat the test before taking any other action.

SUBSOIL

While topsoil can be altered, or even replaced, with reasonable effort, subsoil usually cannot and should not. The ability of the subsoil to retain water, which is related to particle size, is a major factor in determining what will grow on that site. Subsoil consisting mainly of clay drains poorly and causes the upper soil layers to remain saturated longer following precipitation or flooding, often resulting in somewhat swampy conditions. In contrast, sandy or gravelly soils are made of larger particles through which water drains freely, mimicking drought conditions at the surface, even in areas of moderate precipitation. Soil types may also fall anywhere between these two extremes.

The easiest way to determine which type of subsoil is under your site is to dig a hole and examine it. The darker topsoil will yield to paler subsoil, usually within ½ to 2 feet of the surface in most parts of the continent. The finer the particles, the more the soil will act like putty as you mold and smear it in your hands. This technique also applies to topsoil.

Choosing a Theme

Your wildflower garden will look most attractive if it is planned with a theme in mind. The theme should mimic a natural habitat compatible with the factors we've previously discussed, including rainfall, climate, microclimate, exposure to sunlight, temperature, and others.

If your site is wooded, marshy, or otherwise undeveloped, the simplest and soundest course is simply to build upon the natural habitat that's already in place. Replace the lawn in wooded areas with native shrubs, ferns, and wildflowers, and you've got a woodland wildflower garden! Rather than fill in that wet spot, stock it with native wetland species and create a miniature marsh, pond, or even bog! Always try to work with what you've already got. An

open "lawn," on the other hand, allows you maximum flexibility in selecting a theme, because any of several different natural habitats can be created on that site with about the same amount of effort. In any case, the key to implementing a theme successfully is to select plants that occur together naturally. Select a habitat compatible with the conditions on your site, learn which species are normally found there, and work only with them.

Wildflower gardens can be any size, from a window box on up, and it's okay to have more than one theme as long as they are kept separate. A combination of themes can make your property seem larger and creates the impression of a natural ecosystem composed of distinct, yet interrelated, habitats.

Elements of a Wildflower Garden

A wildflower garden does not have to be all wildflowers and nothing else. Many other features can be incorporated to make it more attractive and functional.

FEATURES

Paths. Whether consisting of brick, gravel, wood chips, or simply bare soil, paths allow access to the inner areas of your garden, while reducing the chance that delicate plants will be trampled. Meandering paths will look more natural than straight ones.

Ponds and Streams. Either natural or artificial ponds can create soothing focal points, while at the same time providing conditions for wetland and aquatic plants. Anyone fortunate enough to have a stream flowing through his or her garden can excavate a portion of the streambed to combine the tranquil nature of a pool with the mesmerizing effect of flowing water.

Bridges and Boardwalks. You will need to provide some means of crossing any wet places in your garden. Flat, stable stepping stones make an attractive stream crossing, or you can construct a wooden bridge, keeping it simple and unobtrusive. A wetland more than a few square yards in size may require a small boardwalk to provide access to the middle of it.

ABOVE *and* RIGHT
Wildflowers grow and look their best in a natural landscape with features like boulders, ponds, and fallen logs. Gravel or wood chip paths provide access while blending with the habitat.

LEFT *and* BELOW
Wooden, earth-tone
benches set
inconspicuously along
paths invite garden
visitors to linger and
enjoy the beauty. Large,
flat-topped boulders or
ledges also provide
resting places while
anchoring the
landscape.

Benches and Chairs. If you expend the effort to construct a sizable wildflower garden, plan to spend some leisure time there as well. An occasional bench or a pair of Adirondack chairs along the path or atop a vantage point will invite you to linger and admire your creation.

Rocks and Logs. These can enhance the natural appearance of your garden while creating attractive accents. They also provide a foundation upon which other organisms, such as mosses, lichens, and fungi, may grow. Use them judiciously, however, as they may look unnatural in gardens with certain themes, such as a wildflower meadow.

BELOW *Perennial*
borders, though more
formal in appearance,
are also attractive and
may incorporate
wildflowers as well as
domestic species.

ARRANGEMENT OF FLOWERS

Deciding where one plants a given species of wildflower in a garden has as much to do with aesthetics as it does with soil and other factors. Use the following guidelines to help you arrange your wild garden.

● Wildflowers that are normally found growing together in the wild will simulate their natural environment if intermingled in your wild garden.

● Avoid the neat, orderly rows of plants common to some formal gardens. The pattern of nature is randomness, and this is how wildflowers should be planted in a garden.

● Species of wild plants are often found in

27

clusters rather than scattered evenly across the landscape, so try to copy this tendency as well.

● Odd-numbered groups of a certain species are, for some reason, more aesthetically pleasing than clusters with an even count.

● You will want your wildflowers to be easily seen, so plant smaller and more delicate species closest to the path and progressively larger plants farther away. If the garden is to be viewed from opposite sides, plant the tallest species in the middle.

GROUNDCOVERS

True to the axiom that "less is more," a few individuals of your showiest wildflower spe-

. . . .

BELOW *Virginia bluebells and white-phase purple trilliums create a groundcover that is both attractive and functional, as do large-flowered trilliums (bottom).*

cies will be more impressive than hundreds of the same. To fill the gaps in between, you may want to incorporate groundcovers. These are plants that, by virtue of creeping runners, stolons, or rhizomes, form a low, self-spreading carpet of greenery that prevents the erosion of soil as well as shields it from desiccating wind and sun.

Groundcovers are most applicable to eastern deciduous forests, moist western coniferous forests, and clearings. Desert habitats are characterized by areas of bare soil interspersed with clumps of plants, so trying to establish an extensive groundcover here would be impractical. Likewise, the floors of drier coniferous forests found in certain areas of the South and West are covered more by fallen needles than by green plants.

There are scores of North American wildflower species that make good groundcovers. Some that are listed in the Wildflower Directory are:

Arctostaphylos uva-ursi	Bearberry
Campanula rotundifolia	Harebell
Chimaphila umbellata	Common pipsissewa
Clintonia borealis	Bluebead lily
Clintonia uniflora	Queen's cup
Coptis groenlandica	Goldthread
Cornus canadensis	Bunchberry
Dicentra cucullaria	Dutchman's-breeches
Dicentra canadensis	Squirrel-corn
Dicentra eximia	Fringed bleeding heart
Dicentra formosa	Western bleeding heart
Epigaea repens	Trailing arbutus
Gaultheria hispidula	Creeping snowberry
Gaultheria procumbens	Wintergreen
Geranium maculatum	Wild geranium
Linnaea borealis	Twinflower
Mahonia repens	Creeping Oregon grape
Maianthemum canadense	Canada mayflower
Mertensia virginica	Virginia bluebells
Mitchella repens	Partridgeberry
Phlox spp.	Phlox
Podophyllum peltatum	Mayapple
Polygonatum biflorum	Small Solomon's seal
Sanguinaria canadensis	Bloodroot
Smilacina racemosa	False Solomon's seal
Smilacina stellata	Starry false Solomon's seal
Tiarella cordifolia	Foamflower
Trillium spp.	Trilliums
Uvularia spp.	Bellworts
Viola spp.	Violets

ATTRACTING WILDLIFE

One of the many benefits of wild gardening is the resulting increase in wildlife on your property. The most plentiful of these is likely to be the insect species that feed as larvae, nymphs, or adults on the plants you incorporate into your garden. These include important pollinators such as butterflies, moths, bees, wasps, flies, and beetles. Hot on their heels will come the insectivores, including predatory insects, spiders, scores of bird species, bats, and amphibians. Some birds and small mammals will be drawn by the fruits and seeds of the wildflowers themselves, and hummingbirds will relish the abundant sources of nectar.

You can further attract wildlife to your property by incorporating food-producing trees and shrubs in your landscape, erecting nest boxes, creating brush piles for shelter, providing a water source, and many other techniques. For more information on this aspect of wild gardening, consult the excellent references listed in the Bibliography.

• • • • • • • • • • • • • • • • • •

ABOVE *Wildflowers can enhance your landscape year-round. After blooming, they set seed and attract birds.*

BELOW *While neither the red-eyed vireo (left) nor the yellow warbler (right) have any direct relationship with wildflowers, they are typical of the wildlife that is attracted by the many amenities of a natural landscape.*

Obtaining Plants

The time has passed when people could do as they pleased without regard to the effects of their actions upon our environment. There are no new worlds to which we can move when the old one fails, so we must take care of what's left. The human population threatens to overrun the Earth, and many plants are in danger of extinction.

Wildflower enthusiasts once collected most of their specimens from the wild because the consequences of their actions were less severe and not realized at the time. Today we know that such indiscriminate collecting, coupled with the problem of habitat loss discussed earlier, has indeed driven some plant species to extinction and pushed others to the brink. The removal of a plant from its natural habitat means there is one less plant with a chance to reproduce successfully and maintain its wild population. Not only that, but the shock of transplanting, or the lack of proper conditions, may kill the very plants collectors hope to propagate, and they will often gather more to try again. Realizing that it is in our best interests to preserve as many species as possible, environmentalists have defined acceptable means of obtaining plants (see box).

This is not to say that one may never collect wild plants. There are many species so plentiful that there is no foreseeable threat in collecting them. Many of these are referred to as "aliens," plants introduced to North America from other continents, usually Europe or Asia. These have coexisted with humans for many thousands of years and have evolved so as to thrive in the wake of civilization, which has become their "habitat." Alien plant species are generally those found in disturbed sites and waste soil, such as roadsides, railroad beds, construction sites, old fields, or pastures. Aliens are not usually found in natural habitats such as woodlands, wetlands, prairies, or deserts because they are not adapted to the specific conditions found there. These alien plants are so successful around human habitation that they are generally considered nuisances and labeled "weeds." Many will not wait to be collected but will volunteer themselves to your lawn or garden. Weeds are only nuisances when they grow where they are not wanted, and they can actually be attractive in the right setting.

Another instance in which collecting wild plants is acceptable is when they are facing

ABOVE *and* RIGHT
Trailing arbutus and fringed gentian are examples of wildflowers that are rare in their native habitats and should not be collected from the wild as mature plants. However, one may judiciously collect a few of their seeds without serious consequence to the species.

• • • • • • • •

ABOVE *Collecting and sowing seeds is an acceptable, although sometimes slow, method of propagating plants. Whenever possible, collect seeds of a given species over a wide region and do not take all of an individual plant's seeds. Seeds may be obtained from dry winter "weeds" by placing them in a paper bag and shaking vigorously.*

WILDFLOWER GARDENER'S CREED

● Do not take native plants from the wild unless they are threatened by development or other human activity, and then get the property owner's permission in writing before proceeding.
● Do not take live plants not threatened by human activity from the wild unless you know them to be extremely common over a wide geographical area, such as the alien "weeds" of roadsides and waste places. When in doubt, leave it.
● Whenever possible, obtain mature plants from a friend's garden, from a nursery that propagates its own stock, or from one that sells stock propagated by another nursery.
● Do not patronize nurseries you suspect of selling plants collected from the wild.
● When collecting seeds, take only what you need. Take only a few from each plant, and never take all of an individual's seeds. Try to collect the seeds of a given species over a large area. Better still, collect seeds from plants in your own garden or in a friend's garden.

imminent destruction from development. In this case, it is justifiable to take any plant species and give it a chance of survival elsewhere. Rare species, however, should be transplanted to the best possible site (within reason), whether or not that happens to be your garden. Of course, you should get the property owner's permission in writing before undertaking a "plant rescue," but many will not object if the site is slated for construction.

PURCHASING PLANTS

Gardeners should exercise great care to ascertain that the wild plants they buy were nursery-propagated and not collected in the wild. Reputable nurseries will readily volunteer the origin of their plants, and if plants were acquired from other nurseries or a wholesaler, your dealer should be able to find out how they were produced. Evasiveness or ambiguous answers to inquiries regarding the origin of nursery stock should trigger caution, and you should take your business elsewhere.

Despite assurances that the plants you want are nursery-propagated, trust your eyes when potential profits are involved. Look for the following warning signals suggesting that a plant may have been taken from its natural habitat:
● Poor or abnormal color
● Sparse foliage
● Weak stems or wilted leaves
● Legginess
● Scars
● Large size or obvious maturity, especially in slow-growing plants
● Off-centered potting
● A mixture of salable species in the same pot
● Plants potted with large stones, different soils in the same pot, or compacted clay, rather than uniformly textured potting soil

For the names and addresses of reputable nurseries in your area, contact your local native plant society, listed in Contacts.

PROPAGATING PLANTS

Depending upon the species, plants may be propagated from seeds, stem cuttings, root division, or root cuttings. Only seeds should be routinely procured from wild plants, and even that should be done sparingly. Seeds, rootstock, or stem cuttings may be obtained from plants in your own garden or that of a friend. Many commercial seed companies sell wildflower seeds, and certain nurseries will handle wildflowers as mature plants or rootstock.

Propagation from Seed

SEED COLLECTION

Pick larger seeds or fruits one at a time (1). Crush pods or dry seed heads by hand (2), or place in a bag and shake vigorously (3) to detach seeds. Contain airborne seeds, or those that are forcibly ejected, in a clear plastic sandwich bag as they mature (4) to prevent their loss.

Growing wildflowers from seed can be quite challenging and rewarding, but, except in the case of annuals and biennials, it is not for gardeners wanting quick results. The seeds of many species germinate slowly or with difficulty, and often the seedlings, especially those with fleshy, rootlike underground food storage structures like rhizomes, tubers, corms, and bulbs, are slow to mature and may not bloom for several years.

COLLECTING SEEDS

Seed collection can provide an interesting challenge to wildflower gardeners. Since flowering plants are generally easiest to identify when in bloom, it follows that you should seek out desired species during their blooming period, note their exact location in your field notebook, flag the plants with small pieces of brightly colored yarn, and return to collect the seeds about one month after flowering. The rate of seed maturation varies from one species to the next, and even within the same species in the same location from year to year, depending on climatic conditions. Therefore, it pays to closely monitor the plants from which you wish to obtain seeds. Most, but not all, fruits and seeds darken as they mature. Dry seeds are usually mature when the seeds or seedpods become dark, dry, and brittle. Moist seeds are mature when the color of the fruit surrounding them is most distinctly changed to bright or dark colors from its original green. When in doubt, and if the seeds are large enough, cut open one seed from the plant and check for the presence of a moist, white embryo, which indicates maturity.

Collect only a few seeds from each population of a given species. Although plants normally produce many more seeds than are needed to maintain the population, a certain percentage are nonviable, some will not chance to fall on a suitable germination site, and animals such as insects, birds, and rodents will eat others. Collect fruits or seed heads in paper envelopes or clear plastic food storage bags, each labeled with the common and scientific names, location, and date of collection.

Clean seeds by removing them from the flower head, fruit, pod, or capsule in which they developed. Some can be effectively separated by placing the fruits into a paper or plastic bag and shaking vigorously. (Be sure to use a separate bag for each species.) Beating seed heads against the inside of a clean, dry container may also work. Others may require threshing, loosening the seeds by the moderate beating or crushing of the fruiting structure inside a sturdy bag. Still others must be opened individually and removed by hand. Relatively speaking, the seed-bearing structures should come apart fairly easily; if they do not, that's an indication that the seeds themselves may not be mature.

After freeing the seeds, separate them from the debris in order that they may be sown more easily. The best way to do this is to use three or four sieves of different screen sizes. These may be either homemade from wooden frames and different-sized hardware cloth or wire screening, or purchased commercially from a horticultural supply company. Always start with the sieve that has the largest holes, and progress to

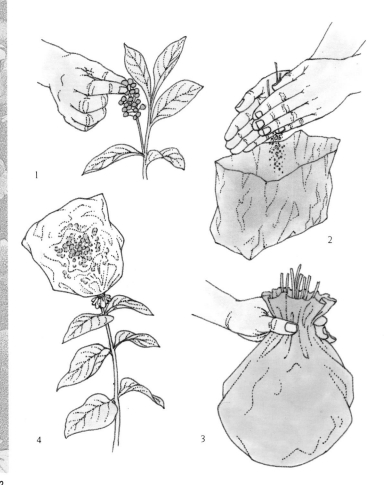

1

4   3   2

process of securing seeds for many species, there are potential pitfalls. Here are a few guidelines to follow if you choose this avenue:

● Write to the seed companies, explain what you want, and ask for a price list. Compare prices, since these can vary significantly from one company to the next. Also, test their knowledge of wildflowers by asking about any special recommendations they may have. Compare their responses with the information in this book and in the references listed in the Bibliography.

● Read the labels on the seed package. Make sure it contains what you want, and follow any special directions for storage or planting.

● Examine the seeds to make sure they are clean and free of insects. If they are not, return them and ask for a refund.

● If the seeds do not germinate within the time designated on the package plus a reasonable period thereafter, write to the company and ask for advice. If most or all of the seeds fail to germinate after you've followed the company's directions, ask for a refund.

● When planting a meadow, beware of commercial seed mixtures which often contain many annuals that give a quick burst of color in their first year but do not reseed themselves very well in your region. Also avoid seed mixtures containing species not native to or naturalized in your area. Instead, you should create your own mixture of six to eight species native to or naturalized in your region. Include a generous amount of native grasses to support the weaker-stemmed wildflowers, and make the whole affair look more natural.

● Whenever possible, purchase seeds from local companies, since the plants will be more likely to be acclimatized to the conditions in your region.

STORING SEEDS

Proper storage techniques vary considerably from one species to the next. The safest and simplest course in propagating plants from collected seeds is to sow them immediately after collection and cleaning in outdoor prepared seedbeds or flats. This will expose them to conditions similar to those they would experience naturally. When storage is necessary, seeds produced in dry pods or seed heads should be stored under cool, dry conditions, preferably in labeled paper envelopes in an airtight container with a small muslin sack containing silica gel, corn meal, dry sand, or another desiccant. Seeds, though dormant, are alive, and refrigeration will slow their rate of

SEED CLEANING

Some seeds are best separated manually or with tweezers (1). Mash pulpy fruit, place in a jar of warm water for a few days, then decant the pulp and water after the seeds have sunk (2). Crush seedpods or heads containing fine seeds and shake through increasingly fine sieves (3).

those with increasingly smaller openings. A small amount of litter will inevitably remain with the seeds, but this is not significant.

Seeds encased in moist, pulpy fruits should be separated as soon as the fruits ripen to avoid spoilage. Free the seeds by soaking the fruits in water overnight to soften them, mashing them gently with a wooden spoon or rolling pin and washing them through the sieves under a gentle stream of water. Any remaining pulp may be separated by means of a flotation technique in which the seed-pulp mixture is placed in a jar or bucket of water. The pulp will float while the heavier seeds sink, and the water and pulp may be poured off to retrieve the seeds. Seeds produced in moist fruit should be sown promptly and not allowed to dry out.

PURCHASING SEEDS

Many commercial seed companies now sell wildflower seeds. Though this simplifies the respiration and keep them fresh longer. Seeds produced inside moist fruits or those of wetland plants should be stratified in a moist medium inside an airtight container and refrigerated at 34° to 41°F. Place such seeds in a single layer between two damp paper towels, and sandwich these alternately between layers of moist sphagnum moss, peat moss, or sand inside an airtight container. Use separate containers for individual species.

SOWING SEEDS

It is best to sow perennial and biennial wildflower seeds outdoors, either in flats or prepared seedbeds, as soon as they mature, so that they are most likely to experience the environmental conditions that trigger germination. Sow the seeds of annuals directly in their desired locations. If you decide to sow wildflower seeds in the spring, wait until after the average date of the last killing frost in your area. It is not unusual for seeds to take two or more years to germinate, so be patient and do not discard uncooperative flats too soon.

A recommended potting soil for wildflowers consists of 1 part sharp sand or vermiculite, 1 part damp peat moss, 2 parts rich compost, and 2 parts loam. Add about 2 tablespoons of slow-release complete fertilizer per bushel of mixture, and sulfur or lime as necessary to correct the pH. Scatter fine seeds sparsely on top of moist soil and leave them uncovered, or cover them with a very thin sprinkling of soil. Sow larger seeds in rows at intervals of no less than ½ inch and cover with a layer of soil no thicker than twice their diameter. Remember to label each species with its name and the date seeds were sown. Water flats from the bottom, keeping the soil surface constantly moist but never wet, since seeds require oxygen and will die in saturated soil.

Seedlings planted in flats should remain there for at least three or four weeks following germination, until they have developed their second or third set of true leaves. They may then be transplanted to individual containers for at least another five or six weeks. Apply a weak liquid fertilizer, according to the directions on the label, to the soil around each seedling to prevent transplant shock. Those planted in seedbeds will need to be thinned or separated in order to avoid crowding. Seedlings should be transplanted to the garden while dormant, usually in their first fall. In colder climates, biennial or perennial seedlings should spend the winter in cold frames or under a heavy mulch.

SEED DORMANCY

The seeds of many wildflower species become dormant when they mature and, in order to germinate, must experience very specific environmental conditions, such as a period of alternate freezing and thawing, that are difficult to imitate. Dormancy is a safeguard which, through chemical or physical mechanisms, ensures that seeds germinate in the proper season so that they do not face harsh conditions, such as winter or drought, as vulnerable seedlings. Occasionally, wildflower gardeners are likely to encounter a species whose seeds do not germinate readily when planted under favorable conditions. The dormancy of such seeds can often be broken by using one of the following techniques:

● *Scarification*, tedious but effective, involves making a cut in the hard coat of each seed or scratching it with a file. Water is absorbed through this opening, the embryo swells, and the seed coat ruptures, resulting in germination. A short-cut method of scarification is to rub the seeds briskly between two sheets of medium-grit sandpaper.
● *Immersion* in hot water, 170° to 212°F, which is then allowed to cool overnight, will soften seed coats and help to deactivate any chemical inhibitors to germination. The seeds of some species respond favorably to immersion following scarification.
● *Stratification*, in which seeds are layered in a moist medium and refrigerated at 34° to 41°F for four to eight weeks, may destroy chemical germination inhibitors (see above under "Storing Seeds").
● *Alternate* freezing and thawing of the seeds. Freeze for seven days, thaw for one day, freeze for six days, thaw for two days, and so on.
● *Exposure* to light may also work. Sow problem seeds on top of moist soil in flats and leave them uncovered in full sun for several days; then move any woodland or shade-tolerant species to an area of partial shade.

Always withhold at least half of the seeds of any untried species until those planted have successfully germinated, thus ensuring a backup supply in case any of the above techniques needs to be employed. If all of the suggested methods fail to induce germination, experiment with them in combination. If you find, through experience, that certain plants undergo a dormant period, try collecting and sowing seeds just before they have fully ripened and developed hard seed coats or other germination inhibitors.

Vegetative Propagation

Obtaining new plants by root division, root cuttings, and stem cuttings from existing plants is known as vegetative, or asexual, propagation. These methods are generally easier and faster than propagation from seed. Even when done properly, they pose a small risk to the original plant, however, and should generally be restricted to those plants that have been growing in your garden or that of a friend for at least one year. Since the new plants will be clones of the original, it is important to choose a healthy, vigorous stock plant.

PROPAGATION BY ROOT DIVISIONS AND CUTTINGS

Dividing large clumps of plants growing from the same rootstock is probably the easiest and fastest method of plant propagation, since the divisions are essentially mature plants with fully developed root systems. Simply unearth the plant with a spade or trowel, wash the excess soil from the roots, and pull or cut apart rooted sections of the plant between the crowns, or upward projections of the rootstock. Rhizomes, rootlike underground stems, may be divided similarly. Dust cut surfaces with sulfur before planting the divisions separately in your garden.

Clumping perennials may be divided every few years to prevent overcrowding and to keep them healthy and vigorous. Spring-flowering plants should be divided while dormant in fall, and vice versa, so as not to interfere with flower and seed production.

Plants with very fleshy roots can often be propagated by cutting the root into sections, each of which will produce a new plant. Unearth and wash the roots as described above, then cut 2- to 4-inch sections from the larger root branches, being careful to leave enough of the root system to serve the parent plant. When planting these sections, it's important to orient them exactly as they originally grew so that the new roots and shoots grow in the right directions. To mark the sections for correct orientation, cut the end nearest the root crown straight across and the end farthest from the crown at an angle. Dipping the angled end into a commercial rooting compound, which contains hormones that stimulate root growth, will accelerate root production.

Plant the cuttings in flats containing a well-drained medium, such as a mix of equal parts of peat moss and sand. The straight end

ROOT CUTTINGS

Prune back aboveground in dormant season, unearth roots, wash, and sever a few young, pencil-size roots near the crown.

Mark the end closest to the crown with a perpendicular cut and the end farthest from the crown with a diagonal cut. Dab the diagonal cut in rooting hormone.

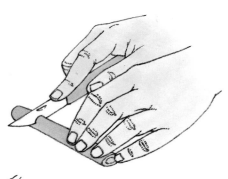

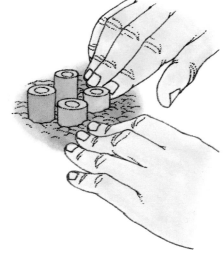

should be at the surface of the peat moss-sand mixture, which is then covered with about ½ inch of sand, tamped down, watered, covered with glass or plastic to maintain high humidity, and sunk in a cold frame or propagation frame located in filtered sunlight. You can also place 1- to 2-inch sections of fine roots horizontally on the peat moss-sand mixture,

Replant the parent plant at its original depth. Orient the root cuttings as they originally grew, with the perpendicular cut at the surface, in a moist, well-drained rooting medium. Keep humid in bright shade or filtered sunlight during their first growing season.

rather than embed them vertically, but the rest of the procedure is identical. Once the new shoots reach a height of about 3 inches, transplant them into individual containers to grow until they are large enough to plant in your garden. Add a weak liquid fertilizer, according to the directions on the label, when transplanting young plants to avoid shock. Mulch young plants for winter protection.

Bulbous plants can often be reproduced from bulb scales by following the same planting procedure for root cuttings, as can corms and tubers, which may be cut into pieces with one or two buds, or "eyes," per piece. Bulbs may also reproduce themselves in the garden, and the extra offsets may simply be dug up and planted elsewhere.

Like root division, root cutting should be performed during the plant's dormant season, preferably in fall or early spring. Mulch new plants for winter protection. While perennials with fibrous roots will often bloom in their first year, those with fleshy roots may take three or more years.

PROPAGATION BY STEM CUTTINGS

The best time to make stem cuttings is usually late June or July, before the plants have set any buds. A recommended medium for stem cuttings consists of 1 part vermiculite or sharp sand, 1 part damp peat moss, 1 part compost, and 2 parts loam, with about 1 cup of bonemeal added to every 20 quarts of the mixture. Equal parts of peat moss and vermiculite, peat moss and sand, or sand and vermiculite also work well, as does plain, moist sand. Plant stem cuttings in individual pots containing the rooting medium.

Remove no more than 10 percent of the aboveground portion of the parent plant if you wish to preserve it. Each stem cutting should include at least four leaf nodes, the lower two of which will be planted below the soil surface. Clip the leaves from the two lower nodes without disturbing the buds in the leaf axils. New shoots will develop from these axillary buds. Clip the terminal bud to stimulate root development and growth from the axillary buds. Dip the two lower nodes in rooting compound, insert the stem in a small hole in the rooting medium, fill the hole with sharp sand, and tamp down the surface. Water the pots from the bottom until the soil surface is moist, then place them in a glass- or plastic-covered cold frame or propagation frame (a rectangular aquarium works well) to maintain humidity, misting them as needed. Never

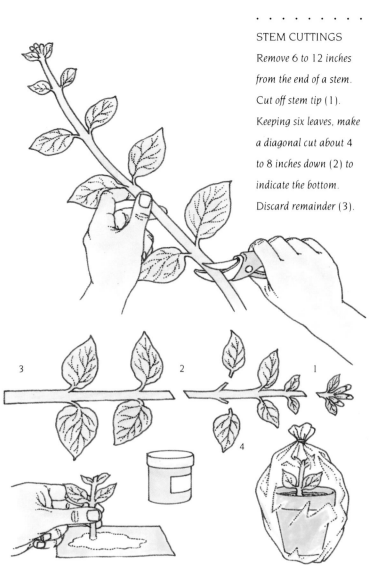

STEM CUTTINGS

Remove 6 to 12 inches

from the end of a stem.

Cut off stem tip (1).

Keeping six leaves, make

a diagonal cut about 4

to 8 inches down (2) to

indicate the bottom.

Discard remainder (3).

Remove lower two leaves (4), but leave their axillary buds. Dab lower half of stem in rooting hormone. Finally, insert stem about halfway (past nodes of the last two leaves removed) into moist rooting medium. Keep humid in bright shade until the new roots are at least 1 inch long.

let stem cuttings or the rooting medium dry out. Locate the frame in filtered, not direct, sunlight, and ventilate occasionally.

When the roots are 1 to 2 inches long, begin "hardening" the cuttings by watering less, ventilating the frame more often, and moving the frame into stronger light every few days, all over a period of about two weeks. When transplanting to permanent locations, use a weak liquid fertilizer applied according to the directions to help prevent transplant shock. Mulch young plants for winter protection. Those that have not made good progress after about four weeks should be kept in the propagation frame or a cold frame and mulched over the winter. Transplant them in the spring and water regularly until they are thoroughly well-established.

Maintaining a Wildflower Garden

In general, wildflower gardens require a minimal amount of maintenance – occasional pruning, thinning, transplanting, and weeding. However, it is important to bear the following points in mind:

● *Never* use herbicides, for they are likely also to kill the plants you are trying to establish. Weed by hand to eliminate unwanted species or individuals.

● *Never* use pesticides, for they will kill a multitude of beneficial species, such as pollinators and predatory insects, as well as the so-called "pest." If a particular species gets out of hand, seek a biological control specific for your problem. Remember that biological diversity is healthy, and avoid the compulsion to eliminate every individual of any species.

BELOW One of the *wonderful aspects of wildflower gardens is that, once established, they require much less maintenance than a formal garden*.

● Artificial fertilizers are generally unnecessary. They tend to encourage the growth of "weeds" at the expense of native species. In order to increase fertility, amend soil with natural additives like compost, peat moss, or leaf mold.

● Select species suited to the conditions in your garden, and avoid those native only to other parts of North America.

● Confine the roots of invasive species with metal or plastic edging strips sunk in the soil to a depth of 6 inches or more, or plant them in bottomless cans or drums sunk in the ground.

● Except for groundcovers and certain colonial species, give plants plenty of room in order to avoid a crowded, "weedy" look. Mulch bare spots to control unwanted growth.

How to Use the Wildflower Directory

The Wildflower Directory is arranged by general habitat to help gardeners find species likely to thrive on their property without having to page through the entire directory. Some of these habitat designations, specifically "Eastern Woodlands," "Prairies" (includes Great Plains), "Western Woodlands," and "Deserts" (includes southwestern grasslands), also correspond roughly to geographic areas of North America, while "Wetlands" and "Fields and Roadsides" are ubiquitous. Note that, since wildflowers don't read books like this, it is not unusual to find certain species in habitats or areas other than those in which the Wildflower Directory describes them.

Within each habitat, species are arranged by families (which in turn are listed in alphabetical order), because learning the characteristics that define each family is the surest way to make positive identifications. Remember that *Wildflowers* is intended to be used in conjunction with a good field guide. Even if the species in question is not listed in this book, knowing that members of the same family growing in the same region and similar habitats often have very similar cultivation and propagation requirements will enable a gardener to make at least an educated guess as to the species' needs.

Each habitat in the directory is preceded by a couple of introductory spreads describing it and listing basic gardening tips for its wildflowers. These descriptions should clear up any doubts as to which habitat you are dealing with at any given site. General range maps are included for all but the widespread "Wetlands" and "Fields and Roadsides," but

be aware that the ranges of many individual species are much more restricted and determined by their hardiness, moisture requirements, and other criteria.

In addition to the botanical name (**1**), common name (**2**), and family (**3**), each entry in the directory usually includes the following:

4 Description. A description of the plant's more noticeable features may include the flower's color, shape, size, and number and arrangement of petals; leaf size, margin, and arrangement; plant height; stem and leaf texture; and other criteria. Dimensions given are usually an approximate range and not absolute.

5 Blooming. The earlier date refers to the blooming of a species in the southern part of its range or at lower elevations, while the later date indicates the end of the flowering season in its northern limits and at higher elevations. Radical microclimates can alter these dates significantly.

6 Soil. Requirements include moisture, fertility, and specific needs such as high humus content and/or good drainage. Moisture content is designated as submerged, wet (when several drops of water can be wrung from a handful of soil), moist, dry, or arid. Fertility is designated as rich, average, or poor. Soil criteria listed indicate the ideal requirements for each species, but gardeners should be aware that most plants will survive, if not thrive, in less-than-ideal conditions.

7 Range. Geographic ranges generally start by roughly defining the northern boundary, listing the northwestern corner, occasionally mid-

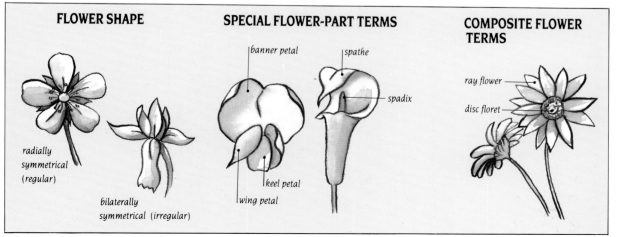

FLOWER SHAPE

radially symmetrical (regular)

bilaterally symmetrical (irregular)

SPECIAL FLOWER-PART TERMS

banner petal

spathe

spadix

keel petal

wing petal

COMPOSITE FLOWER TERMS

ray flower

disc floret

points, and the northeastern corner. The area encompassed by the range lies south of that line to the points indicated, usually the southeastern corner, sometimes followed by mid-points, and the southwestern corner. Those species restricted to the Pacific coastal areas list the northern terminus first, followed by the southern limit, and usually do not extend inland more than a few hundred miles. The boundaries of a range are rarely straight lines and often have many convolutions not evident in a simple verbal description. In addition, sites with microclimates significantly different from the surrounding area can host species well outside of their native range.

8 Propagation. Propagation by seed only is suggested for annuals and most biennials. Propagation of perennials may include dividing clumps of a single species, making root cuttings or stem cuttings, and sowing seeds. Propagation by seed occasionally is not listed because the seeds are too difficult to collect and easier methods exist. The intervals and depths recommended for sowing seeds or planting rootstock are merely average estimations, and most plants will tolerate moderate deviation from these figures.

9 Cultivation. This section lists the general criteria for maintaining healthy individuals. Symbols for hardiness zones, exposure to sunlight, and soil pH (acidity or alkalinity) are located at the bottom of each entry and follow the master key. The range of hardiness zones either is a composite of those listed in various references or, if not obtained from sources listed in the Bibliography, was determined by comparing the species' geographic range to the Hardiness Zone Map of North America compiled by the United States Department of Agriculture (see page 20). If the ranges err at all, it is on the side of moderation. Symbols for exposure and pH indicate the ideal criteria for each species, but like the other soil conditions discussed above, plants will often do well under less-than-ideal conditions.

10 Uses. When given, these recommend general locations for a particular species.

11 Similar species. Occasionally, a species similar in appearance and habitat requirements is listed.

12 Attracts. Symbols for seed- or fruit-eating birds or for pollinators, such as butterflies and moths, bees, and hummingbirds, that are attracted to the plant are shown at the end of the entry, when applicable. Occasionally, wildlife that eat other parts of the plant are also listed, even though they usually don't come in droves, the way pollinators do.

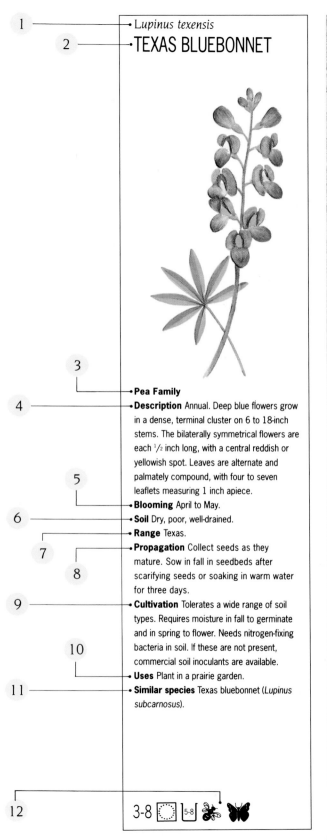

1 *Lupinus texensis*

2 **TEXAS BLUEBONNET**

3 **Pea Family**

4 **Description** Annual. Deep blue flowers grow in a dense, terminal cluster on 6 to 18-inch stems. The bilaterally symmetrical flowers are each $1/2$ inch long, with a central reddish or yellowish spot. Leaves are alternate and palmately compound, with four to seven leaflets measuring 1 inch apiece.

5 **Blooming** April to May.

6 **Soil** Dry, poor, well-drained.

7 **Range** Texas.

8 **Propagation** Collect seeds as they mature. Sow in fall in seedbeds after scarifying seeds or soaking in warm water for three days.

9 **Cultivation** Tolerates a wide range of soil types. Requires moisture in fall to germinate and in spring to flower. Needs nitrogen-fixing bacteria in soil. If these are not present, commercial soil inoculants are available.

10 **Uses** Plant in a prairie garden.

11 **Similar species** Texas bluebonnet (*Lupinus subcarnosus*).

12 3-8 5-8

1

EASTERN WOODLANDS

Eastern Woodlands encompasses all the forest types east of the Great Plains, as well as the vast boreal forest that stretches from Alaska to Labrador.

Large-flowered trillium

In the eastern deciduous forests of North America, life for most wildflowers is a race, a classic case of the early bird getting the worm, or, in this case, getting the sunlight. As deciduous trees awaken from their winter dormancy and unfurl their new leaves, they inadvertently plunge the forest floor into shade, blocking out as much as 95 percent of the available sunlight before it can reach the herb layer, that ground-level stratum of the forest where nearly all of its wildflowers grow. Wildflowers have responded to this environmental pressure by co-evolving so that many emerge before the trees leaf out. They work quickly to convert the early spring sunshine into food, to be stored or used immediately for growth and the development of flowers and fruit. Most eastern woodland wildflowers are perennials, and by the time leaves fill in the forest canopy, the majority will have already grown, flowered, and stored enough energy, in their underground stems or roots, to develop fruit and sustain the plant until the following spring. The others either stick to woodland borders or clearings, where direct sunlight remains available, or they are more shade-tolerant and able to sustain themselves on indirect light.

Eastern forests are generally moist places. They receive relatively high levels of precipitation, distributed fairly evenly throughout the

• • • • • • • • •

ABOVE *and* LEFT

Round-lobed hepatica
and trout lily are two of
the more common early
spring wildflowers in
eastern deciduous
woodlands. Dry forests
suit round-lobed
hepatica, while trout lily
prefers a rich, moist
habitat.

year, so normally there is no dry season with which plants must contend. Dense vegetation creates an effective windbreak, greatly reducing the volume of moisture-robbing air flowing through eastern woodlands. The forest canopy reflects a large percentage of sunlight, keeping both the woodland soil and air cooler and reducing the potential for evaporation. Finally, the thick layer of leaf mold, carpeting the forest floor, presents a barrier that allows moisture to seep through to the soil fairly quickly, but inhibits its evaporation back to the air.

Soil in eastern forests is usually quite fertile. Plant roots, moving imperceptibly, act as a giant churn, slowly but steadily contributing to the weathering of rock into soil, yet holding it firmly in place once formed. There is also a continuous flow of organic debris dropping onto the forest floor, from dead trees to animal carcasses, as well as the annual shedding of deciduous leaves. Since decomposing microorganisms slow down in cooler temperatures and virtually cease operations below freezing, the recycling of organic matter in temperate regions proceeds at a rate that allows a high amount of humus, or partially decomposed organic matter, to remain in the topsoil.

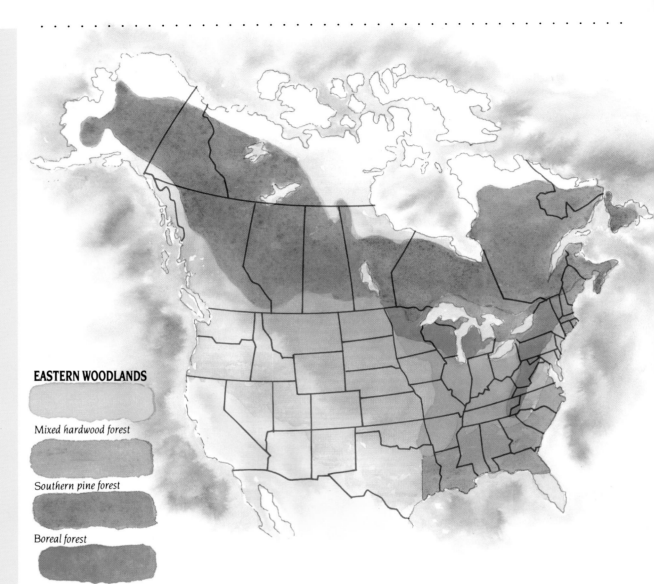

EASTERN WOODLANDS

Mixed hardwood forest

Southern pine forest

Boreal forest

Northern hardwood forest

Humus soaks up and retains water like a sponge, prevents soil from compacting and suffocating plant roots, and provides vital nutrients not available from other sources.

"Eastern forests" is a very broad category that encompasses many smaller yet sizable forest types, each with its own characteristic plant community, determined by the combined effects of geography, climate, soil type, and previous vegetation. There is, for example, the boreal forest, that great spruce/fir-dominated woodland that stretches in a wide band across most of Canada and Alaska, but ventures into the eastern United States only in the northernmost regions of Minnesota, Michigan, New York, and New England, and southward on

LEFT Bloodroot, common along deciduous woodland streams, is named for the red juice in its rhizome. Once used medicinally, this juice is caustic, so avoid contact with skin.

GARDENING TIPS

● Provide summer shade. If a wooded area is not available, many woodland plants can be grown successfully in the shade of a structure such as a house or trellis.

● Work the soil thoroughly to a depth of at least 12 inches.

● Introduce plenty of organic matter into the soil. Composted leaves, grass clippings, vegetable scraps, and manure work well, as does peat moss.

● Add sand to clay soils to improve drainage.

● Create a layer of leaf mold, if none exists, by depositing fallen leaves on the garden each autumn. While contributing humus to the soil, the leaf mold functions as a mulch to retain soil moisture and for protection from the winter cold and summer sun.

● Encourage fungi, which help to recycle nutrients for woodland plants.

● Incorporate other elements of a forest into the garden, such as rocks, logs, and fallen branches.

LEFT *Cheerful and elegant, wild columbine is a favorite source of nectar for hummingbirds and bumblebees. It is partial to rocky, deciduous woodlands, clearings, and meadows.*

ABOVE *Virginia bluebells frequent moist, deciduous floodplain forests of the central Appalachian region, sometimes growing in spectacular masses.*

the highest Appalachian mountains. South of the boreal forest, the northern hardwood forest, characterized by a preponderance of beech, maples, and birches, cuts a broad swath through southern Ontario and the northeastern United States. Farther south, we find the mixed hardwood forest, composed mainly of oaks and hickories. Then there are the cove forests of the southern Appalachians, which are veritable melting pots of plant species, and to the east and south along the coastal plain lie the southern pine forests. Forest types also vary with elevation; while climbing a 4,000-foot mountain in Georgia, one passes through the same forest types as if traveling 1,200 miles to the north at the same elevation!

Zephyranthes atamasco
ATAMASCO LILY

Amaryllis Family

Description Perennial. Basal leaves are 8 to 14 inches long, shiny, grooved, grasslike, and grow from an underground bulb. Single stem is leafless, 8 to 12 inches tall, and bears a funnel-shaped white flower tinted with pink.

Blooming April to June.

Soil Moist, rich, high humus.

Range Virginia south to Florida and Mississippi.

Propagation Sow seeds in outdoor flats or seedbeds upon collection, or in flats indoors or in cold frames in late winter, and cover with 1/4 inch of soil. Transplant from flats to small pots after eight to ten weeks, when roots are about 1 inch long. Divide bulb clusters of mature plants near the end of the growing season, replant 2 inches deep, and water thoroughly.

Cultivation Grows under a variety of conditions, but prefers woodland borders with at least a few hours of direct sun every day and moist, acidic loam or sandy soil. Space new plants and divisions 6 inches apart. In colder climates, store bulbs in a cool indoor location over winter. Deter burrowing rodents by planting in a large pot and sinking that in the soil.

7-10 6-7

Arisaema triphyllum
JACK-IN-THE-PULPIT

Arum Family

Description Perennial. One or two long-stemmed compound leaves, each 6 to 24 inches tall with three leaflets, form a canopy over this unusual flower. A ridged, hooded spathe striped with purplish brown or pale green encloses an erect, brown spadix covered with miniscule male or female flowers. Sex of flowers may change from year to year.

Blooming April to June.

Soil Wet, rich, high humus.

Range Minnesota to New Brunswick, south to Louisiana and northern Florida.

Propagation Remove seeds from red berries in August or September and plant immediately 1/2 inch deep in a woodland garden, in seedbeds, or in flats to be left out over winter. Transplant seedlings from flats to pots at the end of the first growing season, and into garden at the end of the second growing season. Divide corms in fall and space pieces at least 6 inches apart at depths three times their diameter.

Cultivation Requires constantly moist or wet, humus-rich soil in moderate shade. Mulch in colder regions.

Uses Strictly for shady woodland gardens.

3-9  5-6 🐦

Podophyllum peltatum
MAYAPPLE

Barberry Family

Description Perennial. A single, nodding flower, 2 inches wide, with six to nine waxy, white petals, arises on a short stalk from the crotch between twin umbrella-like, deeply lobed leaves. It grows 12 to 18 inches tall.

Blooming April to June.

Soil Moist, rich, high humus.

Range Southern Minnesota, southern Ontario, and southern New Hampshire south to Georgia and eastern Texas.

Propagation Divide rhizomes in fall, leaving at least one bud per piece. Plant rhizome segments horizontally, about 1 inch deep and 12 inches apart, with bud pointing upward. Mulch with 1 inch of deciduous leaf litter. Propagation from seeds is difficult. Remove seeds as soon as fruit ripens, July through September, and plant 1/2 inch deep in outdoor flats. Transplant to pots at the end of the first growing season and into the garden at the end of the second growing season.

Cultivation Soil must be constantly moist. Grows only in deciduous woodlands. Mulch with deciduous leaves over winter.

Uses Excellent groundcover for shady woodlands, but aggressive and may crowd out more delicate species.

4-8  4-7 🐝

Jeffersonia diphylla
TWINLEAF

Barberry Family

Description Perennial. Solitary white flower, 2 inches wide, eight petals, on a leafless stalk 6 to 12 inches tall. Long-stemmed basal leaves, each deeply divided into two lobes.

Blooming April to May.

Soil Moist, rich, high humus.

Range Southern Wisconsin, southern Ontario, and western New York south to Virginia and Iowa.

Propagation Sow seeds immediately after collection in June or July; do not allow to dry! Sow in shaded outdoor flats or seedbeds in well-drained soil rich in humus, and keep evenly moist throughout the growing season. Germination may take two years. Transplant slow-growing seedlings into the garden after their second growing season. Near the end of the growing season, divide rhizomes into large segments, each with at least two buds and several roots, and replant horizontally, buds facing upward. Plant singly for accents or space 6 inches apart to form colonies.

Cultivation Prefers alkaline soils. If soil is acidic, dust once a year with lime around the base. Requires constant moisture and a soil rich in humus. Mulch with compost or leaf mold before and after the growing season.

Lobelia siphilitica
GREAT LOBELIA

Bluebell Family

Description Perennial. Bright blue flowers are located in leaf axils on the upper portion of a leafy 1 to 4-foot stem. Flowers, 1 inch long, are composed of two lips, the upper one having two lobes and the lower, three lobes. Leaves are 2 to 6 inches long, opposite, toothed, and oval with wavy or irregularly toothed margins.

Blooming August to September.

Soil Wet, rich.

Range Minnesota to Vermont, south to eastern Virginia, western North Carolina, northern Alabama, and eastern Kansas.

Propagation Collect seeds in early fall and sow in outdoor flats. Transplant to pots or garden after the first growing season. Seeds self-sow in wet areas. Divide clumps of stringy, white, fibrous roots in spring. Prune roots to 2 to 3 inches and replant with crowns at soil surface, spaced 12 or more inches apart.

Cultivation Does best in wet woodland clearings and borders, and also in wet meadows with full sun to light shade. Mulch over in winter.

4-7

Triodanis perfoliata
VENUS'S LOOKING GLASS

Bluebell Family

Description Annual. Star-shaped purplish blue flowers occur singly, in axils of alternate leaves, on the upper portion of a 6 to 20-inch stem. Flowers are 3/4 inch wide with five pointed petals. Leaves are heart-shaped, less than 1 inch wide, and have scalloped margins.

Blooming May to August.

Soil Dry, poor.

pH Unknown.

Range British Columbia to Maine, south to Florida, Texas, and northern California.

Propagation In fall, collect and sow seeds in the garden, seedbeds, or outdoor flats. Transplant seedlings in late spring, if necessary. Self-sows readily.

Cultivation Requires little care. Full to partial sun.

Uses Good, quick filler for spots with poor soil.

4-9

Key

5-6 zone

exposure

full shade

light shade

part sun

full sun

4-5 pH

 attracts

 attracts

attracts

attracts

Mertensia virginica
VIRGINIA BLUEBELLS

Borage Family

Description Perennial. Stems 12 to 24 inches tall terminate with drooping clusters of light blue, trumpet-shaped flowers. Oval, thick-veined leaves with smooth margins alternate on the stem. Stem leaves are 2 to 5 inches long.

Blooming March to June.

Soil Wet, rich, high humus.

Range Minnesota, southern Ontario, and western New York south to North Carolina, northern Alabama, and Arkansas.

Propagation Sow seeds in shaded outdoor flats or seedbeds immediately after collection. Transplant seedlings into the garden near the end of their first growing season. Just as mature plants turn yellow and enter dormancy, divide root mass into clusters 2 to 3 inches across, replant 2 inches deep and at least 18 inches apart, and water immediately.

Cultivation In drier areas, mulch plants with decaying leaves to conserve moisture and for winter protection.

3-7   5-7

Aquilegia canadensis
WILD COLUMBINE

Buttercup Family

Description Perennial. Nodding red and yellow flowers, with five upward-spurred petals, dangle from the tips of branching stems. Long yellow stamens hang below the flower. Leaves are alternate, long-stalked, and compound, divided into lobed leaflets grouped in threes.

Blooming April to July.

Soil Dry, average, well-drained.

Range Minnesota to New Brunswick, south to northern Georgia and northeastern Texas.

Propagation Collect seeds in summer and sow heavily on the surface of outdoor flats or seedbeds (wild columbine seeds will not germinate without exposure to light). Following germination in spring, thin to $1/2$-inch spacing and wait about seven weeks before transplanting to individual pots or garden. Self-sows readily. Mature rootstock is difficult to divide or transplant successfully.

Cultivation Prospers in woodland borders or open deciduous forest, but also does well in meadows. Amend well-drained soil with a moderate amount of humus. Water weekly during drought. Full sun to light shade.

Uses Attractive in rock gardens, against a rock ledge, or above a garden pool.

3-8   5-7

Actaea pachypoda
WHITE BANEBERRY

Buttercup Family

Description Perennial. Dense, oblong terminal cluster of white flowers, each $1/4$ inch wide, on an erect 1 to 2-foot stem. Later, shiny white berries, each borne on a thick red stalk and possessing a black dot, replace the flowers. Compound leaves are composed of oval, coarsely toothed leaflets.

Blooming May to June.

Soil Moist, rich, high humus.

Range Manitoba to Nova Scotia, south to northern Georgia and Oklahoma.

Propagation As soon as the berries ripen in August, sow seeds in seedbeds or outdoor flats and keep moist. Transplant to the garden at the end of the first growing season. Divide rootstock in fall, leaving several buds per segment, and plant segments 1 inch deep and 24 inches apart, and mulch with leaves.

Cultivation Plant in cool shade and keep soil moist. Mulch heavily in fall, preferably with oak or beech leaves.

Uses Berries make nice accents against ferns.

Attracts Chipmunks, white-footed mice.

3-8   5-6

Hepatica americana
ROUND-LOBED HEPATICA

Buttercup Family

Description Perennial. Several fuzzy, leafless stalks bear pink, lavender, blue, or white flowers, each about 1 inch wide with five to nine oval, petal-like sepals and no petals. The basal leaves are leathery, wine-colored on the underside, and have three distinct, rounded lobes. New leaves grow after flowering. Height is 4 to 6 inches.

Blooming March to May.

Soil Moist, rich, high humus.

Range Manitoba to Nova Scotia, south to northern Florida and Alabama.

Propagation Collect seeds as they mature, usually in May or June, and sow 1/4 inch deep in shaded seedbeds or outdoor flats and mulch lightly. Divide rootstocks in fall, taking care not to break off the evergreen foliage, plant divisions 12 inches apart with crowns at the soil surface, and mulch lightly.

Cultivation To encourage self-sowing and establish denser colonies, wait until seeds mature, cover the plants lightly with mulch, and water thoroughly. Mulch plants, preferably with oak or beech leaves, in fall, but remove mulch in early spring.

Uses Good groundcover when grown in large colonies. Attractive in shaded rock gardens.

3-9 ⬚ 4-6

Anemone quinquefolia
WOOD ANEMONE

Buttercup Family

Description Perennial. A solitary flower, white above, pink to purple on the underside, and composed of four to nine petal-like sepals and no petals, rises on a long stalk above a whorl of three deeply divided leaves. Each leaf is palmately divided into three to five segments, each 1 to 1 1/2 inches in length, and sharply toothed. Plant is 3 to 8 inches tall.

Blooming April to June.

Soil Moist, rich.

Range Southern Quebec to Nova Scotia, south to North Carolina, Kentucky, and Ohio.

Propagation Seeds mature quickly after flowering. Sow immediately in outdoor flats or seedbeds. Rhizome will self-propagate, sending up new shoots as it forks. Divide rhizome in fall and plant segments 1 inch deep and 6 inches apart, with buds facing upward. Apply a light mulch about 1 inch thick.

Cultivation Mulch over winter.

Uses Plant in large colonies to create a groundcover.

4-7 ⬚ 5-6

Anemonella thalictroides
RUE ANEMONE

Buttercup Family

Description Perennial. Several long-stalked white, pink-tinged, or lavender-tinged flowers radiate from a whorl of leaflets, each about 1 inch wide with three rounded lobes. Each flower consists of 5 to 10 petal-like sepals and lacks petals. Plant height is 4 to 8 inches.

Blooming April to June.

Soil Dry, average, high humus.

Range Minnesota to southern Maine, south to Georgia and Oklahoma.

Propagation Seeds mature quickly. Sow in outdoor flats or seedbeds as soon as they mature. Divide the cluster of tubers in fall, making sure each has at least one bud. Plant segments 1 inch deep and 4 or more inches apart, and mulch with small or shredded leaves.

Cultivation Will grow in moist or dry soil, but prefers filtered or partial sunlight.

Uses Attractive in rocky terrain.

4-8 ⬚ 5-7

Key

5-6 zone

exposure

⬚ full shade

⬚ light shade

⬚ part sun

○ full sun

4-5 pH

 attracts

 attracts

 attracts

attracts

Cimicifuga racemosa
BLACK COHOSH

Buttercup Family

Description Perennial. Large plant (3 to 8 feet tall) with very tall wands of small white flowers. Flowers are $1/2$ inch wide with four to five petal-like sepals that usually drop off as the flower opens; petals are absent. The large leaves are doubly compound (twice divided) in threes. Each leaflet is soft, hairy, sharply toothed, measures up to 4 inches long, and may or may not have three pointed lobes.

Blooming June to September.

Soil Moist, rich, high humus, well-drained.

Range Wisconsin to Massachusetts, south to northern Georgia, Tennessee, and Missouri.

Propagation Divide rootstock in fall, leaving several buds per division. Space sections 3 feet apart with buds 1 inch deep in soil, and mulch with leaf mold or compost. Sow seeds in flats containing fertile woodland soil, and transplant seedlings to permanent locations in the garden when dormant in fall. Seedlings take three to four years to bloom.

Cultivation Requires constant moisture and light to deep shade. Mulch with leaves over winter.

Uses Place in the back of mixed plantings; also good for borders or rock gardens.

5-7 5-6

Aster macrophyllus
BIGLEAF ASTER

Daisy Family

Description Perennial. Flat-topped clusters of violet or lavender composite flowers with yellow to reddish centers crown 1 to 4-foot stems. Alternate leaves are broad and heart-shaped, and the lower leaves may be 8 or more inches wide.

Blooming August to September.

Soil Moist, average, high humus.

Range Minnesota to Nova Scotia, south to western North Carolina and Illinois.

Propagation Divide root clumps in fall, and replant 12 inches apart, with crowns at soil surface. Sow seeds as they mature, in September or October, in outdoor flats.

Cultivation Prefers woodland edges in partial sun to light shade. Drought-tolerant.

Uses Plant in colonies in filtered sunlight or bright shade to bloom, or in deep shade for a non-blooming groundcover.

Similar species White wood aster (*Aster divaricatus*), New York aster (*Aster novi-belgii*).

3-6 5-6

Dicentra cucullaria
DUTCHMAN'S-BREECHES

Fumitory Family

Description Perennial. Readily recognized by its delicate, compound, fernlike basal foliage and its unique blooms that resemble white pantaloons hanging upside down from arched stems, 4 to 12 inches tall. Occasionally, the flowers have a pinkish hue.

Blooming April to May.

Soil Moist, rich, high humus.

Range North Dakota to Nova Scotia, south to northern Georgia, Alabama, and Missouri. Also along the Columbia River valley in Idaho, Washington, and Oregon.

Propagation Divide tubers in early fall, separating kernels from the main tuber. Replant segments 6 inches apart and $1/2$ inch deep, and mulch with deciduous leaves. Sow seeds $1/4$ inch deep in outdoor flats as soon as they ripen, mulch lightly, and keep them moderately moist. If germination is slow, maintain the flats for two years. Transplant seedlings to individual pots about ten weeks after germination, and move into the garden near the end of summer.

Cultivation Requires constant but not excessive moisture. Mulch with deciduous leaves in fall.

3-7 6-7

Dicentra canadensis
SQUIRREL CORN

Fumitory Family
Description Perennial. White heart-shaped flowers, $1/2$ to $3/4$ inch long, dangle from 6 to 12-inch stems, and the compound, finely cut, fernlike basal leaves strongly resemble those of Dutchman's-breeches.

Blooming April to June.

Soil Moist, rich, high humus.

Range Minnesota to southwestern Quebec, south to North Carolina and Missouri.

Propagation Divide cornlike tubers in late summer, replant segments 6 inches apart and 2 inches deep, and mulch with deciduous leaves. Sow seeds $1/4$ inch deep in outdoor flats as soon as they ripen, mulch lightly, and keep them moderately moist. If germination is slow, maintain the flats for two years. Transplant seedlings to individual pots about ten weeks after germination, and move into the garden near the end of summer.

Cultivation Locate plants where they will receive direct or filtered spring sun. Cover dormant plants with hardware cloth to discourage rodents from stealing tubers. Prefers deep layer of leaf mold.

4-7  6-7

Dicentra eximia
FRINGED BLEEDING HEART

Fumitory Family
Description Perennial. Pink heart-shaped flowers dangle in clusters from arching stems. Like squirrel corn and Dutchman's-breeches, the compound leaves of fringed bleeding hearts are finely cut and fernlike. Flowers are $3/4$ inch long, and the plant stands about 10 to 18 inches tall.

Blooming May to August.

Soil Moist, rich.

Range New York south to Georgia and Tennessee.

Propagation Divide rootstock in fall, separating the crowns and making sure each division has several buds. Replant divisions so that buds are about 1 inch below the soil surface. Immediately after collection, sow seeds in outdoor flats. Transplant seedlings to individual pots about ten weeks after their germination in the following spring, and wait four weeks before transplanting to the garden. Space plants 24 inches apart.

Cultivation Divide rootstock every second or third year to promote vigorous blooming. Prefers well-worked woodland soil. Mulch in fall with deciduous leaves. Do not crowd individual plants.

5-8  4-5 🐝 🦋 🐦

Geranium maculatum
WILD GERANIUM

Geranium Family
Description Perennial. Loose clusters of lavender, five-petaled, inch-wide flowers rise on long branches above a pair of leaves, each with three to five distinct palmate lobes and coarse teeth. The grayish leaves are 4 to 5 inches wide, while the plant stands 12 to 24 inches tall.

Blooming April to May.

Soil Moist, rich.

Range Southern Manitoba to Maine, south to northern Georgia and Kansas.

Propagation Sow seeds in shaded outdoor flats or seedbeds immediately after collection in June or just as the pod turns black. If germination is poor, maintain the flats or seedbeds for a second year. Transplant seedlings in fall when they become dormant. In fall, cut rhizomes into pieces, each with two to three buds and several roots, and replant 1 inch deep and 12 inches apart with buds facing upward.

Cultivation Mulch with decaying leaves in early spring and again in fall. Keep soil moist. Plant in areas sheltered from strong winds. Partial sun to light shade.

3-7  5-6 🐝

Key

5-6
zone

exposure

full shade

light shade

part sun

full sun

4-5
pH

attracts

attracts

attracts

attracts

Geranium robertianum
HERB ROBERT

Geranium Family

Description Biennial. Pinkish purple flowers arise in pairs from the axils of decoratively lobed leaves. The five-petaled flowers measure about $1/2$ inch wide, and the plant stands 8 to 24 inches tall.

Blooming May to October.

Soil Moist, rich.

Range Southern Manitoba to Nova Scotia, south to Maryland and Illinois.

Propagation By seed only. Sow seeds as they mature in outdoor flats, seedbeds, or directly in the garden. Since the plant is biennial, sow for two or more consecutive years to ensure a yearly blooming population. Transplant seedlings to permanent locations in garden in the middle to latter part of their first growing season. Self-sows readily under suitable conditions.

Cultivation Thrives in light shade or filtered sunlight. Mulch with deciduous leaves in fall. Will not tolerate low pH.

Uses Provides constant color through the growing season.

3-6 6-7

Aralia nudicaulis
WILD SARSAPARILLA

Ginseng Family

Description Perennial. An umbrella-like, doubly compound basal leaf shades three dome-shaped clusters of greenish white flowers growing on a leafless stem. Flowers have five small reflexed petals and five green stamens, and ultimately transform into purplish black berries. Leaves are 6 to 15 inches tall and divide into three leaflets, each with three to five oval, finely toothed leaflets.

Blooming May to July.

Soil Dry, average.

Range British Columbia to Newfoundland, south to Georgia, Missouri, Colorado, and Idaho.

Propagation Divide rootstock in fall when plants are dormant. Replant rhizomes horizontally, 12 inches apart with crowns at soil surface. Plant seeds in fall in outdoor flats or seedbeds, and transplant to the garden near the end of the first growing season. Seedlings mature slowly.

Cultivation Mulch for winter protection. Requires little care once established. Plants spread aggressively via underground rhizomes and may need to be contained by burying underground edging strips.

Uses Colonies make good groundcover.

3-7 5-6

Gaultheria procumbens
WINTERGREEN

Heath Family

Description Perennial. White, nodding, bell-shaped flowers grow singly or in groups of two or three from the leaf axils of the creeping woody stem, and later ripen into bright red berries. The alternate leaves are dark green, shiny, oval, finely toothed, evergreen, and 1 to 2 inches long.

Blooming April to May.

Soil Dry, poor, high humus.

Range Southern Manitoba to Newfoundland, south to northern Georgia and northern Alabama.

Propagation Make cuttings of stems and stolons in July, dip ends in rooting hormone, and plant in outdoor flats containing a moist sand-peat moss combination. Transplant the following spring to permanent locations. Seeds should be collected in fall, sown densely in outdoor flats, and thinly covered with peat moss. Cover with hardware cloth to discourage rodents from eating seeds. If germination is slow, maintain flats for at least two springs.

Cultivation Grows under a wide range of conditions, but requires relatively acidic soil with a fair humus content.

Uses Great groundcover.

3-7 4-6

Epigaea repens
TRAILING ARBUTUS

Heath Family
Description Perennial. Clusters of pink or white, fragrant, trumpet-shaped flowers grow in leaf axils, near the tips of trailing stems. The five lobes of the corolla flare to about $1/2$ inch wide. Leaves are oval, leathery, and 1 to 3 inches long.
Blooming March to May.
Soil Moist, average, high humus, well-drained.
Range Saskatchewan to Labrador, south to Florida and Mississippi.
Propagation Stem cuttings should be made in the fall, the cut end dipped in rooting hormone, planted in flats in a moist sand-peat moss mixture, mulched lightly, and kept in a cold frame over winter. If a cold frame is unavailable, make cuttings in early spring. Keep in flats for two years before transplanting to the garden, taking care not to damage the delicate roots.
Cultivation Prefers oak or pine woodlands, with lots of humus in the thin upper topsoil and a high percentage of sand below, to facilitate good drainage.
Attracts Ants seek seeds for food.

2-8

4-5

Lonicera sempervirens
TRUMPET HONEYSUCKLE

Honeysuckle Family
Description Perennial. Whorled clusters of trumpet-shaped flowers, scarlet outside and yellow inside, grow at the ends of climbing vines. Flowers are 1 to 2 inches long and five-lobed. Leaves are oblong, 1 to 3 inches in length, and the bases of the endmost leaves are fused, so that the stem seems to pierce them.
Blooming April to September.
Soil Moist, rich.
Range Iowa to Massachusetts, south to Florida and Texas.
Propagation Take stem cuttings in spring, dip the cut end in rooting hormone, and plant in individual pots in a moist sand-peat moss mixture. Transplant to garden in midsummer. Collect seeds as they mature and sow immediately in outdoor flats.
Cultivation Plant in full or partial sun at the base of trees, shrubs, stone walls, or other objects it can climb.
Uses Good plant for woodland borders.

5-9

5-6

Erythronium americanum
TROUT LILY

Lily Family
Description Perennial. A pair of mottled green leaves clasps the base of a 4 to 10-inch stem bearing a single yellow flower. Six stamens protrude from the flower, which has three petals and three sepals, all reflexed. The leaves are 3 to 8 inches long, narrowly oval, with smooth margins.
Blooming March to May.
Soil Moist, rich, high humus.
Range Minnesota to Nova Scotia, south to northern Georgia and northeastern Oklahoma.
Propagation Separate root offsets from corms in late summer, replant 3 inches deep in garden, and mulch well. Replant parent corms at their original depth with the narrow end up. Collect seeds as they mature, and sow $1/4$ inch deep in individual pots, filled with a mixture of sand, compost, and garden soil. Place pots where they will receive spring sun. Transplant seedlings to permanent locations at the end of their first full growing season. Immature plants have only one leaf, will not bloom for four to seven years, and take eight to ten years to produce root offsets.
Cultivation Plant in areas that receive lots of spring sunlight.
Uses Attractive spring groundcover.

3-7

5-7

Trillium grandiflorum
LARGE-FLOWERED TRILLIUM

Lily Family

Description Perennial. A single white flower with three waxy petals and six yellow stamens is borne on a stalk, above a whorl of three roundish leaves, on an erect stem 10 to 18 inches tall. Flower is funnel-shaped, 2 to 4 inches wide, and turns pink with age. Leaves are roughly diamond-shaped and heavily veined.

Blooming April to June.

Soil Moist, rich, well-drained, high humus.

Range Minnesota, southern Ontario, and southern Quebec to Maine, south to Georgia and Arkansas.

Propagation Collect seeds as they mature in July or August, and immediately sow $\frac{1}{4}$ inch deep in a mixture of sand, loam, and compost in outdoor flats or seedbeds. Mulch with deciduous leaves and keep moist. Transplant to the garden, when the plants go dormant next summer. Takes three to ten years to produce flowering plants from seed. Divide rhizomes in late summer, replant horizontally 3 inches deep and 12 inches apart, and mulch with deciduous leaves.

Cultivation Ideally planted in sandy loam with lots of humus, where it remains consistently moist and receives spring sun.

3-8 ▨ |5-7」

Trillium erectum
PURPLE TRILLIUM

Lily Family

Description Perennial. A solitary, seminodding red or maroon flower perches on a stalk above a whorl of three rounded, diamond-shaped leaves. Flower is 2 to 3 inches wide with six pale yellow stamens. Height is 8 to 16 inches.

Blooming April to June.

Soil Moist, rich, high humus.

Range Michigan and southeastern Ontario to Nova Scotia, south to northern Georgia and Tennessee.

Propagation Collect seeds as they mature in late summer, sow immediately $\frac{1}{4}$ inch deep in outdoor flats or seedbeds of humus-rich loam, and mulch with oak or beech leaves. If germination is slow, maintain flats for two years. Divide rhizomes in midsummer, removing small, new rhizomes from the parent, and plant segments 2 inches deep in individual pots or in garden 6 inches apart or farther. Mulch with oak or beech leaves.

Cultivation Plant in light to deep shade where there is plenty of leaf mold, but where plants will receive spring sun. Mulch with a 2-inch layer of oak or beech leaves for winter protection.

Attracts Flesh flies.

3-7 ▨ |5-6」

Trillium viride var. luteum
YELLOW TRILLIUM

Lily Family

Description Perennial. Appearing closed because of its erect petals, the solitary lemon-scented flower of yellow trillium is stalkless and sits directly above a whorl of egg-shaped leaves mottled with patterns of brown and green.

Blooming May to June.

Soil Moist, rich, high humus.

Range Missouri to North Carolina, south to Georgia and Louisiana.

Propagation Immediately after collection, sow seeds $\frac{1}{4}$ inch deep in humus-rich loam in outdoor flats or seedbeds, and mulch with deciduous leaves. Transplant to garden after one full growing season. Divide rhizomes in late summer, replant segments 2 inches deep and 6 inches apart, and mulch with deciduous leaves.

Cultivation Needs filtered sunlight in spring and light to deep shade thereafter. Mulch for winter protection.

6-8 ▨ |5-7」

Trillium undulatum
PAINTED TRILLIUM

Lily Family

Description Perennial. A rosy red V and thin reddish veins radiating toward the wavy edges of each of the three white petals, along with six pink and white stamens, make this a most attractive woodland wildflower. Each plant has a solitary flower perched on an erect stalk above a whorl of three dark green, egg-shaped leaves.

Blooming April to June.

Soil Wet, rich, high humus.

Range Manitoba to Nova Scotia, south to northern Georgia and Missouri.

Propagation As they mature, immediately sow seeds $1/4$ inch deep in flats or seedbeds with a high percentage of peat moss mixed into the soil, and keep them damp. Transplant into the garden after the first full growing season. Divide in midsummer and randomly plant 3 inches deep and at least 12 inches apart.

Cultivation Select cool, shady, damp sites. Fertile, humus-rich soil is best. Mulch for winter protection.

Uses Plant singly or in groups of two to three.

2-6 ▨ ⌊4-5⌋

Amianthium muscitoxicum
FLY POISON

Lily Family

Description Perennial. A tall, 12 to 36-inch stem culminates in a clublike cylindrical cluster of white flowers that turn greenish bronze with age. Flowers are about $1/2$ inch wide with three petals, three petal-like sepals, and six stamens. Basal leaves are 12 inches or longer, grasslike, and blunt at the tip.

Blooming June to July.

Soil Moist, average, well-drained.

Range Missouri to southeastern New York, south to Florida and Oklahoma.

Propagation Divide bulbs in late summer, and replant in the garden at their original depth and 12 or more inches apart. Sow seeds in well-drained outdoor seedbed, and cover with a sprinkling of soil. Transplant to the garden after the second growing season.

Cultivation Plant in open woodland where filtered or partial sunlight reaches the floor. Prefers sandy soil.

Uses Pulp from crushed bulb was once mixed with sugar to poison flies.

6-8 ▨ ⌊4-5⌋

Trillium cernuum
NODDING TRILLIUM

Lily Family

Description Perennial. A nodding white flower dangles beneath the whorl of three diamond-shaped leaves. The three white petals of the flower are reflexed to expose fully six stamens with rose or maroon anthers. Dimensions are: flower, $1^1/2$ inches wide; leaves, $2^1/2$ to 4 inches long; and height, 8 to 20 inches.

Blooming April to June.

Soil Moist, rich, high humus, well-drained.

Range Manitoba to Newfoundland, south to Georgia and Missouri.

Propagation Divide rhizomes in fall, plant 2 inches deep and 6 inches apart in seedbeds, and mulch with leaves. Transplant to the garden after one or more growing seasons. Sow seeds immediately after collection in outdoor flats or seedbeds. Transplant seedlings to the garden at the end of their first growing season.

Cultivation Prefers sun in spring and light shade in summer. Soil should be moist and humus-rich. Mulch with maple leaves.

3-7 ▨ ⌊5-6⌋

Key

5-6 zone

exposure

▨ full shade

▨ light shade

◩ part sun

◌ full sun

⌊4-5⌋ pH

🐝 attracts

🦋 attracts

🐦 attracts

🐦 attracts

Clintonia borealis
BLUEBEAD LILY

Lily Family

Description Perennial. The steel-blue berries adorning this plant in late summer are more distinctive than its loose cluster of greenish yellow, nodding, bell-shaped flowers. It stands 6 to 15 inches tall and has shiny, oblong, basal leaves 5 to 8 inches long.

Blooming May to July.

Soil Moist, rich, high humus.

Range Manitoba to Labrador, south to Georgia and Tennessee.

Propagation Divide rhizomes in fall and plant in individual pots or in the garden. Place segments horizontally and ¹/₂ inch deep with the shoot tips at soil level and pointing in different directions. Immediately after collection, sow seeds ¹/₄ inch deep in outdoor flats, and transplant to permanent locations after the second growing season.

Cultivation Grows where summer temperatures routinely remain below 75°F, usually more than 1,000 feet above sea level. Requires cool, shady, moist sites. Mulch with a thick layer of pine needles and oak leaves.

Uses Excellent groundcover for deep shade.

2-7 | 4-5

Lilium philadelphicum
WOOD LILY

Lily Family

Description Perennial. Upright, cup-shaped orange-red flowers spotted with purplish brown adorn the erect, 12 to 36-inch stem, along with whorled, lance-shaped leaves. Flowers are about 2 inches wide and include three petals, three petal-like sepals, and six stamens. Leaves are 1 to 4 inches long.

Blooming June to August.

Soil Dry, average, high humus, well-drained.

Range British Columbia to Maine, south to North Carolina, Arkansas, and New Mexico.

Propagation Divide bulb in late summer, plant offsets 3 inches deep in permanent locations, and mulch with oak leaves and pine needles. Bulb scales may be planted in outdoor flats, containing a mixture of loam, sand, and peat moss. Mulch well or winter in cold frames, and transplant into the garden after the following growing season. Sow seeds as they mature in outdoor flats and transplant to the garden after the first growing season.

Cultivation Mulch over winter with pine needles and oak leaves.

Uses Plant along woodland borders and in clearings.

4-7 | 4-6

Maianthemum canadense
CANADA MAYFLOWER

Lily Family

Description Perennial. A zigzag stem only 2 to 6 inches tall is topped by a 1 to 2-inch cluster of minute white flowers, each less than ¹/₄ inch long. Each flower has two petals and two petal-like sepals. The 1 to 3-inch-long alternate leaves have heart-shaped bases, smooth margins, and clasp the stem.

Blooming May to June.

Soil Moist, poor.

Range Manitoba to Labrador, south to Maryland and Iowa, and in mountains to northern Georgia.

Propagation Divide rhizomes in fall into 2-inch pieces, each with at least one bud, plant segments 1 inch deep and 6 inches or more apart in outdoor flats or the garden, water and mulch. Collect seeds in late summer and immediately sow ¹/₄ inch deep in outdoor flats or peat pots. Transplant the following summer.

Cultivation Needs moist, acidic, humus-rich soil, but thrives in sun or shade. Spreads readily. Mulch with conifer needles or oak, beech, maple, or birch leaves.

Uses An excellent north woods groundcover.

Attracts Mice, chipmunks.

2-7 | 4-6

Uvularia grandiflora
LARGE-FLOWERED BELLWORT

Lily Family

Description Perennial. Lemon yellow flowers, 1 to 2 inches in length, dangle bell-like from downturned stems. Alternate oblong leaves with smooth margins and downy white undersides clasp the stem at their bases. Reaches a height of 6 to 20 inches.

Blooming April to June.

Soil Moist, average.

Range North Dakota to Quebec, south to northern Georgia and Kansas.

Propagation Divide root clumps in midsummer and transplant individual plants 12 inches apart with rhizomes 1 inch deep and the crowns at the soil surface. Sow seeds as soon as they mature in outdoor flats or seedbeds and transplant the following summer.

Cultivation Mulch with a generous layer of beech, maple, or birch leaves. Transplant regularly to form new clumps. Needs partial sun in spring.

Uses Long-lasting foliage.

3-7 ◨ 6-7

Uvularia sessilifolia
WILD OATS

Lily Family

Description Perennial. One or two pale yellow, slender, bell-shaped flowers droop from the top of an angled stem. Flowers are 1 inch long and have three petals, three petal-like sepals, and six stamens. Oblong leaves are 2 to 3 inches long and have smooth margins. Plant height is 6 to 12 inches.

Blooming April to June.

Soil Moist, average, high humus.

Range North Dakota to New Brunswick, south to Georgia and Arkansas.

Propagation Divide rhizomes in fall and replant 12 inches apart with the rhizome 1 inch deep and the crown just below the soil surface. Sow seeds as they ripen in individual peat pots and transplant to the garden in the following summer.

Cultivation Work plenty of humus into the garden soil. Mulch with deciduous leaves.

Uses Plant in colonies.

3-7 ◨ 5-6

Medeola virginica
INDIAN CUCUMBER ROOT

Lily Family

Description Perennial. Several nodding yellow flowers arch on short stalks from a whorl of three to five oval leaves at the top of an erect, hairy, 12 to 24-inch stem. Another whorl of five to ten oval leaves, each 3 to 5 inches long, occurs about midway on the stem. Three petals and three petal-like sepals, all recurved, and six stamens compose the $1/2$-inch flowers.

Blooming May to June.

Soil Moist, rich, high humus.

Range Minnesota to Nova Scotia, south to Florida and Louisiana.

Propagation Divide the tubers in spring and replant segments horizontally 2 inches deep and 6 inches apart. Sow seeds in peat pots as soon as they mature and leave out over winter.

Cultivation Plant in deciduous woodland where soil is consistently moist.

3-8 ◨ 4-5

Key

5-6 zone

exposure

◨ full shade

◨ light shade

◨ part sun

☐ full sun

4-5 pH

 attracts

attracts

attracts

attracts

55

Camassia scilloides
WILD HYACINTH

Lily Family
Description Perennial. A leafless 6 to 24-inch stem sports bluish lavender flowers in a loose elongated cluster. Flowers are 1 inch wide with three petals, three petal-like sepals, and six stamens. Basal leaves are 8 to 16 inches long, grasslike, and have a distinct keel.
Blooming May to June.
Soil Wet, rich.
Range Southern Wisconsin to southern Ontario, south to South Carolina, Georgia, Alabama, eastern Texas, and eastern Kansas.
Propagation Divide bulbs in fall and replant 4 inches deep and 6 inches apart. Collect seeds when they mature and sow in outdoor flats. Transplant to the garden after the second growing season.
Cultivation Thrives in damp areas with full or partial sun. Mulch with deciduous leaves or compost.
Uses Suitable for open woods, woodland borders, clearings, or meadows.

5-8 6-7

Disporum maculatum
NODDING MANDARIN

Lily Family
Description Perennial. Creamy or yellowish flowers speckled with purplish brown dangle singly or in pairs opposite the last leaf on forked stems. The alternate leaves are 2 to 4 inches long and egg-shaped, with hairy undersides and distinct parallel veins. Six stamens project beyond the 1-inch-long flowers, which have three petals and three petal-like sepals, widely separated at their narrow bases.
Blooming April to May.
Soil Moist, rich, high humus.
Range Southern Michigan and Ohio, south to North Carolina, Georgia, and Alabama.
Propagation Divide rootstock clump in fall, replant individuals 1 inch deep and 12 or more inches apart, and mulch. Sow seeds in outdoor flats as they mature, and transplant after the next growing season.
Cultivation Requires constant moisture and a deep layer of humus. Mulch generously in fall.

5-7 6-7

Polygonatum biflorum
SMALL SOLOMON'S SEAL

Lily Family
Description Perennial. One to four, but usually paired, greenish yellow flowers dangle from the lead axils on an arching stem 12 to 36 inches long. Flowers are $1/2$ to $3/4$ inch long and bell-shaped with three petals, three sepals, and six stamens. Alternate leaves are 2 to 6 inches long, oval, parallel-veined, clasp the stem, and have smooth margins.
Blooming May to June.
Soil Moist, rich, high humus.
Range Nebraska to southern Ontario and Connecticut, south to Florida and eastern Texas.
Propagation In fall, divide rhizomes into pieces with at least one bud each, replant horizontally with buds upward, 1 inch deep and 18 inches apart. Collect seeds after fruit has turned black, immediately sow them $1/2$ inch deep in outdoor flats, mulch with compost or deciduous leaf mold, and keep moist over winter.
Cultivation Tolerates a wide variety of conditions, from partial sun to deep shade, and dry to moist soil. Mulch generously in fall with pine needles or oak leaves.
Uses Appropriate groundcover around the base of larger trees.

5-8 4-7

Allium tricoccum
WILD LEEK

Lily Family

Description Perennial. A 6 to 16-inch leafless stem, topped by a hemispherical cluster of creamy white flowers, emerges after the two or three long, canoe-shaped leaves wither in the shade cast by the new spring leaves of deciduous forest canopies. Individual flowers are ¼ inch wide, with three petals and three petal-like sepals, and the clusters are approximately 1½ inches in diameter. Leaves are 8 to 12 inches long and 1 to 2 inches wide with smooth margins.

Blooming June to July.

Soil Moist, rich, high humus.

Range Minnesota to Nova Scotia, south to north Georgia, Tennessee, Illinois, and Iowa.

Propagation Separate bulb offsets in summer, replant 1½ inches deep and 6 inches apart, and mulch with compost. After collection in August or September, sow seeds ½ inch deep in outdoor flats containing a loam-compost mixture. Transplant during the next summer, following the same procedure as for bulb offsets.

Cultivation Locate plants where they will receive direct spring sunlight. Work an abundant amount of compost into the soil. Mulch with deciduous leaves for winter.

4-7 [full shade] 6-7

Mitchella repens
PARTRIDGEBERRY

Madder Family

Description Perennial. Trailing evergreen herbaceous plant. Tubular flowers, ½ inch long with four spreading lobes, paired at the ends of branches. Leaves are opposite, round, shiny green with white veins. Adventitious roots form along the stem, where nodes touch moist soil.

Blooming June to July.

Soil Moist, rich, high humus.

Range Minnesota to Newfoundland, south to Florida and eastern Texas.

Propagation Most easily propagated by stem cuttings. Cut a 6 to 12-inch section from the leading tip of the plant in early spring, unearth roots carefully, and replant with roots ½ inch deep in well-worked soil containing compost, peat moss, and sand. Keep soil moist, and weight stem at various points with small stones to encourage new root growth. Propagation from seed is much slower. Collect fruit in October, separate seeds, plant ¼ inch deep in outdoor flats, and mulch thinly with pine needles. Transplant seedlings in fall.

Cultivation Prospers in cool, moist, humus-rich soil in shady locations. Mulch lightly, with leaves or needles, in fall.

3-9 [full shade] 4-6

Polygala paucifolia
FRINGED POLYGALA

Milkwort Family

Description Perennial. Two lateral sepals of this magenta flower flare into large wings, while the three petals form a tube with a finely fringed yellow or pink tip. The oval, smooth-edged leaves are about 1 inch long and crowded near the tip of the stem.

Blooming May to June.

Soil Dry, rich.

Range Saskatchewan to New Brunswick, south to northern Georgia and Illinois.

Propagation Take stem cuttings in early summer, dip cut ends in rooting hormone, and plant in peat pots, using a mixture of sand, loam, peat moss, and compost; grow in propagation frames or cold frames. Transplant to permanent locations, 6 inches apart in the garden, after the second growing season, and mulch with shredded leaves. Collect seeds in July or August and sow in outdoor flats.

Cultivation Plant in colonies. Apply light mulch of oak leaves in fall.

3-7 [part sun] 5-6

Scutellaria incana
DOWNY SKULLCAP

Mint Family

Description Perennial. Short, loose clusters of blue, two-lipped flowers decorate the ends of fuzzy, square, branching stems. The opposite leaves are egg-shaped and coarsely toothed. Plant is 12 to 48 inches tall.

Blooming June to September.

Soil Dry, average, high humus.

Range Iowa to southwestern New York and New Jersey, south to Georgia and Louisiana.

Propagation Divide rhizomes in spring and replant individuals at least 12 inches apart with crowns 2 inches deep. Take stem cuttings in midsummer, dip in rooting hormone, plant in peat pots, and keep in propagation frames until the following June. Collect seeds in fall, sow in outdoor flats, and transplant to the garden at the end of the next summer.

Cultivation Mulch in fall. Also does well in light shade and moist soil.

5-8 5-6

Scutellaria integrifolia
HYSSOP SKULLCAP

Mint Family

Description Perennial. Lavender flowers with arched upper lips and flared lower lips cluster atop finely haired square stems. The opposite leaves are 1 to 3 inches long and elliptical with smooth margins.

Blooming May to July.

Soil Moist, rich.

Range Missouri to Connecticut, south to Florida and Alabama.

Propagation Divide rhizomes in spring and replant 12 inches apart with crowns 2 inches deep and rhizomes horizontal. Take stem cuttings in midsummer, dip in rooting hormone, plant in peat pots, and keep in propagation frames until the following June. Collect seeds in fall, sow in outdoor flats, and transplant to garden at the end of the next summer.

Cultivation Does well in full sun to light shade, but prefers constant moisture. Mulch in fall.

Uses Good on sunny side of woodland border or in clearings. Plant in colonies.

6-8 6-7

Pycnanthemum incanum
HOARY MOUNTAIN MINT

Mint Family

Description Perennial. Small white or lavender flowers grow densely clustered in the axils of the opposite leaves, and at the top of the 12 to 36-inch stem. The irregular flowers are $1/4$ to $1/2$ inch long and two-lipped, with purple spots on the lower lip. Flower clusters are 1 to $1^1/2$ inches in diameter. Leaves are oval, toothed, and whitish underneath.

Blooming July to September.

Soil Moist, average, high humus.

Range Southern Michigan to Maine, south to northern Florida and eastern Texas.

Propagation In fall, divide root clumps into sections 3 to 4 inches wide, replant shallowly in the garden, and water. Take stem cuttings in June, dip the ends in rooting hormone, plant in individual pots containing a sand-vermiculite mixture, place in propagation frames, mist several times per day for three to seven weeks, and transplant to the garden in fall. Sow seeds in outdoor flats in fall, transplant to individual pots in the following July, and transplant to the garden in fall.

Cultivation Plant in woodland borders. Work ample humus into the soil, and mulch in spring. Spreads aggressively.

5-8 5-6

Dentaria diphylla
TOOTHWORT

Mustard Family

Description Perennial. Topping the 8 to 14-inch stem is a loose cluster of white four-petaled flowers. Two compound leaves, each composed of three oval, coarsely toothed leaflets, arise nearly opposite each other, about midway up the unbranched stem.

Blooming April to June.

Soil Moist, rich, high humus.

Range Minnesota to New Brunswick, south to South Carolina and Kentucky.

Propagation Divide rhizomes in fall, keeping the soil intact around the roots. Plant in individual pots for one year before transplanting to the garden, 1 inch deep and 12 inches apart. Upon collection, sow seeds in shaded outdoor flats or seedbeds, keep moist, and transplant seedlings to the garden in their second fall.

Cultivation Does not tolerate direct sunlight. Weed out aggressive neighbors and mulch lightly with deciduous leaves in early spring and fall.

4-7 ⬛ 5-7

Dentaria laciniata
CUT-LEAVED TOOTHWORT

Mustard Family

Description Perennial. A loose terminal cluster of white or pink four-petaled flowers, each ³/₄ inch wide, crowns an 8 to 16-inch stem. Midway up the stem is a whorl of three deeply divided, toothed leaves.

Blooming April to June.

Soil Moist, rich, high humus.

Range Minnesota to western Quebec, south to Florida and Louisiana.

Propagation Divide rhizomes in fall, keeping the soil intact around the roots. Plant in individual pots for one year before transplanting to garden, 1 inch deep and 12 inches apart. Upon collection, sow seeds in shaded outdoor flats or seedbeds, keep moist, and transplant seedlings to the garden in their second fall.

Cultivation Does not tolerate direct sunlight. Weed out aggressive neighbors and mulch lightly with deciduous leaves in early spring and fall.

4-9 ⬛ 6-7

Cypripedium calceolus
YELLOW LADY'S SLIPPER

Orchid Family

Description Perennial. Leafy stems bear one or two flowers, each consisting of a yellow pouch-shaped lip, 2 inches long. They are flanked by two petals and two greenish brown, twisted sepals. Leaves are 6 to 8 inches long, elliptical, with parallel veins and smooth margins.

Blooming April to July.

Soil Wet, rich, high humus.

Range British Columbia to Newfoundland, south to Georgia and Arizona.

Propagation May be difficult due to the plant's symbiotic relationship with a soil fungus that must be present. Scatter seeds in woodland garden, or sow in individual pots containing rich woodland soil mixed with copious quantities of compost. Transplant seedlings to the garden after several years, keeping the soil intact around the roots. Divide rhizomes in fall, and replant 1 inch deep in the garden with some original soil.

Cultivation Plant 12 inches apart in groups of three or randomly. Mulch well with decaying deciduous leaves. Keep moist.

Special note Exercise caution when obtaining plants. Many of those commercially available were probably collected in the wild.

4-7 ⬛ 6-7

Key

5-6
zone

exposure

⬛ full shade

⬛ light shade

◩ part sun.

☐ full sun

4-5 pH

🐝 attracts

🦋 attracts

🐦 attracts

🐦 attracts

Cypripedium acaule
PINK LADY'S SLIPPER

Orchid Family

Description Perennial. Each leafless stem, 6 to 15 inches tall, bears a single pink bloom. The flower has two petals and two sepals, both greenish brown and twisted, and a pouch-shaped lip, 2^1/$_2$ inches long and heavily veined. Each plant has a pair of basal leaves up to 8 inches long, parallel-veined, with silvery hair underneath.

Blooming April to June.

Soil Dry, rich, high humus.

Range Saskatchewan to Nova Scotia, south to northern Georgia and Tennessee.

Propagation Up to ten years required to produce blooming plants. May be difficult due to symbiotic soil fungus that must also be present. Scatter seeds in oak or pine woodland, or sow in individual pots, transplanting seedlings after several years. Divide rhizomes of clumps in fall and replant 1 inch below the soil surface in the garden.

Cultivation Roots must be kept moist for several years after transplanting. Mulch in fall with 2 inches of oak leaves, pine needles, or a combination of the two.

Special note Exercise caution when obtaining plants. Many of those commercially available were probably collected in the wild.

Lupinus perennis
WILD LUPINE

Pea Family

Description Perennial. Blue flowers grow in an elongated terminal cluster on an erect, unbranched stem 10 to 24 inches tall. The five-petaled flowers are pealike, each ^{1}/$_2$ to ^{3}/$_4$ inch long with a broad upper "banner," two lateral "wings," and two bottom petals fused to form the "keel." The alternate leaves are palmately compound, each with 7 to 11 leaflets measuring 1 to 2 inches.

Blooming April to July.

Soil Dry, average, well-drained.

Range Minnesota to Maine, south to Florida and Louisiana.

Propagation Upon collection, soak seeds in lukewarm water for 12 hours, then sow in individual pots containing a mixture of peat moss and sand. Transplant seedlings to garden after the third leaf has developed, placing them 12 inches apart with the crown at the soil surface. Keep the soil around the seedlings moist until they are established.

Cultivation Do not attempt to transplant mature plants. Plant needs full sun, and does best in meadows, open woodland, woodland borders, or clearings.

Uses Lupines enhance the fertility of soil by fixing nitrogen from the atmosphere.

Phlox divaricata
WILD BLUE PHLOX

Phlox Family

Description Perennial. A loose cluster of pale blue or light violet flowers, each ^{3}/$_4$ to 1^1/$_2$ inches wide, crowns a hairy, sticky stem 10 to 20 inches tall. The five, widely flared, notched petals are united at the base to form a tube. Leaves are opposite, 1 to 2 inches long, narrowly egg-shaped, and have smooth margins.

Blooming April to June.

Soil Moist, fertile, high humus.

Range Minnesota to Quebec, south to Florida and southeastern Texas.

Propagation Divide clumps in late summer, making sure each has several stems and a mass of roots, then replant and water immediately. Take 6-inch stem cuttings in late spring, dip in rooting hormone, plant in individual pots containing a mixture of sand and peat moss. Keep moist and out of direct sunlight, mist, then transplant to the garden in fall. Sow seeds in pots outdoors. They will germinate the following spring and may be transplanted to the garden in fall.

Cultivation Cut back the flower stalks after the seeds have been dispersed. When transplanting, set plant with the first one or two leaf nodes buried.

Silene stellata
STARRY CAMPION

Pink Family

Description Perennial. Five deeply fringed, white petals compose individual flowers which form loose clusters on 24 to 36-inch erect stems. Smooth-margined leaves, 2 to 4 inches long, occur mostly in whorls of four.

Blooming July to September.

Soil Dry, average, well-drained.

Range Minnesota to Massachusetts, south to Georgia and eastern Texas.

Propagation Sow seeds immediately upon collection in outdoor flats and cover thinly with soil. Moisten soil, but allow it to dry between waterings to prevent fungal infections. Transplant seedlings to pots after they have developed six leaves, and to the garden at summer's end. Take stem cuttings after flowering, dip in rooting hormone, place in pots in a propagation frame, and mist often. Transplant cuttings to the garden in late summer. In late fall, the root clump of mature plants may be divided. Replant and water immediately.

Cultivation Locate in open woodlands, borders, or clearings, where the plants can get full or partial sun. Needs sandy, well-drained soil. Apply a gravel or bark mulch.

Uses Thrives in marginal soils.

Silene virginica
FIRE PINK

Pink Family

Description Perennial. Loose terminal clusters of crimson flowers, each $1^1/_2$ inches wide with five slender, notched petals, adorn weak stems. Stem leaves are opposite, canoe-shaped, and up to 6 inches long with smooth margins.

Blooming April to June.

Soil Dry, average, well-drained.

Range Minnesota to southern Ontario, south to Georgia and Oklahoma.

Propagation Sow seeds immediately upon collection in outdoor flats and cover thinly with soil. Moisten soil, but allow it to dry between waterings to prevent fungal infections. Transplant seedlings to pots after they have developed six leaves, and to the garden in fall. Take stem cuttings after flowering, dip in rooting hormone, place in pots in a propagation frame, and mist often. Transplant cuttings to the garden in late summer. Divide the root clump of mature plants in late fall, and replant and water immediately.

Cultivation Locate where the plants can get full or partial sun. Needs sandy, well-drained soil. Apply a gravel or bark mulch.

Uses Thrives in marginal soils.

Sanguinaria canadensis
BLOODROOT

Poppy Family

Description Perennial. Solitary white flowers, $1^1/_2$ inches wide with eight to ten petals and golden stamens, grow on smooth, 6 to 10-inch leafless stalks. The round basal leaves are deeply lobed and wrap around the stalks of young plants, unfurling with age.

Blooming March to May.

Soil Moist, rich, high humus, well-drained.

Range Manitoba to Nova Scotia, south to northern Florida and eastern Texas.

Propagation Divide rhizomes in late summer, replant segments horizontally $^3/_4$ inch deep, with the buds at the soil surface, and about 6 inches apart, and mulch lightly with deciduous leaves. Immediately after collection, sow seeds on the surface of outdoor flats containing loam, cover with $^1/_2$ inch of peat moss-compost mixture, cover flats with hardware cloth to discourage rodents, and keep moist. Transplant seedlings to the garden late in the summer.

Cultivation Needs direct sunlight in early spring, but will thrive later in full sun to light shade. Work ample amounts of peat moss and sand into the soil. Mulch lightly with deciduous leaves in fall.

Uses Great groundcover.

Key

5-6
zone

exposure

full shade

light shade

part sun

full sun

4-5
pH

attracts

attracts

attracts

attracts

CELANDINE POPPY
Stylophorum diphyllum

Poppy Family

Description Perennial. Yellowish orange flowers grow singly or in small clusters on top of a 10 to 18-inch stem, above a pair of opposite, compound, deeply lobed leaves. The plant may also have basal leaves, and all leaves measure 4 to 10 inches long. Flowers are up to 2 inches wide with four petals.

Blooming March to May.

Soil Moist, rich, high humus.

Range Wisconsin to western Pennsylvania, south to Virginia and Missouri.

Propagation In fall, divide rhizomes into segments with at least two buds apiece, and replant 12 inches or farther apart with the buds 1 inch below the soil surface. Collect seeds as they mature, sow immediately in outdoor flats or pots, and transplant to the garden in midsummer.

Cultivation Mulch in fall with deciduous leaves. Thrives in full sun to light shade, but requires constant moisture. Work plenty of humus into soil.

5-6 5-7

STARFLOWER
Trientalis borealis

Primrose Family

Description Perennial. One to three, but usually two, white flowers arise on slender stalks from a whorl of five to nine leaves. The flowers usually have seven pointed petals, seven stamens with golden anthers, and are 1/2 inch wide. Leaves are 2 to 4 inches long and canoe-shaped with smooth margins. Plant height is 4 to 9 inches.

Blooming May to June.

Soil Moist, rich, high humus.

Range Saskatchewan to Labrador, south to Virginia, Illinois, and Minnesota.

Propagation As soon as seeds mature, sow them 1/2 inch deep in individual peat pots in soil with a high leaf mold content. Mulch with conifer needles for winter protection. So as not to disturb the roots, transplant seedlings in their pots to a lightly shaded portion of the garden in midsummer, after germination the following spring.

Cultivation Plant in colonies, spacing individual plants 6 to 9 inches apart, or intermingle with other species. Mulch with sphagnum moss and conifer needles.

Uses Good groundcover. Spreads rapidly but not aggressively.

2-6 4-5

SHOOTING STAR
Dodecatheon meadia

Primrose Family

Description Perennial. Pink, lilac, or white flowers with strongly reflexed petals nod on arching stalks in a rather flat-topped cluster. Flowers are 1 inch long, with five petals and five yellow stamens that protrude and unite to form a cone. The basal leaves are dark green with reddish bases, spoon-shaped, and have smooth margins.

Blooming April to June.

Soil Dry, rich, well-drained, high humus.

Range Wisconsin to Pennsylvania, south to Georgia and eastern Texas.

Propagation Divide mature plants in late summer. Separate the crowns into segments, each with one or more buds and at least 3 inches of roots. Replant in the garden, spacing plants 12 inches apart with the buds 1/2 inch below the soil surface and the roots well-spread. Sow seeds in individual peat pots outdoors as soon as they mature, and wait until the seedlings are two years old before transplanting to the garden.

Cultivation Mulch in fall. Requires direct sun in spring. Needs moisture while blooming, but otherwise drought-tolerant.

Uses Showcase along walkways or in rock gardens. Do not crowd with other species.

5-8 5-7

Spring Beauty

Claytonia virginica

SPRING BEAUTY

Purslane Family

Description Perennial. White flowers, having five petals striped with rose-pink and five anthers with pink stamens, grow in loose clusters on 6 to 12-inch stems. A pair of dark green, narrowly canoe-shaped leaves occur opposite each other about midway on the stem.

Blooming March to May.

Soil Moist, rich, high humus.

Range Minnesota to southern Quebec, south to Georgia and Texas.

Propagation Tubers of this plant are only pea-sized, so mark the plant locations exactly while they bloom. Then, in fall, divide tubers into two or more segments, each with several buds, and replant them 2 inches deep and 4 inches apart in colonies in the garden. Seeds are difficult to collect, and should be sown in outdoor flats as soon as they mature.

Cultivation Mulch with oak or beech leaves in fall, and remove mulch in spring. Work lots of humus into soil.

Uses Beautiful but short-lived spring groundcover. Plant in masses, and intermingle with other flowers.

4-8 ▨ 5-7

Foamflower

Tiarella cordifolia

FOAMFLOWER

Saxifrage Family

Description Perennial. Ten long, filamentous stamens per flower give a feathery appearance to the elongated, terminal cluster of white flowers. Each flower is five-petaled and $1/4$ inch wide, and the plant is 6 to 12 inches tall. The basal leaves are maplelike, coarsely toothed, and 2 to 4 inches long.

Blooming April to June.

Soil Moist, rich, high humus.

Range Michigan to Nova Scotia, south to northern Georgia and Alabama.

Propagation Divide rhizomes in fall and replant segments 12 inches apart, with the crowns at the soil surface and the roots spread. Add a thin top layer of compost, mulch with shredded leaves, and keep soil moist until established. Collect seeds as soon as they mature and sow them $1/4$ inch deep in outdoor flats in a moist mixture of sand, compost, and peat moss. Following germination in spring, transplant seedlings to the garden in fall.

Cultivation Mulch with deciduous leaves in fall.

Uses Excellent woodland groundcover.

3-8 ▨ 5-6

Downy False Foxglove

Gerardia virginica

DOWNY FALSE FOXGLOVE

Snapdragon Family

Description Biennial. Funnel-shaped yellow flowers with five flared lobes grow in the axils of opposite leaves, forming a terminal cluster on top of a 24 to 60-inch downy stem. The downy leaves are 2 to 5 inches long, narrowly egg-shaped near the top of the stem, and pinnately lobed near the bottom.

Blooming June to August.

Soil Dry, rich.

Range Michigan to New Hampshire, south to northern Florida and Louisiana.

Propagation When seeds have matured in late fall, sow near the base of oak trees in the garden. Sow seeds for at least two consecutive years, to assure a continuing population. Usually does not survive transplanting.

Cultivation Mulch generously with oak leaves in fall.

Uses Must be planted near oaks, as the plant is partially parasitic on the roots of oaks.

4-8 ▨ 5-6 🦋

63

Campsis radicans
TRUMPET CREEPER

Trumpet Creeper Family

Description Perennial. Trumpet-shaped, orangish red flowers grow in large terminal clusters on a woody, climbing vine. Leaves are opposite and pinnately compound with 7 to 11 leaflets, each 2 to 3 inches long, egg-shaped, and toothed. The flowers are 3 inches long with five spreading lobes.

Blooming July to September.

Soil Dry, rich, high humus.

Range Michigan to Massachusetts, south to Florida and Texas.

Propagation Sow seeds outdoors in individual peat pots when they mature in fall, and transplant to permanent locations in midsummer. Take stem cuttings in spring, dip in rooting hormone, insert in a deep pot with a moist sand and peat moss mixture, and place inside a rooting chamber or sealed clear plastic bag for four weeks. Overwinter in cold frames, and transplant in spring. Runners of older plants that have terminated in a new shoot may be divided in fall, but be sure to keep the soil around the roots intact.

Cultivation Mulch generously with leaf mold, and water during droughts. Attach young vines to the tree or another structure on which it will climb until it can support itself.

Viola papilionacea
COMMON BLUE VIOLET

Violet Family

Description Perennial. Bilaterally symmetrical flowers with five petals, the lowest one longer with a rearward spur, and the two lateral petals hairy. Solitary blue to white flowers grow on individual stalks, and the basal leaves are heart-shaped with scalloped margins. The plant grows to a height of 3 to 8 inches.

Blooming March to June.

Soil Moist, average.

Range North Dakota to Maine, south to Florida and Texas.

Propagation Divide rhizomes in fall, replant in the garden 12 inches apart with the crown $1/2$ inch below the soil surface, and keep moist until established. Collect seeds in early summer and sow immediately in seedbeds or outdoor flats. Transplant seedlings in the following summer.

Cultivation Grows virtually anywhere in full sun to light shade, rich to poor soil, and dry to wet conditions. May need to be contained in the garden by an underground barrier.

Uses Excellent groundcover for marginal sites. Plant with taller species that will provide competition and shade.

Attracts Rabbits.

Viola pensylvanica
SMOOTH YELLOW VIOLET

Violet Family

Description Perennial. Several yellow bilaterally symmetrical flowers may grow on long stalks from the axils of alternate leaves. The plant is 4 to 12 inches tall and usually has one to five basal leaves. Leaves are heart-shaped with scalloped margins.

Blooming April to June.

Soil Moist, rich, high humus.

Range Manitoba to Nova Scotia, south to North Carolina and Oklahoma.

Propagation Divide rhizomes in fall, and replant 6 inches apart with the crowns just below the soil surface. Sow seeds in outdoor flats as soon as they mature, water and mulch with shredded leaves, and do not transplant seedlings to the garden until the fall after their second growing season.

Cultivation Can be grown in light shade to full sun, but requires moderate moisture. Work leaf mold into soil in early spring. Mulch with deciduous leaves in fall.

Uses Plant in colonies, intermingled with other flowers.

Viola blanda
SWEET WHITE VIOLET

Violet Family
Description Perennial. Solitary white bilaterally symmetrical flowers, with upper petals twisted rearward, rise on reddish leafless stalks from an underground rhizome. The basal leaves are dark green, shiny, and heart-shaped with scalloped margins.
Blooming April to June.
Soil Moist, rich, high humus.
Range Minnesota to Quebec, south to northern Georgia and Tennessee.
Propagation Divide rhizomes in fall, replant 6 inches apart with the crowns at the soil surface, and mulch generously with decaying deciduous leaves. Collect seeds in early summer and sow immediately in outdoor flats. Transplant seedlings to the garden after their first growing season.
Cultivation Mulch with deciduous leaves in fall. Spreads readily where leaf mold is deep. Tolerates full sun to light shade.
Uses Good groundcover.
Attracts Rabbits.

4-7 ▨ 5-6 🦋 🐦

Phacelia bipinnatifida
FERN-LEAVED PHACELIA

Waterleaf Family
Description Biennial. Loose terminal clusters of purplish blue flowers form on the branched stem. Flowers are five-petaled and 1 inch wide. The long-stalked leaves are pinnately compound with deeply lobed leaflets.
Blooming April to May.
Soil Wet, rich, high humus.
Range Iowa to Virginia, south to Georgia and Arkansas.
Propagation Collect seeds as they mature and sow in outdoor flats, seedbeds, or directly in the garden. Sow at least two years in a row to ensure constant blooming. Transplant seedlings late in their first growing season.
Cultivation Plant in low, wet areas of your woodland. Mulch in fall.
Uses Plant in large masses.

5-8 ▨ 6-7

Pyrola elliptica
SHINLEAF

Wintergreen Family
Description Perennial. An elongated cluster of nodding, greenish white flowers is supported on a 5 to 10-inch stem. On each $1/2$-inch flower, five waxy petals surround 10 stamens with yellow anthers and a curved, elongated pistil. Leaves are 3 to 4 inches long, oval-shaped, dark green with reddish stalks, and arranged in a basal rosette.
Blooming June to August.
Soil Moist, rich, high humus.
Range Southern Ontario to Labrador, south to Maryland, West Virginia, Ohio, and northern Illinois. Isolated ranges also in southern British Columbia, southern Manitoba and Saskatchewan, western South Dakota and Nebraska, and southwestern New Mexico.
Propagation Divide rhizomes in fall and replant 12 inches apart, with the buds at the soil surface. Collect mature seeds and sow immediately on the surface of seedbeds or outdoor flats filled with equal parts loam, sand, compost, and peat moss. Cover with a sprinkling of soil and keep moist. Transfer seedlings to permanent locations in fall.
Cultivation Tolerates dry to moist soil and light to deep shade. Work plenty of peat moss and conifer needles into the soil.

2-6 ▨ 5-6

Key

5-6 zone

exposure

▨ full shade

▨ light shade

▨ part sun

▢ full sun

4-5 pH

🐝 attracts

🦋 attracts

🐦 attracts

🐦 attracts

2

WESTERN WOODLANDS

Western Woodlands describes the montane and coastal woodlands west of the Great Plains. Height and orientation affect the type of forest.

Yellow fawn lilies

Like their eastern counterparts, the western forests of North America can differ greatly. Unlike eastern forests, however, the differences in the west are determined largely by the amount of rainfall the forests receive. This, in turn, depends on their location on mountains or in valleys.

Warm air can hold more water vapor than cold air, and air cools as it travels higher. When the relatively warm, moist winds of the Pacific Ocean strike North America, they are quickly forced higher by the coastal mountain range. As it travels upward, the air cools, and there is less and less room in it for the water vapor it carries. When it has cooled to its saturation point, it carries as much water vapor as possible at that temperature. If the saturated air is forced still higher and cools even more, it must shed the extra moisture, usually in the form of rain or snow. As the air passes over the highest peaks and begins to descend, it again warms up, but having lost some of its moisture on the

ABOVE The state flower of Colorado, blue columbine can often be found in aspen groves of the central Rocky Mountains.

LEFT Rich in wildflowers, western woodlands are frequently interspersed with meadows or clearings, which also host a myriad of wildflowers.

LEFT *Clearings of mountain forests in the northern Rockies and Cascades host yellow fawn lilies known for their habit of springing into bloom as the snowpack melts in spring.*

other side of the mountain, it is now drier, and sometimes extremely so.

What this means is that, since the winds generally travel from west to east over North America, the western sides of the taller mountain ranges tend to be wetter than the eastern slopes. Therefore, the kinds of forests that require very moist conditions will grow on western slopes, while those that favor drier conditions will be found to the east. In fact, the lower elevations on eastern slopes may be too dry for most trees to grow, and the forest will yield to grasslands. Lower still, one may actually find a desert.

Sunlight also affects western forest communities. South-facing mountain slopes receive

WESTERN WOODLANDS

Western woodlands

stronger sunlight than those facing north, and are therefore warmer and drier. Combined with rainfall patterns, this means that the western forests that require the coolest, wettest environment will be found on the northwestern side of a mountain, while those needing very warm, dry conditions will grow on the southeastern side.

So what do forest types have to do with wildflowers? Like trees, wildflowers have particular needs that must be met in order for them to grow. The same conditions that encourage certain species of trees to grow will also favor particular kinds of wildflowers. With a little practice, you can learn which wildflowers to expect in a lodgepole pine forest, an Engelmann spruce forest, a ponderosa pine forest, and so on.

Most western forests are composed largely of evergreen, needle-leaved trees like pines, spruces, and firs. Those that grow closely together tend to be shadier, which helps determine the species of wildflowers that can live there. Aspen forests, on the other hand, are deciduous, and so may admit more sunlight to warm the soil in spring before the new leaves emerge, encouraging the growth of more sunloving spring wildflowers.

. . . .

LEFT *Bear grass inhabits higher open woods and clearings.*

BELOW *Many factors, including tree species, determine the types of wildflowers in a forest.*

GARDENING TIPS

● Soils in coniferous forests tend to be moderately or strongly acidic, while those in aspen stands are generally less so. Lower the pH of soils in coniferous woodland gardens by working in lots of conifer needles.

● Soils in pine forests, especially those on south-facing slopes, generally are poorer, drier, and contain less humus than those in spruce or fir forests or aspen stands, so select wildflower species for your garden accordingly.

● Soils should, in most cases, be fairly well drained and contain moderate proportions of sand, gravel, or small rocks.

● Pay attention to microclimates in your garden. In mountainous terrain, conditions at sites just a few yards from one another may differ significantly.

Mahonia repens
CREEPING OREGON GRAPE

Barberry Family

Description Perennial. Dense, branched clusters of yellow flowers grow at the ends of short stems 4 to 12 inches tall. Each flower is $^1/_2$ inch wide with six petals and six stamens. The leaves are pinnately divided into five to seven leathery, hollylike leaflets, each 1 to 3 inches long, egg-shaped, and very coarsely toothed.

Blooming March to June.

Soil Dry, rich, high humus, well-drained.

Range Southern British Columbia to southwestern North Dakota, south to western Texas and northeastern California.

Propagation Collect mature seeds and sow immediately $^1/_4$ inch deep in outdoor flats or in their permanent locations, and keep cool and moist. Maintain the flats for two years if germination is slow. Transplant the seedlings to pots after the first growing season and move to the garden after the second. Divide creeping underground stems in spring into sections, each having ample roots, and replant 12 inches apart, with the creeping stem just below the soil surface.

Cultivation Tolerates full sun. Do not plant near saltwater or roads that are salted in winter. Drought-tolerant.

Eriogonum umbellatum
SULFUR FLOWER

Buckwheat Family

Description Perennial. Spherical clusters of yellow or creamy white flowers, turning reddish to maroon with age, rise from one point near the top of a 4 to 12-inch stem, below which is a whorl of spoon-shaped leaves with wooly undersides. A cluster of similar but larger leaves occurs at the base of the plant. Individual flowers are about $^1/_4$ inch long with six petal-like sepals, while clusters are generally 2 to 4 inches across.

Blooming June to August.

Soil Dry, average, well-drained.

Range British Columbia to Montana, south to Colorado and southeastern California.

Propagation Collect seeds as they mature and immediately sow them thickly in outdoor flats of sandy soil. Transplant the seedlings to their permanent locations six to eight weeks after germination in spring. Mature plants are very difficult to transplant.

Cultivation Prefers limestone soils. Drought-tolerant, but occasional watering during drought prolongs blooming period.

Uses Plant in dry meadows, clearings, or woodland borders.

Aquilegia caerulea
BLUE COLUMBINE

Buttercup Family

Description Perennial. White and bluish violet flowers with five backward-spurred petals are borne on the tips of branching stems that may reach 36 inches in height. Long, hollow spurs extend between spreading blue sepals from the base of each of five white, scoop-shaped petals. Many yellow stamens protrude from the flower. The compound leaves are alternate, long-stalked, and divided into three deeply lobed leaflets.

Blooming June to August.

Soil Moist, average, high humus, well-drained.

Range Idaho to Montana, south to New Mexico and Arizona.

Propagation Collect seeds in summer and sow heavily on the surface of outdoor flats or seedbeds. Following germination in spring, wait six weeks before transplanting from the flats to the individual pots or the garden. Self-sows readily. Mature rootstock is difficult to divide or transplant successfully. To do so, divide the several crowns with a sharp knife, taking care not to break any roots.

Cultivation Prospers in aspen groves or meadows. Amend well-drained soil with a moderate amount of humus. Tolerates full sun.

Aconitum columbianum
WESTERN MONKSHOOD

Buttercup Family

Description Perennial. Deep blue-violet flowers grow in a loose, elongated cluster on 12 to 72-inch stems. The bilaterally symmetrical flowers are composed primarily of five petal-like sepals, the uppermost of which forms a large, arched hood. Leaves are alternate, 2 to 8 inches wide, and palmately lobed into sections with large, irregular teeth.

Blooming June to August.

Soil Moist, average.

Range Alaska to British Columbia and Montana, south to New Mexico and eastern California.

Propagation Immediately after collection in fall, sow seeds ¼ inch deep in outdoor flats or seedbeds and keep moist. Transplant the seedlings from the flats to the individual pots eight weeks after germination, and move to the garden in fall. Collect any bulblets from leaf axils in late summer and follow the same procedure as with the seeds. Divide offsets from tubers in fall or spring and replant 24 inches apart at their original depth.

Cultivation Thrives in full to partial sun.

Uses Plant in the rear of a border or scattered throughout a forest clearing.

4-9

Actaea rubra
RED BANEBERRY

Buttercup Family

Description Perennial. A short terminal cluster of small white flowers tops an erect 12 to 24-inch stem. Flowers are ¼ inch wide, and the narrow petals drop off shortly after it opens. Deep red, shiny berries replace the flowers in August and September. Alternate compound leaves are divided into 9 to 27 oval, coarsely toothed leaflets.

Blooming May to June.

Soil Moist, rich, high humus.

Range British Columbia to Labrador, south to northern Georgia, Oklahoma, and California.

Propagation As soon as the berries ripen in August, sow seeds in seedbeds or outdoor flats and keep moist. Transplant to the garden at the end of the first growing season. Divide rootstock in fall, leaving several buds per segment, and plant segments 1 inch deep and 24 inches apart or at random, and mulch with leaves.

Cultivation Plant in cool shade and keep soil moist. Mulch heavily in fall, preferably with oak or beech leaves.

Uses Berries make nice accents against ferns.

2-7

Arnica cordifolia
HEART-LEAVED ARNICA

Daisy Family

Description Perennial. One or more yellow flower heads crown a 6 to 24-inch stem. Each flower head is 2 to 3 inches wide and composed of 9 to 15 ray flowers encircling a central cluster of disc florets. The opposite leaves are 2 to 5 inches long, heart-shaped, and coarsely toothed.

Blooming May to August.

Soil Moist, rich.

Range Alaska to Montana, south to California and New Mexico.

Propagation As soon as seeds are mature, collect and sow in seedbeds or outdoor flats and keep moist. Transplant the seedlings from the flats to the garden in fall after their first growing season. Divide clumps in fall and replant 12 inches apart, with the crowns at the soil surface.

Cultivation Does well in light shade or partial sun.

Uses Plant with other perennials under stands of lodgepole pines, ponderosa pines, or quaking aspen, or along woodland borders or roads.

3-8

Key

5-6 zone

exposure

full shade

light shade

part sun

full sun

4-5 pH

attracts

attracts

attracts

attracts

Wyethia amplexicaulis
MULE'S EARS

Daisy Family

Description Perennial. From one to five yellow flower heads terminate the branches of a stem that stands 12 to 30 inches tall. Each flower head is 3 to 5 inches wide and has 13 to 21 ray flowers and numerous disc florets. The basal leaves are 8 to 24 inches long and elliptical with smooth margins, while those alternating on the stem are similar but smaller.

Blooming May to July.

Soil Moist, average, well-drained.

Range Washington to Montana, south to Colorado and Nevada.

Propagation Divide rhizomes in fall into sections with at least one bud apiece and replant these 12 inches apart, with the buds just below the soil surface. Collect mature seeds in late summer and promptly sow $1/4$ inch deep in the desired locations or in outdoor flats. Transplant the seedlings from the flats to their permanent sites in the following fall.

Cultivation A controlled burn of mule's ears stands every two to three years will enhance their growth.

Uses Plant in woodland clearings with other perennials.

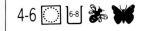

Erigeron speciosus
OREGON FLEABANE

Daisy Family

Description Perennial. Pink, lavender, or white ray flowers surrounding a yellow central disc compose the 1 to 2-inch flower heads that terminate short branches near the top of a 12 to 36-inch stem. The leaves are 3 to 6 inches long, egg-shaped, and clasping.

Blooming June to September.

Soil Moist, rich, well-drained, high humus.

pH Unknown.

Range British Columbia to Montana and South Dakota, south to New Mexico and California.

Propagation Divide clumps in early spring and replant 12 inches apart, with the crowns at the soil surface. Sow seeds thickly in outdoor flats as soon as they mature, and keep moist. Transfer the seedlings to individual pots about six weeks after germination, then move to the garden in fall.

Cultivation Tolerates full sun to light shade and dry soil. Divide clumps every two to three years.

Uses Plant in open woodlands, clearings, meadows, or borders.

4-9

Cornus canadensis
BUNCHBERRY

Dogwood Family

Description Perennial. What appears to be a single flower atop the stem is actually a cluster of small, greenish yellow flowers surrounded by four creamy white, petal-like bracts. A whorl of satiny, oval leaves, 2 to 3 inches long, occurs about midway up the 4 to 8-inch stem. Develops a cluster of bright orange-red berries in late summer.

Blooming May to July.

Soil Moist, rich, high humus.

Range Alaska to Labrador, south to Maryland, Illinois, Minnesota, in the Rockies to Colorado, and along the Pacific coast to northern California.

Propagation Remove seeds from the mature fruit in fall and plant $1/2$ inch deep in outdoor flats containing mixed sand and peat moss. Keep soil moist and transplant the seedlings to their permanent locations in the following fall. Maintain flats, as some seeds do not germinate for two or three years. In fall, cut rhizomes into 6-inch segments, each with one or more buds, plant horizontally with buds facing up, $1/4$ inch deep and 12 inches apart, and mulch lightly with conifer needles.

Cultivation Plant in colonies and keep soil evenly moist. Partial sun to deep shade.

Oenothera caespitosa
TUFTED EVENING PRIMROSE

Evening Primrose Family
Description Perennial. Low-growing plant with white flowers 2 to 4 inches wide that turn to pink and then to red with age. The four-petaled flowers grow directly from the rootstock, as do the 2 to 6-inch basal leaves, which are covered with silky hair and have irregularly toothed or lobed margins.

Blooming May to July.

Soil Dry, poor, well-drained.

Range Eastern Washington to southern Saskatchewan, south to southern California and western New Mexico.

Propagation As soon as the seeds mature, sow 1/4 inch deep in outdoor flats or in the desired garden locations. Keep the soil around the seedlings moist until they mature.

Cultivation Prefers sandy, gravelly, or rocky slopes.

Dicentra formosa
WESTERN BLEEDING HEART

Fumitory Family
Description Perennial. Rose-pink flowers dangle in clusters from arching stems 8 to 18 inches long. The long-stalked, bluish green, basal leaves are pinnately compound and finely cut into fernlike leaflets. Flowers are heart-shaped and 3/4 inch long.

Blooming March to July.

Soil Moist, rich, high humus, well-drained.

Range Southwestern British Columbia south to central California.

Propagation Divide rhizomes in fall, separating the crowns and making sure each division has several buds. Replant divisions 24 inches apart, with buds about 1 inch below the soil surface, and mulch. Collect seeds as soon as they mature and sow immediately 1/4 inch deep in outdoor flats filled with a mixture of equal parts compost, sand, and loam. Maintain flats for at least two years if germination is slow. Transfer seedlings to individual pots about ten weeks after germination in spring. Transplant in fall.

Cultivation Divide rootstock every second or third year to promote vigorous blooming. Prefers well-worked woodland soil. Mulch in fall with leaves. Do not crowd individual plants. Tolerates partial sun.

Geranium viscosissimum
STICKY CRANESBILL

Geranium Family
Description Perennial. Several purplish pink flowers, 1 inch wide with five broad petals and a downy mass of hair near the center, form loose clusters at the tops of multiple stems. The leaves are mostly basal, covered with downy hair, and have five to seven palmate lobes that are very coarsely toothed.

Blooming May to August.

Soil Moist, average.

pH Unknown.

Range Southern British Columbia to southern Saskatchewan, south to western South Dakota, Colorado, and northern California.

Propagation Sow seeds in lightly shaded outdoor flats or seedbeds immediately after collection. If germination is poor, maintain the flat or seedbed for a second year. Transplant seedlings in fall when they become dormant. Divide rhizomes in fall and replant 12 inches apart and 1 inch deep with buds facing upward.

Cultivation Tolerates full sun to light shade. Keep soil moist.

Uses Plant in open woodlands, sunny meadows, or clearings.

3-5

Key

5-6
zone

exposure

full shade

light shade

part sun

full sun

4-5
pH

attracts

attracts

attracts

attracts

Gaultheria hispidula
CREEPING SNOWBERRY

Heath Family

Description Perennial. Tiny white flowers grow intermittently along short, trailing stems that form a delicate mat. The flowers are nodding and bell-shaped, and the alternate leaves are round or egg-shaped and roughly the same size as the flowers. Stems are 3 to 12 inches long.

Blooming May to June.

Soil Moist, rich, high humus.

Range British Columbia to Labrador, south to western North Carolina, Pennsylvania, Michigan, Minnesota, and Idaho.

Propagation Take 6-inch stem cuttings in late spring or early summer, prune leaves from the lower third, dip the cut ends in rooting hormone, insert the cuttings 2 inches deep in a moist mixture of peat moss and sand, and mist regularly. Pot the cuttings in peat pots filled with equal parts peat moss, compost, soil, and sand. Mulch heavily or store in a cold frame in fall, remove the mulch in spring, and transplant into the garden at 12-inch intervals in the following fall, taking care not to disturb the roots.

Cultivation Locate in a cool, moist site. Will not tolerate direct sunlight.

Uses Groundcover for moist, shady sites.

2-7 4-6

Arctostaphylos uva-ursi
BEARBERRY

Heath Family

Description Perennial. Small terminal clusters of tiny white or pink flowers grow on a woody, trailing stem up to 10 feet long, with branches 6 to 12 inches tall. The flowers are roughly $1/4$ inch long and bell-shaped. Evergreen leaves alternating on the stem are $1/2$ to $1 1/2$ inches long, leathery, and somewhat spoon-shaped with smooth margins.

Blooming March to July.

Soil Dry, poor.

Range Alaska to Labrador, south to Virginia, Minnesota, New Mexico, and California.

Propagation Take 6-inch stem cuttings in late summer, prune leaves from the lower third, dip the cut ends in rooting hormone, insert 2 inches deep in a moist mixture of peat moss and sand, and mist regularly. Pot the cuttings in peat pots filled with equal parts soil and sand. Mulch heavily or store in a cold frame in fall, remove the mulch in spring, and transplant at 12-inch intervals in the following fall, taking care not to disturb the roots. Sow the seeds as soon as they mature in outdoor flats of sandy soil, pot the seedlings in fall, and move to the garden in the following fall.

Cultivation Tolerates full sun to light shade.

Uses Excellent groundcover for dry sites.

1-7 4-6

Linnaea borealis
TWINFLOWER

Honeysuckle Family

Description Perennial. From a creeping evergreen stem shoot upright branches, 3 to 6 inches tall and each bearing a pair of nodding white or pinkish bell-shaped flowers at the tip. The flowers are five-lobed and about $1/2$ inch long. The opposite, light green leaves are round or oval, measure $1/2$ inch in diameter, and are finely toothed.

Blooming June to August.

Soil Wet, rich, high humus.

Range Alaska to Labrador, south to Maryland, West Virginia, Indiana, Wisconsin, Minnesota, South Dakota, New Mexico, and northern California.

Propagation Take stem cuttings in spring while the plant is dormant, dip the cut ends in rooting hormone, and plant in individual pots containing a very moist peat moss-sand mixture. If possible, keep in a cold frame for two years before transplanting. Take care not to damage the delicate roots when transplanting. Seeds are difficult to collect and germinate slowly, and seedlings mature slowly. Sow in individual pots and keep cool and moist in a shaded location.

Cultivation Plant in a cool, wet, shaded area with plenty of humus worked into the soil.

1-5 ▨ 4-5

Iris douglasiana
DOUGLAS'S IRIS

Iris Family

Description Perennial. Flower color ranges from rose-purple to pink, cream, or white, with purple veins on the three downward-arching petal-like sepals. The three petals are erect and narrower than the sepals, which they join to form a tube at the flower's base. Two to five flowers per stem grow on short, branched stalks amid a dense clump of swordlike leaves measuring 12 to 36 inches.

Blooming February to May.

Soil Moist, rich, high humus, well-drained.

Range Along the Pacific Coast from southern Oregon to central California.

Propagation Divide rhizomes in late summer, and replant segments horizontally, with the crowns just below the soil surface. Collect seeds as the pods dry, and sow them ¼ inch deep in their permanent locations or in outdoor flats containing equal parts sand, peat moss, and loam. Transplant the seedlings to the garden after their first growing season.

Cultivation Tolerant of widely varying moisture, sunlight, soil, and pH conditions, but must be brought inside during winter in areas colder than Zone 8.

Uses Plant in clearings or open woodlands.

8-10

Smilacina stellata
STARRY FALSE SOLOMON'S SEAL

Lily Family

Description Perennial. An arching, zigzag stem, 12 to 24 inches tall, produces a terminal plumelike cluster of white star-shaped flowers. The three petals and three petal-like sepals create a six-pointed star ¼ inch wide. Alternate, pointed leaves folded along the midrib are a distinctive feature.

Blooming May to June.

Soil Moist, rich, well-drained.

Range Alaska to Labrador, south to Virginia, Kansas, New Mexico, and California.

Propagation Divide rhizomes at their forks in fall, making sure each segment has at least one new bud, and replant horizontally 12 inches apart and 1 inch deep, with the bud near the soil surface. Aim segments in different directions so that they extend outward to form a colony. Collect seeds as they mature, sow immediately ¼ inch deep in outdoor flats or in their permanent locations, and apply a 1-inch mulch of decaying deciduous leaves. If germination is slow, maintain the flats for at least two years. Transplant the seedlings to the garden after their first full growing season.

Cultivation Spreads readily with little care. Tolerates dry soil and full sun to light shade.

2-7 5-6

Smilacina racemosa
FALSE SOLOMON'S SEAL

Lily Family

Description Perennial. A conical cluster of very small (⅛ inch wide) white flowers develops at the end of an arching 12 to 36-inch stem. Alternate egg-shaped leaves, 3 to 7 inches long with smooth margins, clasp the stem. Brown-speckled green berries replace the flowers and later turn translucent red.

Blooming March to July.

Soil Moist, rich, high humus.

Range British Columbia to Nova Scotia, south to Georgia, Missouri, New Mexico, and central California.

Propagation Divide rhizomes in fall, leaving at least one bud per segment, and replant horizontally 12 inches apart and 2 inches deep, with the bud facing upward. Sow seeds immediately upon collection at a depth of ¼ inch in outdoor flats or in permanent locations, and mulch heavily with deciduous leaves. Maintain the flats for two years if germination is slow. Transplant the seedlings to the garden in fall after their first growing season.

Cultivation Mulch heavily in fall. Grows best where leaf mold is deep.

Uses Good woodland groundcover.

Attracts Ruffed grouse.

2-8 5-6

Key

5-6 zone

exposure

full shade

light shade

part sun

full sun

4-5 pH

attracts

attracts

attracts

attracts

Clintonia uniflora
QUEEN'S CUP

Lily Family

Description Perennial. A solitary white flower rises on a short, leafless stalk above two to three basal, canoe-shaped, shiny leaves. Three petals and three petal-like sepals, all with rounded tips, form a somewhat funnel-shaped flower about 1 inch wide that later becomes a lustrous steel-blue berry. The plant is 4 to 8 inches tall.

Blooming May to July.

Soil Moist, rich, high humus.

Range Alaska to western Montana, south to central California.

Propagation Divide rhizomes in fall and plant in individual pots or in garden. Place segments horizontally, $1/2$ to 1 inch deep, with the shoot tips at soil level and pointing in different directions. Immediately after collection, sow seeds $1/4$ inch deep in outdoor flats and transplant to their permanent locations after the second growing season.

Cultivation Requires cool, shady, moist sites. Mulch with a thick layer of conifer needles.

Uses Excellent groundcover for deep shade.

4-8 4-5

Erythronium grandiflorum
YELLOW FAWN LILY

Lily Family

Description Perennial. One to five yellow, nodding flowers dangle from the top of a 6 to 12-inch leafless stem, arising from a pair of bright green, 4 to 8-inch basal leaves. The bell-shaped flowers, 1 to 2 inches wide, are formed by three petals and three sepals, strongly recurved to the base of the flower.

Blooming March to July.

Soil Moist, rich, high humus, well-drained.

Range Southern British Columbia, south to Colorado, Utah, Idaho, and northern California.

Propagation Separate root offsets from corms in late summer, replant 3 inches deep in the garden, and mulch well. Replant parent corms at their original depth. Collect the seeds as they mature, and sow $1/4$ inch deep in individual peat pots filled with a mixture of sand and compost. Locate the pots outdoors, where they will receive partial sunlight, and keep them moist. Transplant the seedlings to their permanent locations, 3 inches deep and 6 inches apart, at the end of their first full growing season.

Cultivation Apply a thin layer of compost and mulch in fall. Needs cool summers.

Uses Plant in colonies as a groundcover.

3-6 5-6

Lilium pardalinum
LEOPARD LILY

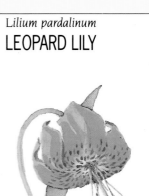

Lily Family

Description Perennial. Several bright orange, nodding flowers dangle on arching stalks on a 24 to 84-inch stem. Three petals and three petal-like sepals, strongly recurved and flecked with maroon, make up a flower 2 to 4 inches wide, with six long anthers suspended below them. Canoe-shaped leaves, 3 to 6 inches long with smooth margins, grow in whorls of 9 to 15.

Blooming May to July.

Soil Moist, rich, well-drained, high humus.

Range Western Oregon to northern California.

Propagation Separate the outer rows of scales and the offsets from the parent bulb in late summer or early fall, replant 4 to 6 inches deep and 18 inches apart. Collect the seeds as soon as they ripen and plant them immediately in seedbeds or outdoor flats. Transplant seedlings to their permanent locations after second full growing season.

Cultivation Prepare a deep, fertile, well-drained soil by working a generous amount of humus and sand to a depth of 12 inches. Mulch generously in spring with decomposing leaves. Tolerates full sun to light shade, but requires deep topsoil.

5-9 6-7

Xerophyllum tenax
BEAR GRASS

Lily Family

Description Perennial. Stems standing 12 to 60 inches tall support dense, clublike clusters of small, creamy white flowers, each measuring less than $1/2$ inch long. The stem rises from a thick clump of basal, grasslike, sharp-edged leaves 12 to 30 inches long, and is itself covered densely with similar, shorter leaves.

Blooming May to August.

Soil Dry, average, well-drained.

Range British Columbia to western Montana, south to western Wyoming and northern California.

Propagation Divide rhizomes in fall into sections with at least one bud apiece and replant 24 inches apart, with the buds upward. Separate the offsets from the roots in fall and replant 24 inches apart, with the crowns at the soil surface. Collect the mature seeds in late summer and sow immediately $1/4$ inch deep in outdoor flats or seedbeds. Transplant the seedlings to their permanent locations after their first growing season.

Cultivation Grows well in full sun to light shade.

Uses Plant in woodland borders or clearings.

4-10 ⬜ ⌊6-8⌋

Trillium chloropetalum
GIANT TRILLIUM

Lily Family

Description Perennial. The three erect petals of the solitary, 1 to 3-inch flower vary in color from burgundy with white bases to greenish yellow. This bloom rests directly above a whorl of three mottled, broadly oval leaves measuring about 6 inches long.

Blooming February to May.

Soil Moist, rich, well-drained, high humus.

Range Western Washington to central California.

Propagation Collect seeds as soon as they mature and sow immediately in outdoor flats filled with equal parts sand, compost, peat moss, and soil. Keep moist and lightly shaded, and transplant the seedlings to the garden after their second growing season. Divide rhizomes in late summer, replant horizontally 3 to 4 inches deep and 12 inches apart, and mulch.

Cultivation Mulch in fall. Tolerates partial sun.

Uses Plant in a moist, coniferous woodland garden.

6-9 ▨ ⌊5-6⌋

Streptopus roseus
ROSY TWISTED-STALK

Lily Family

Description Perennial. Small mauve flowers dangle on thin stalks from the leaf axils of an arching, branched, zigzag stem 6 to 36 inches long. The flowers are bell-shaped, about $1/2$ inch long, and composed of three petals and three petal-like sepals. Alternate, egg-shaped leaves, 2 to 6 inches long with smooth margins, and clasping bases.

Blooming April to July.

Soil Moist, rich, high humus.

Range Alaska to New Brunswick, south to New Jersey, in mountains to northern Georgia, also to Michigan, Minnesota, along the Pacific coast to Oregon.

Propagation In fall, divide rhizomes into pieces with at least one bud each, plant horizontally with buds upward, 1 inch deep and 12 inches apart. Collect the seeds as they mature, sow immediately $1/4$ inch deep in outdoor flats, mulch with compost or decaying leaves, and keep moist over winter. Maintain the flats for two years if germination is slow. Transplant the seedlings to the garden in fall after their first growing season.

Cultivation Grows best where leaf mold is deep. Mulch generously in fall.

Uses Good woodland groundcover.

3-7 ▨ ⌊5-6⌋

Key

5-6 zone

exposure

▨ full shade

▨ light shade

▨ part sun

☐ full sun

⌊4-5⌋ pH

 attracts

attracts

 attracts

attracts

Allium cernuum
NODDING WILD ONION

Lily Family

Description Perennial. A nodding cluster of pink flowers hangs from the downturned tip of an erect 8 to 24-inch stem. Each flower is $1/4$ inch wide with three petals and three petal-like sepals. The basal leaves are grasslike and may reach 18 inches in length.

Blooming June to August.

Soil Moist, average, well-drained.

Range British Columbia to New York, south to northern Georgia, Texas, New Mexico, and Oregon.

Propagation Divide bulb offsets from the mature bulbs in fall and replant 1 inch deep and 6 inches apart. Collect mature seeds in fall and sow promptly $1/4$ inch deep in outdoor flats filled with equal parts compost, sand, and loam. Transplant the bulbs of seedlings to the desired locations in fall after their first growing season. Self-sows readily.

Cultivation Thrives in full sun to light shade. Divide clumps every third year to alleviate overcrowding.

Uses Plant in an open woodland garden, woodland border, clearing, or meadow.

3-8 [5-8]

Glechoma hederacea
GILL-OVER-THE-GROUND

Mint Family

Description Perennial. Upright stems rising 4 to 12 inches hold whorls of blue-violet flowers in the axils of opposite leaves. Flowers are tubular, bilaterally symmetrical, and about $1/2$ inch long, with a two-lobed upper lip and a three-lobed lower lip, the middle lobe of which is significantly larger than that on either side. Leaves are $1/2$ to $1 1/2$ inches long and heart- or kidney-shaped with scalloped margins.

Blooming March to July.

Soil Moist, average.

Range Throughout most of North America.

Propagation Take stem cuttings in July and insert them in a moist sand-vermiculite mixture. Move them to the garden when well-rooted. Divide the rooted sections of the vine and replant them 12 inches apart, with the crowns at the soil surface. Self-sows readily.

Cultivation Thrives in nearly all soil conditions and full sun to deep shade.

Uses Good groundcover, especially in marginal areas. May become a pest in lawns.

3-9 [4-8]

Cypripedium montanum
MOUNTAIN LADY'S SLIPPER

Orchid Family

Description Perennial. A leafy stem bears one to three bilaterally symmetrical flowers, each consisting of a white pouch-shaped lip 1 inch long and flanked by two petals and two sepals, all bronze and twisted. Leaves are 2 to 6 inches long, elliptical, parallel-veined with smooth margins, and clasping bases.

Blooming May to July.

Soil Wet, rich, high humus.

Range Alaska to Alberta, south to northern California and northwestern Wyoming.

Propagation May be difficult due to the plant's symbiotic relationship with a soil fungus that must be present. Scatter seeds in a woodland garden, or sow in individual pots containing rich woodland soil mixed with copious quantities of compost. Transplant the seedlings to the garden after several years, keeping the soil intact around the roots. Divide rhizomes in fall, and replant 1 inch deep in the garden with some of the original soil left intact.

Cultivation Mulch well with decaying leaves in fall. Constant moisture is required.

Special note Exercise caution when purchasing plants. Do not remove from the wild.

3-7 [6-7]

Lupinus polyphyllus
BLUE-POD LUPINE

Pea Family

Description Perennial. Blue-violet flowers grow densely in long, spiked clusters atop 24 to 60-inch stems. The bilaterally symmetrical flowers are $^1/_2$ inch long and typically pealike, with one banner petal, two wings, and two petals forming the keel. Leaves are alternate and palmately compound, with 9 to 15 canoe-shaped leaflets, each 2 to 4 inches long with smooth margins.

Blooming May to August.

Soil Moist, rich.

Range British Columbia to Alberta, south to Colorado and central California.

Propagation Collect seeds as they mature, scarify by rubbing between two sheets of sandpaper, and sow immediately $^1/_4$ inch deep in the desired locations or in outdoor flats containing rich soil. Transplant from the flats to the permanent locations six to eight weeks after germination.

Cultivation Needs nitrogen-fixing bacteria in soil. If these are not present, commercial soil inoculants are available. Thrives in partial shade as well as full sun. Needs cool summers.

Uses Plant in moist meadows or woodland gardens or along stream banks.

Polemonium viscosum
SKY PILOT

Phlox Family

Description Perennial. Loose clusters of violet flowers crown a 4 to 18-inch stem. The funnel-shaped flowers are $^1/_2$ inch wide, with five rounded lobes and five stamens with orange anthers. Leaves are up to 6 inches long and compound, pinnately divided into many small, lobed leaflets.

Blooming June to August.

Soil Dry, average, well-drained.

Range British Columbia to Alberta, south to Arizona and New Mexico.

Propagation Sow recently matured seeds on the surface of outdoor flats of sandy soil in fall, and cover with a very light sprinkling of soil. Keep moist, and move the seedlings to their permanent locations in late summer.

Cultivation Tolerates partial or very light shade.

Uses Plant in alpine or subalpine meadows or along woodland borders.

Silene californica
CALIFORNIA INDIAN PINK

Pink Family

Description Perennial. Scarlet flowers appear at the end of branches on a 6 to 18-inch stem. Deep lobes on the five petals spreading from a tubular calyx create the illusion of more on the 1-inch-wide flowers. Leaves are opposite, 1 to 3 inches long, and somewhat egg-shaped with clasping bases.

Blooming March to August.

Soil Dry, average, well-drained.

Range Western Oregon to southern California.

Propagation In Zones 7 to 10, collect the seeds as they mature and sow promptly on the surface of deep flats or pots outdoors. Carefully transplant to the desired locations in fall after the first growing season, spacing the plants 12 inches apart with the crown just below the soil surface. In Zone 6 or colder, sow seeds in pots in spring after the last frost and bring the potted plants indoors before the first frost of fall.

Cultivation Thrives in full sun or partial shade.

Uses Plant in open woodland gardens or clearings.

Key

5-6 zone

exposure

full shade

light shade

part sun

full sun

4-5 pH

attracts

attracts

attracts

attracts

Lewisia rediviva
BITTER ROOT

Purslane Family

Description Perennial. One to several relatively large flowers, ranging from deep to pale pink, grow on short stalks directly above a basal rosette of leaves. The flowers are 2 to 3 inches wide and include 12 to 18 petals and numerous stamens. Leaves are narrow, succulent, and up to 3 inches long.

Blooming May to July.

Soil Dry, average, well-drained.

Range Southern British Columbia, south through western Montana and eastern Washington to Colorado and central California.

Propagation Gather seeds as they mature and sow ¼ inch deep in deep flats or pots filled with sandy or gravelly soil. Transplant the taproots of the seedlings during their summer dormancy to their permanent locations, with the buds just above the soil surface. Divide the taproot of mature plants after the flowers and leaves wither during summer dormancy, and replant the vertical sections 6 inches apart.

Cultivation Keep the soil dry during summer dormancy, covering it if necessary, but remove the covering in late summer.

Uses Great rock garden plant.

3-10

Tellima grandiflora
FRINGE CUPS

Saxifrage Family

Description Perennial. Pale pink to creamy white flowers grow in several loose, elongated clusters on a 12 to 36-inch stem. The flowers are ½ inch wide and have five fringed petals. Leaves are alternate or basal, 1 to 4 inches wide, and rather roundish with shallow lobes and coarse teeth. Those at the base have long stalks.

Blooming April to July.

Soil Moist, rich.

pH Unknown.

Range Alaska south to western Montana and central California.

Propagation Divide rhizomes in fall and replant the segments 12 inches apart, with the crowns at the soil surface and the roots spread. Mulch and keep the soil moist until established. Collect the seeds as soon as they mature and sow them ¼ inch deep in outdoor flats in a moist mixture of sand, compost, and peat moss. Transplant the seedlings to the garden in fall after the first growing season.

Cultivation Mulch with leaves in fall.

Uses Excellent woodland groundcover.

4-9

Penstemon strictus
ROCKY MOUNTAIN PENSTEMON

Snapdragon Family

Description Perennial. A one-sided cluster of blue to violet flowers occupies the upper half of a 12 to 30-inch stem. The tubular, two-lipped flowers are bilaterally symmetrical and 1 to 1½ inches long, with two lobes on the upper lip and three on the lower. Appearing opposite each other on the stem, the leaves are 1 to 4 inches long and either narrow and grasslike or egg-shaped.

Blooming June to July.

Soil Dry, poor, well-drained.

Range Central Wyoming south through western Colorado and eastern Utah to northwestern New Mexico and northeastern Arizona.

Propagation Collect the seeds when they have matured and sow immediately in the desired locations or in outdoor flats of sandy soil, and keep moist. Transplant the seedlings to the garden in the following fall. Divide rhizomes in early spring into sections with at least one bud each and replant 12 inches apart, with the buds at the soil surface.

Cultivation Tolerates full sun to light shade. Drought-tolerant, but occasional watering during droughts will enhance flowering.

Uses Open woodland and clearings.

4-5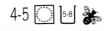

Viola canadensis
CANADA VIOLET

Violet Family

Description Perennial. White flowers hang facing outward from stalks arising from leaf axils on 4 to 16-inch stems. The flowers are bilaterally symmetrical and 1 inch wide. Each of the five petals has a yellow base, the lowest one has purple veins, and the two upper ones have lavender on their backs. The leaf blades are 2 to 4 inches long, heart-shaped, toothed, and may be long-stalked.

Blooming April to July.

Soil Moist, rich, high humus.

Range Alaska to Quebec, south to western South Carolina, northern Alabama, North Dakota, New Mexico, Arizona, and Oregon.

Propagation Gather the mature seeds and sow in the desired locations or outdoor flats filled with a mixture of loam, compost, and peat moss. Transplant the seedlings from the flats near the end of their first growing season. Divide rhizomes in fall, replant them in the garden 6 inches apart with the crown just below the soil surface, and keep moist.

Cultivation Requires moderate moisture. Work leaf mold into soil in early spring. Mulch in fall.

Uses Plant in colonies in shaded woodland gardens.

3-7 ⌊6-7⌋

Chimaphila umbellata
COMMON PIPSISSEWA

Wintergreen Family

Description Perennial. Pink or white flowers nod in a loose cluster at the top of a 4 to 12-inch stem. The five petals that make up the 1/2-inch-wide flowers are rounded, cupped, and waxy. Midway up the stem is a whorl of 1 to 3-inch leaves that are egg-shaped, wider at the tip than at the base, and toothed.

Blooming June to August.

Soil Moist, rich.

Range Alaska to Quebec, south to northern Georgia, Ohio, Illinois, Minnesota, New Mexico, Arizona, and California.

Propagation Divide rhizomes in fall into sections with one or more buds and replant them 6 inches apart and 1/2 inch deep. Sow the seeds in outdoor flats in fall, keep moist, and transplant them to the garden six to eight weeks after germination in spring.

Cultivation Tolerates light shade. Mulch with leaves in winter and remove in spring.

Uses Plant in cool, shady woodland garden.

2-7 ▨ ⌊4-5⌋

Oxalis oregana
REDWOOD SORREL

Wood Sorrel Family

Description Perennial. A white or rose-pink flower tops each 2 to 6-inch flower stalk. Deep lavender veins run the length of the five petals, and there are yellow spots at the bases. Each basal leaf is divided palmately into three heart-shaped leaflets and resembles a shamrock.

Blooming March to September.

Soil Moist, rich, high humus.

Range Coastal forests from Vancouver Island to central California.

Propagation Divide rhizomes in early spring into sections with one or more buds, and replant the sections 1/2 inch deep and 12 inches apart. Collect the mature seeds by tying a fine mesh sack around the developing fruit, and sow promptly in the desired locations or in flats. Keep the seedlings moist and transplant them from the flats to the garden in the following fall.

Cultivation Does well in light or deep shade.

Uses Plant as a groundcover in moist, cool, shady settings.

8-10 ▨ ⌊4-6⌋

Key

5-6
zone

exposure

▨ full shade

▨ light shade

▨ part sun

☐ full sun

⌊4-5⌋ pH

🐝 attracts

🦋 attracts

🐦 attracts

🐦 attracts

WETLANDS

Wetlands includes any freshwater area that is perpetually wet, from swamps and bogs to streams and pond perimeters.

Fragrant water lily

While it's commonly known that plants take in carbon dioxide and release oxygen while manufacturing their own food through the process of photosynthesis, many people don't realize that green plants must also take in oxygen in order to convert their self-made food into energy needed for growth and reproduction. Although water is essential to all plant life, too much of it in the soil can prevent oxygen from reaching important parts of a plant, such as the roots, and it can drown just as an animal can. Wetland wildflowers have had to develop means to overcome this problem in order to take advantage of waterlogged habitats. One common solution has been the evolution of air ducts within the stems and leaves that conduct oxygen-rich air to the submerged parts that, if growing on dry land,

. . . .

BELOW *Perhaps the most brilliant red to be found in nature, the searing scarlet of cardinal flower is a sure indicator of wet soil. Cardinal flowers are a favorite nectar source for hummingbirds.*

GARDENING TIPS

● Create your wetland garden in a naturally wet area, if possible.

● If a naturally wet area is not available, create an artificial wetland by excavating a shallow depression and lining it with a tarp or plastic sheet to retard drainage. Fill the depression with soil, amended generously with peat moss or other humus to retain moisture.

● Locate a wetland garden in a sunny area and well away from the septic system, house foundation, and underground utility lines.

● Conserve water and save on water bills by rerouting the downspout from your roof to the wetland garden.

ABOVE LEFT

Arrowhead grows in marshes and around lakes and ponds.

ABOVE RIGHT

Pitcher plants are found in bogs.

LEFT *Spotted jewelweed.*

would receive oxygen through the microscopic gaps between soil particles.

Too much water can create other challenges as well. It washes mineral nutrients required for plant growth out of the soil, slows the release of new minerals from the soil, slows the production of nitrogen (another important plant nutrient) by soil bacteria, and slows the decomposition of dead plants and animals, and therefore the recycling of nutrients, by microorganisms. All of these challenges required special adaptations to be evolved in the structure and biology of wetland plants, and those that have not evolved to cope with wet conditions are restricted to drier habitats.

Most wetland plants require lots of direct

CREATING A BOG GARDEN

Plants such as sundews and pitcher plants require constantly moist conditions. One way of achieving this is to construct a bog garden. Use a large container, such as a tub, dishpan, or child's wading pool. Make several drainage holes located four inches from the rim. The container can be buried in the ground or left on the surface with soil banked around it to create a mound. Make sure that the ground is level. Fill with a mixture of sand and peat moss, then gently fill with water until it begins to leak out the drainage holes. Check the water level weekly during droughts.

sunlight to grow, and since wetlands are generally free of trees and other shading obstructions, their wildflowers tend to bloom later in the spring and summer than do woodland wildflowers. Those that grow in swamps, however, do need to cope with shade, and thus bloom earlier or make do with less light.

Wetlands are generally considered to be areas where the soil is either saturated with water or submerged under shallow, standing water. In the context of this book, however, wetlands are areas that are perpetually wet, but not necessarily saturated, and wetland wildflowers are generally those that require constantly moist or wet conditions and are not drought-tolerant. "Wet" soil is that from which drops of water can be squeezed by hand.

BELOW *Water hyacinth is an introduced tropical plant that has made a nuisance of itself by clogging southern waterways. It belongs to the same family as pickerel weed.*

RIGHT *Each spring, marsh marigold graces wet areas across Canada and the northern United States. In the context of this book, wetlands are not necessarily submerged but have consistently wet or moist soil.*

85

Symplocarpus foetidus
SKUNK CABBAGE

Arum Family

Description Perennial. A most unflowerlike wildflower. A hooded shell-like spathe, 3 to 6 inches tall and mottled with brownish purple and green, surrounds a knoblike spadix bearing tiny flowers. Leaves 12 to 24 inches long and up to 12 inches wide appear later on a separate stalk.

Blooming February to April.

Soil Wet, rich, high humus.

Range Manitoba to Quebec, south to northern Georgia, Tennessee, and Iowa.

Propagation Sow seeds in permanent locations or outdoors in deep peat pots containing three parts peat moss to one part loam, and keep constantly wet. Transplant seedlings from pots to permanent locations several feet apart with the crown at soil level in fall. Readily self-sows. In fall, divide the large rhizome, which reaches about 2 feet into the soil, into pieces with one or two buds apiece and replant horizontally 4 inches deep and several feet apart.

Cultivation Requires no care if planted in low, wet areas. Will tolerate direct sunlight in the northern part of its range. Mature plants are difficult to transplant.

Uses Thrives in swampy conditions.

3-7 | 5-7 | ▨

Calla palustris
WATER ARUM

Arum Family

Description Perennial. A broad white spathe, 2 inches long, partially surrounds a spadix, 1 inch long, bearing tiny yellow flowers. The long-stalked basal leaves are dark green, glossy, heart-shaped, and 2 to 6 inches long.

Blooming May to August.

Soil Submerged, average, high humus.

Range Alaska to Newfoundland, south to Pennsylvania, Minnesota, Colorado, and northern California.

Propagation When seeds mature, sow immediately in peat pots containing peaty muck and set in a pan of water. Take cuttings in early summer and set them in the same medium as you would seeds. When transplanting to garden, set the rootstock just below the soil surface.

Cultivation Mulch in fall for winter protection. Requires very wet soil or still, shallow water no more than a few inches deep.

2-5 | 5-6 | ⬚

Arisaema dracontium
GREEN DRAGON

Arum Family

Description Perennial. A long spadix (4 to 8 inches) covered with tiny greenish yellow flowers protrudes well beyond the pointed spathe surrounding it. A solitary basal leaf is divided into 5 to 15 leaflets. Height ranges from 12 to 48 inches.

Blooming May to June.

Soil Wet, rich, high humus.

Range Minnesota to southern Quebec, south to Florida and southeastern Texas.

Propagation Separate offsets from corms in fall and plant in permanent locations 2 inches deep, either randomly or in small groups. Collect seeds when they mature in fall and sow immediately 4 inches apart in outdoor seedbeds, flats, or peat pots. Transplant seedlings to permanent locations in fall after their second growing season.

Cultivation Mulch with compost in late winter. Tolerates full sun to light shade.

Uses Showcase along a path, garden pond, or against a ledge.

4-9 | ▨ | 6-7

Lobelia cardinalis
CARDINAL FLOWER

Bluebell Family

Description Perennial. Brilliant red flowers grow in an elongated cluster atop a 24 to 48-inch stem. The tubular flowers have a three-lobed lower lip, a two-lobed upper lip, and stamens united into a tube protruding between the two upper lobes. The alternate leaves are canoe-shaped, toothed, and 2 to 6 inches long.

Blooming July to September.

Soil Wet, average.

Range Southeastern California to Minnesota to New Brunswick, south to Florida and Arizona.

Propagation Collect seedpods as they mature and immediately sow on top of humus-rich soil in outdoor flats. Cover with a hardware cloth, mulch lightly, and keep the soil moist. Remove mulch in spring, and transplant seedlings to individual peat pots ten weeks after germination and to permanent locations in fall after their first growing season. Divide rootstock in early spring and replant 9 inches apart with crowns at the soil surface.

Cultivation Mulch in fall. Tolerates full sun and drier conditions as long as soil is always slightly damp.

Uses Stream banks and wet borders.

Myosotis scorpioides
FORGET-ME-NOT

Borage Family

Description Perennial. Small, sky blue five-petaled flowers with yellow centers grow in loose clusters on a hairy stem 12 to 24 inches tall. Tightly coiled branches unfurl as the flowers open. The hairy alternate leaves are oblong with smooth margins.

Blooming May to August.

Soil Wet, poor.

Range Throughout North America.

Propagation Divide large plants in spring and replant at their original depth and 12 to 24 inches apart. Take stem cuttings in July, dip the ends in rooting hormone, and insert in a damp mixture of equal parts sand and vermiculite. Mist cuttings several times per day, and transfer to individual pots after about four weeks. Move to garden in late summer.

Cultivation Tolerates partial shade, but demands constant moisture.

Uses Good groundcover for wet places.

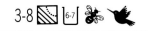

Mertensia ciliata
MOUNTAIN BLUEBELLS

Borage Family

Description Perennial. Loose, drooping clusters of pink buds open to form sky blue bell-shaped flowers that grow atop clumps of leafy stems 12 to 48 inches tall. Leaves are 2 to 6 inches long, alternate, smooth, and canoe-shaped with smooth margins.

Blooming May to August.

Soil Wet, rich.

Range Central Oregon to western Montana, south through western Colorado to New Mexico and northeastern California.

Propagation Upon collection in fall, sow seeds $1/4$ inch deep in outdoor flats, seed beds, or permanent locations. (Germination rate is reportedly increased by seed scarification, achieved by rubbing seeds lightly between sheets of sandpaper.) Keep soil moist and transplant seedlings to permanent locations in the following fall. In fall, divide rhizomes into 3-inch segments and replant them 1 inch deep and 12 inches apart.

Cultivation Needs constantly wet soil with a high humus content, but will tolerate full sun to light shade. Mulch generously with leaves or compost in spring to retain soil moisture.

Coptis groenlandica
GOLDTHREAD

Buttercup Family

Description Perennial. Solitary white flowers and glossy basal leaves rise 3 to 6 inches from a golden threadlike underground stem. Flowers are 1/2 inch wide with five to seven petal-like sepals. Leaves are compound and palmately divided into three leaflets with coarsely toothed margins.

Blooming May to July.

Soil Wet, rich, high humus.

Range Manitoba to Labrador, south to New Jersey, western North Carolina, and Iowa.

Propagation Sow seeds outdoors in individual peat pots set in a pan of water. Transplant seedlings to the garden in late summer. Take 3-inch root cuttings in fall and replant them shallowly 6 inches apart.

Cultivation Mulch lightly with conifer needles in fall. Tolerates deep shade.

Uses Beautiful groundcover for wet, shady areas.

2-7 ▨ 4-5

Caltha palustris
MARSH MARIGOLD

Buttercup Family

Description Perennial. A thick, branching stem 12 to 24 inches tall bears shiny yellow flowers and lustrous, dark green, heart-shaped or kidney-shaped leaves. Stem leaves are alternate, and both they and the long-stalked basal leaves are 2 to 7 inches wide with a lightly scalloped margin. Flowers are bright yellow with five to nine glossy petal-like sepals.

Blooming April to June.

Soil Wet, rich, high humus.

Range Alaska to Labrador, south to South Carolina and Nebraska.

Propagation Divide clumps soon after blooming and replant 18 inches apart with the crown at the soil surface and the roots spread evenly. Sow seeds in peat pots immediately after collection and set the pots in a pan of water outdoors. Transplant seedlings to the garden in the midsummer of their first growing season.

Cultivation Mulch for winter protection. Does well in full sun to light shade.

Uses Line stream banks or plant colonies in wet, sunny locations.

3-7 ▢ 5-7 🐝 🦋

Trollius laxus
SPREADING GLOBEFLOWER

Buttercup Family

Description Perennial. A creamy white or yellowish bowl-shaped flower crowns each 6 to 20-inch stem in the cluster. Flowers are 1 to 1 1/2 inches wide with five to nine broad petal-like sepals. Leaves are about 2 inches wide and are deeply indented into five coarsely toothed palmate lobes.

Blooming May to August.

Soil Wet, rich, high humus.

Range British Columbia and Washington to Connecticut, south to Pennsylvania, Michigan, and Colorado.

Propagation Collect seeds in late summer, sow immediately in peat pots set in a pan, and water from the bottom. Transplant seedlings to the garden in fall after their first growing season. Divide root clumps in fall and replant 12 inches apart with crowns at the soil surface.

Cultivation Tolerates partial shade.

Note Rare or endangered in the East.

4-6 ▢ 5-7

Thalictrum polygamum
TALL MEADOW RUE

Buttercup Family

Description Perennial. Feathery clusters of white flowers terminate the 36 to 96-inch branching stems. Flowers are about $1/2$ inch wide and lack petals. Male flowers consist of starburst clusters of threadlike stamens, while female flowers on the same plant have several pistils. The compound leaves are divided into rounded, bluish green three-lobed leaflets, each about 1 inch in diameter.

Blooming June to August.

Soil Wet, rich.

Range Ontario to Nova Scotia, south to northern Georgia and Tennessee.

Propagation Divide offsets of fibrous rootstock in fall and replant 18 inches apart with crowns at the soil surface. Sow seeds in outdoor flats as soon as they mature, and keep moist. If germination is slow, maintain flats for two years before discarding. Transplant seedlings to the garden in fall after their first growing season.

Cultivation Mulch in spring to retain soil moisture. Will tolerate partial or light shade.

4-7 ▢ 5-6 🐝 🦋

Typha latifolia
COMMON CATTAIL

Cattail Family

Description Perennial. A straight, rigid stem supports a terminal spike of tiny yellowish male flowers directly over a brown, clublike cylinder of female flowers. The swordlike leaves that extend above the flowers are bluish green, up to 1 inch wide, and sheathe the stem alternately with their bases.

Blooming May to July.

Soil Submerged, average.

Range Throughout North America.

Propagation Divide rhizomes in spring and replant 18 inches apart.

Cultivation Requires constant moisture, preferably in still, shallow water or very wet soil. Needs no care. Very aggressive in sunny, wet areas, and may need to be contained.

Uses Ideal for low, wet clearings and borders of streams and large ponds, or as a container plant in small ponds.

Attracts Muskrats.

2-9 ▢ 5-7

Eupatorium maculatum
SPOTTED JOE-PYE WEED

Daisy Family

Description Perennial. A flat-topped cluster of feathery rose-purple flower heads rests atop a purple or purple-spotted stem 24 to 72 inches tall. Clusters of dense flower heads measure 4 to 5 inches wide, and individual flower heads are up to $1/2$ inch wide and consist entirely of ray flowers. Pointed, egg-shaped, coarsely toothed leaves, 3 to 8 inches long, occur in whorls of three to five.

Blooming July to September.

Soil Wet, average.

Range British Columbia to Newfoundland, south to western North Carolina, Nebraska, New Mexico, and Arizona.

Propagation Divide clumps in fall, making sections that include a single stem and roots, trim the roots to 3 to 4 inches, and replant 24 inches apart with the crown just below the soil surface. Upon collection, sow seeds outdoors in peat pots set in a pan of water, cover with a sprinkling of soil, and transplant seedlings to the garden in the following fall.

Cultivation Divide clumps every other year to avoid overcrowding. Work extra humus into the soil for taller plants.

Uses Plant in a wet border.

3-7 ▢ 5-6 🐝 🦋

Key

5-6 zone

exposure

full shade

light shade

part sun

full sun

4-5 pH

attracts

attracts

attracts

attracts

Vernonia noveboracensis
NEW YORK IRONWEED

Daisy Family

Description Perennial. Deep lavender to violet flower heads grow in a loose branching cluster at the top of erect 36 to 72-inch stems. Flower heads are $1/4$ to $1/2$ inch wide, contain 30 to 50 disc florets, and are surrounded at the base by bracts with hairlike tips. The alternate leaves are 4 to 8 inches long, canoe-shaped, and finely toothed.

Blooming August to October.

Soil Wet, rich.

Range Ohio to Massachusetts, south to Georgia and Mississippi.

Propagation Divide clumps in late fall, replant divisions 18 inches apart with crowns at the soil surface, and mulch. Sow seeds thickly in outdoor flats and keep moist. Transplant seedlings to individual peat pots after they have developed a rosette of three to four leaves, and move them to the garden in fall. Take stem cuttings in June or July, dip cut ends in rooting hormone, and insert in equal parts of moist peat moss and sand. Maintain high humidity for four to five weeks, and move to the garden in fall.

Cultivation Tolerates a wide range of soil conditions as long as it remains damp. Also tolerates partial shade.

5-8 ☐ 5-6

Bidens aristosa
TICKSEED SUNFLOWER

Daisy Family

Description Annual. A branched stem 12 to 48 inches tall bears several yellow flower heads, 1 to 2 inches wide and composed of both ray and disc florets. The opposite leaves are pinnately compound, and their segments strongly toothed.

Blooming August to October.

Soil Moist, average.

Range Minnesota to Maine, south to Virginia and Texas.

Propagation Collect seeds in fall after the second frost and sow immediately in a moist garden location. Prepare a seedbed exclusively for this species, as it does not compete well with established perennials and grasses. Self-sows readily in moist, sunny locations. Mow the site in late fall.

Cultivation Tolerates light shade, but this may result in fewer blooms. Also tolerates a wide range of soil conditions, but requires constant moisture. Also tolerates partial or light shade.

4-8 ☐ 5-6 🐝 🦋

Eupatorium perfoliatum
BONESET

Daisy Family

Description Perennial. A stout, hairy stem, 24 to 48 inches tall, supports a flat-topped cluster of off-white flower heads. The opposite leaves, 4 to 8 inches long, have a wrinkled texture, toothed margins, and their bases are fused so that the stem appears to pierce a single leaf.

Blooming July to October.

Soil Wet, average.

Range Manitoba to Nova Scotia, south to Florida and Texas.

Propagation Divide clumps in fall, making sure each section has at least one stem with its roots. Trim roots to a few inches in length and replant 12 inches apart with the crowns at the soil surface. Upon collection, sow seeds outdoors in peat pots set in a pan of water and cover with a sprinkling of soil. Transplant seedlings to the garden in the following fall.

Cultivation Divide clumps every other year to avoid overcrowding. Tolerant of a variety of soil conditions, but requires consistently wet or moist soil.

Uses Plant in wet meadows.

3-9 ☐ 5-7 🐝 🦋

Aster umbellatus
FLAT-TOPPED ASTER

Daisy Family

Description Perennial. A rigid 24 to 84-inch stem terminates in a flat-topped cluster of flower heads, each ³/₄ inch wide with 10 to 15 white ray flowers and numerous pale yellow disc florets that turn purplish with age. Canoe-shaped leaves, measuring 2 to 6 inches long with smooth margins, alternate up the stem.

Blooming August to September.

Soil Moist, average.

Range Minnesota to Newfoundland, south to northern Georgia, Kentucky, and Iowa.

Propagation Collect seeds in fall and sow immediately in outdoor seedbeds or flats. Transplant from flats to pots in midsummer and to the garden in late fall. Set crowns at the soil surface, trim roots to 4 inches, and space 12 inches apart. Self-sows readily.

Cultivation Prefers constant moisture. Mulch in drier locations.

Gentiana andrewsii
CLOSED GENTIAN

Gentian Family

Description Perennial. Deep blue, bottle-shaped flowers crowd into a terminal cluster above a whorl of egg-shaped leaves on a single 12 to 24-inch stem, while other flowers may cluster in the axils of opposite leaves below. The flowers are up to 1¹/₂ inches long and always appear closed. Leaves are 2 to 4 inches long and have smooth margins.

Blooming August to October.

Soil Wet, rich, well-drained, high humus.

Range Manitoba to southern Quebec, south to northern Georgia and Arkansas.

Propagation Divide the root crowns in fall, making sure each new section has at least one bud and several roots, trim roots to 4 inches, and replant 8 to 12 inches apart, with buds 1 inch deep. Sow seeds on the surface of outdoor flats filled with a mixture of equal parts loam, sand, and compost, and lightly sprinkle a very thin layer of peat moss over them. Transplant seedlings to peat pots at the end of their first growing season and to the garden at the end of their second.

Cultivation Tolerates light shade, but blooms more profusely with at least partial sun. Mulch with compost in spring.

Uses Wet meadows, stream and pond banks.

Gentiana saponaria
SOAPWORT GENTIAN

Gentian Family

Description Perennial. Light blue, vase-shaped flowers that turn lavender with age cluster terminally above a whorl of narrowly egg-shaped leaves on a single 12 to 30-inch stem, while other flowers may appear in the axils of opposite leaves below. The flowers are up to 1¹/₂ inches long, slightly open, and appear toothed at their tips. Leaves are 2 to 4 inches long and have smooth margins.

Blooming July to September.

Soil Wet, rich, well-drained, high humus.

Range Minnesota to western New York, south to northern Georgia and Arkansas.

Propagation Divide the root crowns in fall, making sure each new section has at least one bud and several roots, trim roots to 4 inches in length, and replant divisions 8 to 12 inches apart, with buds 1 inch deep. Sow seeds on the surface of outdoor flats filled with a mixture of equal parts loam, sand, and compost, and lightly sprinkle a very thin layer of peat moss over them. Transplant seedlings to peat pots at the end of their first growing season and to the garden at the end of their second.

Cultivation Mulch with compost in spring.

Uses Wet meadows, pond and stream banks.

Key

5-6 zone

exposure

full shade

light shade

part sun

full sun

4-5 pH

attracts

attracts

attracts

attracts

Iris cristata
CRESTED IRIS

Iris Family

Description A single flower, composed of three drooping sepals, three erect petals, and three petal-like styles arching directly over the sepals, tops a 3 to 9-inch slender stem. The flowers are 2^1/$_2$ inches wide, bluish violet, and the sepals are marked by a bearded crest of yellow and white ridges streaked with purple. The wide, flat leaves are 4 to 8 inches long.

Blooming April to May.

Soil Moist, rich, well-drained.

Range Missouri to Maryland, south to Georgia and Oklahoma.

Propagation Divide rhizomes in early fall, leaving at least one fan of leaves and plenty of fibrous roots per division. Replant divisions with the crowns slightly above the soil surface and at least 6 inches apart. Sow seeds immediately after collection in seedbeds or outdoor flats containing a mixture of one part compost or peat moss, one part loam, and two parts sand, and keep moist. Transplant seedlings into pots at two months of age, and move them into the garden in fall.

Cultivation Tolerates full sun to light shade. Work some bonemeal into the soil, and mulch lightly in fall. Best planted on an incline.

Uses Very attractive as a groundcover.

Iris versicolor
BLUE FLAG

Iris Family

Description Perennial. Several bluish violet flowers grow on a stout stem among a basal cluster of swordlike leaves. Each flower is 3 to 4 inches wide with three arching petal-like sepals, three petal-like styles above the sepals, and three erect petals. The sepals have a white and yellow pattern near their base and bold purple veins. Leaves are 8 to 36 inches long and up to 1 inch wide, and the stem is 24 to 36 inches tall.

Blooming May to July.

Soil Wet, rich.

Range Manitoba to Labrador, south to Virginia, Ohio, Michigan, and Wisconsin.

Propagation Divide rhizomes in late summer and replant segments horizontally just below the soil surface and 12 inches apart. Sow seeds immediately upon collection, ^{1}/$_4$ inch deep in permanent locations or in outdoor flats containing equal parts loam and peat moss. Keep moist and transplant seedlings to garden in late spring.

Cultivation Tolerates full sun to light shade and submerged to moderately moist soil. Divide clumps every third year for maximum blooming.

Uses Banks and wet meadows.

Lilium superbum
TURK'S-CAP LILY

Lily Family

Description Perennial. Several nodding orange flowers with strongly recurved petals stand on long stalks above a single erect stem, 36 to 84 inches tall. Long stamens with large brown anthers dangle from a green star at the center of three petals and three petal-like sepals, all speckled with brown. The upper canoe-shaped leaves grow in whorls of three to eight, are 2 to 6 inches long, and have smooth margins.

Blooming July to August.

Soil Wet, rich.

Range New York to southern New Hampshire, south to Georgia and Alabama.

Propagation Separate outer rows of scales from parent bulbs in early fall, replant the parent bulb at its original depth, and plant scales 1 inch deep in outdoor flats or seedbeds. Collect seeds as soon as they ripen and sow immediately in seedbeds or outdoor flats. Transplant 4 inches deep and 12 inches apart in permanent locations after their second growing season.

Cultivation Locate in sheltered spots. Work in a generous amount of humus to a depth of 12 inches. Mulch in spring with decomposing leaves. Tolerates full sun to light shade.

Lilium canadense
CANADA LILY

Lily Family

Description Perennial. Nodding, bell-shaped flowers dangle from the top of a 24 to 60-inch stem. Ranging from yellow to orangish red and spotted with brown, they are 2 to 3 inches wide and have three petals, three sepals, and six long stamens. The canoe-shaped leaves are 3 to 6 inches long and occur in whorls of four to ten on the stem.

Blooming June to July.

Soil Wet, average.

Range Ontario to Nova Scotia, south to western South Carolina and northern Alabama.

Propagation Separate the outer two rows of scales from parent bulbs in late summer or early fall, replant the parent bulb at its original depth, and plant scales 1 inch deep in outdoor flats or seedbeds. Collect seeds as soon as they ripen, sow immediately in seedbeds or outdoor flats. Transplant bulbs or scales 4 inches deep and 12 inches apart in permanent locations after their second growing season.

Cultivation Tolerates full sun to light shade. In full sun, mulch generously with decaying leaves to keep roots cool and conserve soil moisture.

Lilium michiganense
MICHIGAN LILY

Lily Family

Description Perennial. Several nodding, deep orange flowers with strongly recurved petals stand on long stalks above a single erect stem 36 to 60 inches tall. The three petals and three petal-like sepals are flecked with brown, and six long, protruding stamens with large brown anthers dangle from the flower's center. Canoe-shaped leaves, 2 to 6 inches in length, grow in whorls of three to eight and have smooth margins. Similar to Turk's-cap lily, but flowers are larger, lighter, and lack a distinct green star.

Blooming July to August.

Soil Wet, rich.

Range Manitoba to southern Ontario, south to Tennessee and Arkansas.

Propagation Separate clumps by dividing rhizomes between bulbs in late summer or early fall and replant bulbs 4 inches deep and 12 inches apart. Collect seeds as soon as they ripen and sow immediately in seedbeds or outdoor flats. Transplant bulbs at the same depth and interval in permanent locations after their second full growing season.

Cultivation Tolerates full sun to light shade, but requires deep topsoil.

Uses Wet clearings, meadows, or woods.

Lythrum salicaria
PURPLE LOOSESTRIFE

Loosestrife Family

Description Perennial. An elongated cluster of magenta flowers tops a stem that is 24 to 48 inches tall. Four to six, but usually six, wrinkled petals compose each flower. The stalkless leaves are narrowly egg-shaped, 2 to 4 inches long, and have smooth margins.

Blooming June to September.

Soil Moist, rich.

Range Minnesota to Newfoundland, south to North Carolina and Missouri.

Propagation Take stem cuttings in July, dip ends in rooting hormone, and insert in a rooting medium of equal parts peat moss and loam. Mist several times per day or keep in a rooting chamber. Transplant to individual pots after about four weeks, then to the garden in late summer.

Cultivation Requires constant moisture and at least partial sun.

Caution Some experts warn against introducing this alien because it tends to crowd out native wetland plants. Should you wish to grow it for the vibrant color, contain the rootstock with an underground barrier, such as a bottomless 5-gallon bucket, which could accommodate one to three plants. Police for escaped seedlings.

Key

5-6
zone

exposure

full shade

light shade

part sun

full sun

4-5
pH

attracts

attracts

attracts

attracts

Hibiscus moscheutos
SWAMP ROSE MALLOW

Mallow Family

Description Perennial. Huge white flowers with red or purple centers grow on short stalks in the axils of alternate leaves on coarse, multistemmed plants standing 36 to 84 inches tall. The creamy white flowers are 4 to 7 inches wide, with five egg-shaped petals and numerous stamens united to form a column around the style with anthers on the outside. Leaves are about 4 inches long, egg-shaped, and coarsely toothed.

Blooming July to September.

Soil Wet, rich.

pH Unknown.

Range Indiana to Maryland, south to Florida and Texas.

Propagation Gather seeds in fall and sow immediately in outdoor pots. Transplant to garden in late summer. Take stem cuttings in July, dip ends in rooting hormone, and insert in pots of moist sand and vermiculite. Transplant to garden in late summer.

Cultivation Tolerates average soil that is constantly moist to submerged.

Uses A very showy feature plant for sunny, wet areas.

7-9 ▢

Rhexia virginica
VIRGINIA MEADOW BEAUTY

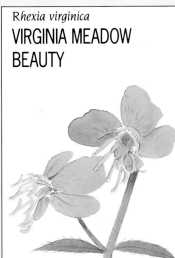

Meadow Beauty Family

Description Perennial. Several reddish pink flowers form a very loose terminal cluster on a 12 to 24-inch, four-sided stem. The flower, $1\frac{1}{2}$ inches wide, is characterized by four lopsided petals and eight prominent stamens with yellow, curved anthers. Leaves are stalkless, 1 to 3 inches long, opposite, and egg-shaped with toothed margins.

Blooming July to September.

Soil Wet, average.

Range Southern Ontario to Nova Scotia, south to Florida and eastern Texas.

Propagation Divide tubers in late fall into sections with at least one bud apiece, and replant 1 inch deep and 12 inches apart. Collect seeds as they ripen and sow immediately in outdoor flats containing equal parts sand and peat moss. Transplant seedlings in fall. Take stem cuttings in July, dip ends in rooting hormone, insert in wet sand and vermiculite, and place in a rooting chamber or mist several times per day. Transplant cuttings to pots after four weeks, and move to garden in spring.

Cultivation Adjust the pH of less acidic soil by adding compost or peat moss, which also helps retain moisture. Tolerates partial shade.

5-9 ▢ 4-5

Asclepias incarnata
SWAMP MILKWEED

Milkweed Family

Description Perennial. Clusters of deep pink flowers rise above the ground on a branching stem 24 to 48 inches tall. Each flower is about $\frac{1}{4}$ inch wide and consists of five strongly reflexed petals and a five-part crown. The opposite leaves are oval with smooth margins and measure 2 to 4 inches in length.

Blooming June to August.

Soil Wet, average.

Range Manitoba to Nova Scotia, south to Georgia and Texas.

Propagation In fall, divide the crown of the rootstock into sections with at least one bud each. Trim the roots to 3 to 4 inches and replant the divisions 24 inches apart with the crowns at the soil surface. Gather seeds in early fall and sow $\frac{1}{2}$ inch deep in outdoor flats and mulch lightly. Transplant seedlings to permanent locations in fall.

Cultivation Tolerates moist soil, but needs full sun.

3-8 ▢ 5-7

Monarda didyma
BEE BALM

Mint Family

Description Perennial. A dense, round, terminal cluster of scarlet flowers crowns a square stem 24 to 48 inches tall. The bilaterally symmetrical flowers are tubular and two-lipped, resembling a gaping pair of jaws, and measure about 1¹/₂ inches long. The dark green, opposite leaves are egg-shaped, coarsely toothed, and 3 to 6 inches long.

Blooming June to August.

Soil Wet, rich.

Range Michigan to New York, south to northern Georgia and Tennessee.

Propagation Divide clumps in early spring before they send up stems, replant 12 inches apart, and water immediately. Sow seeds immediately after collection in outdoor flats, transfer to individual pots seven weeks after germination in spring, and move to the garden in early fall. Take stem cuttings in June or July, dip end in rooting hormone, insert in a wet mixture of sand and vermiculite, and keep in a rooting chamber. Mist several times per day. Transplant rooted cuttings to the garden after five weeks.

Cultivation Requires constant moisture, but tolerates partial sun. Divide annually. Work generous amounts of humus into the soil.

Physostegia virginiana
OBEDIENT PLANT

Mint Family

Description Perennial. At the top of a square, 12 to 48-inch stem is a somewhat elongate cluster of pinkish, two-lipped, inch-long, tubular flowers, each of which has a three-lobed lower lip with the middle lobe spotted purple. The opposite leaves are 3 to 5 inches long, canoe-shaped, and have coarse, curved teeth.

Blooming June to September.

Soil Wet, rich, high humus, well-drained.

Range Minnesota to New Brunswick, south to Florida and Louisiana.

Propagation Divide clumps in fall, replant sections 12 inches apart with the crowns at the soil surface, and mulch. Sow seeds as soon as they ripen in outdoor flats containing equal parts compost and loam, keep moist, and transplant seedlings to permanent locations in the following fall.

Cultivation Requires constant moisture, but tolerates partial sun. Mulch in fall for winter protection.

Pontederia cordata
PICKEREL WEED

Pickerel Weed Family

Description Perennial. Clublike clusters of small purple flowers rise 12 to 24 inches above the water's surface. The flowers, less than ¹/₂ inch long, are two-lipped and funnel-shaped, and the middle lobe of the upper lip has two yellow spots. The basal leaves may be 4 to 10 inches long and heart-shaped.

Blooming June to October.

Soil Submerged, rich.

Range Minnesota to Nova Scotia, south to northern Florida and eastern Texas.

Propagation Divide rhizomes in fall, and replant 36 inches apart in 12 inches of water or less.

Uses Plant just offshore from cattails and arrowhead, but shallower than pond lilies, in lakes and ponds, or use as a container plant in a small garden pond.

Attracts Ducks, geese.

95

Sarracenia purpurea
PITCHER PLANT

Pitcher Plant Family

Description Perennial. A large, solitary, maroon flower rises on a leafless stalk 8 to 24 inches above a basal rosette of red-veined, pitcher-shaped leaves. The flower is about 2 inches wide, with five petals and a style expanded into an umbrellalike structure. Leaves are 4 to 12 inches long with a flared opening covered with stiff hairs.

Blooming May to July.

Soil Wet, poor.

Range Saskatchewan to Labrador, south to Florida and Texas.

Propagation Divide rhizomes in fall and replant 12 inches apart with the crowns at the soil surface. Collect seeds as they mature, sow lightly in peat pots on top of a mixture of equal parts peat moss and vermiculite, and place in a pan of water in a sheltered outdoor location. Use rainwater or distilled water, as pitcher plants are sensitive to salt buildup from evaporating tap water. Transplant seedlings to garden in their second spring.

Cultivation Needs six to eight hours of direct sun, with shade at midday. Needs constant moisture, but should be 4 to 6 inches above the water table. To construct a bog garden see p. 85.

2-9 ⬚ 4-5⌐

Lysimachia terrestris
SWAMP CANDLES

Primrose Family

Description Perennial. An elongated spike of yellow flowers grows terminally on a stem 10 to 24 inches tall. The star-shaped flowers are $1/2$ inch wide and have five separate petals and five stamens. Leaves are opposite, canoe-shaped, 2 to 4 inches long, and have smooth margins.

Blooming June to September.

Soil Wet, rich.

Range Minnesota to Newfoundland, south to northern Georgia and Arkansas.

Propagation Divide clumps in fall and replant rhizomes horizontally, 1 inch deep and 12 inches apart. Sow seeds in outdoor flats or seedbeds as soon as they mature, and transplant to permanent locations in the following fall. Vegetative buds are produced in the leaf axils after flowering, which when sown like seeds, will produce new plants.

Cultivation Mulch in fall.

Uses Plant in large colonies in sunny, wet sites.

4-7 ⬚ 5-6⌐

Potentilla anserina
SILVERWEED

Rose Family

Description Perennial. Solitary golden flowers grow on prostrate stems, while compound basal leaves appear on separate stalks. Flowers measure up to 1 inch wide and have five rounded petals and numerous pistils and stamens. Leaves may be as much as 12 inches long and pinnately divided into coarsely toothed leaflets covered with silvery hairs on the undersides.

Blooming June to August.

Soil Average, moist.

Range Alaska to Newfoundland, south to New York, Illinois, Iowa, New Mexico, and northeastern California.

Propagation Runners root easily to form new plants, so simply divide runners between plants and transplant to desired locations with crowns at soil level. Weight runners with small stones at a few points to encourage rooting where they contact the soil.

Cultivation Constant moisture is a must. Tolerates full sun to light shade.

Uses Spreads quickly to form an attractive groundcover.

2-5 ◨ 5-7⌐ 🐝

Parnassia grandifolia
GRASS-OF-PARNASSUS

Saxifrage Family
Description Perennial. A solitary white flower with green veins crowns an 8 to 24-inch stem, leafless except for a single clasping leaf in the middle. Five stamens with yellow anthers lie alternately between the five petals. All but one of the leaves are basal, long-stalked, egg-shaped or heart-shaped, 2 to 2½ inches wide, with smooth margins.
Blooming July to October.
Soil Wet, rich.
Range Manitoba to New Brunswick, south to Pennsylvania and Illinois, and South Dakota.
Propagation Separate clumps in fall, making sure each crown has as many roots as possible, and replant 12 inches apart. Collect seeds as soon as the seed capsules open and sow them immediately in outdoor flats kept constantly moist. Transplant to individual peat pots when five leaves have formed. Keep pots in a pan in light shade and water regularly from the bottom. Move seedlings to the garden in fall.
Cultivation Regular, light additions of lime (about ¼ teaspoon per plant) are recommended to maintain a high pH. Locate plants on slight mounds above wet soil. Divide clumps every third year.

3-5 ☐ 6-7

Chelone glabra
WHITE TURTLEHEAD

Snapdragon Family
Description Perennial. A terminal cluster of white, inflated, arching, two-lipped flowers grows on 12 to 36-inch stems. The tubular, bilaterally symmetrical flowers, 1 to 1½ inches long, grow nearly perpendicular to the stem and are often tinged with pink or lavender. Leaves measuring 3 to 6 inches long are opposite, canoe-shaped, and coarsely toothed.
Blooming July to September.
Soil Wet, rich, high humus.
Range Minnesota to Newfoundland, south to Georgia, Alabama, and Missouri.
Propagation Divide clumps in late fall and replant 18 inches apart with the crowns at the soil surface. Collect seeds in fall and sow immediately in outdoor flats or seedbeds, keep moist, and transplant to garden in late summer. Take stem cuttings in July before blooming, dip ends in rooting hormone, and insert in a wet sand-peat moss mixture in a rooting chamber, misting regularly. Pot cuttings after five weeks, and transfer to the garden in late summer.
Cultivation Tolerates full sun to light shade. Apply compost to the soil around plants. Mulch with decaying leaves in spring and fall.

3-8 ▨ 5-7 🐝 🐦

Pedicularis groenlandica
ELEPHANT HEADS

Snapdragon Family
Description Perennial. Flowers looking remarkably like miniature replicas of elephant heads grow in a dense elongated cluster at the top of a stem 8 to 30 inches tall. The upper lip of this reddish purple or pink, bilaterally symmetrical flower forms the "trunk," while the lower lip composes the "ears" and "jaw." Leaves are 2 to 10 inches long and pinnately divided into toothed lobes.
Blooming June to August.
Soil Wet, rich.
Range Alaska to Labrador, south in western mountains to California and New Mexico.
Propagation Collect seeds in fall and sow immediately ¼ inch deep in outdoor flats containing a mixture of equal parts loam, compost, and peat moss. Transplant seedlings to permanent locations in the following fall.
Cultivation Needs full sun, wet soil, and cool summers.
Uses Showcase this plant by itself in small colonies.

2-5 ☐ 5-8 🐝

Veronicastrum virginicum
CULVER'S ROOT

Snapdragon Family

Description Perennial. Several dense, fuzzy, spiked clusters of small white flowers appear on top of a 36 to 72-inch stem. The tubular flowers are $1/4$ inch long with two stamens projecting beyond the lips. Leaves are canoe-shaped, sharply toothed, and 2 to 6 inches long. Lower leaves are opposite, while the higher ones occur in whorls of three to nine.

Blooming June to September.

Soil Moist, rich, high humus.

Range Manitoba to Vermont, south to northern Florida and eastern Texas.

Propagation In late fall, divide the rootstock into segments, each with at least one bud, and replant 12 inches apart with the buds 1 inch deep. Collect seeds as they mature in fall, sow in outdoor flats, and transplant seedlings to the garden in the following fall. Take stem cuttings in July, dip ends in rooting hormone, and insert the ends in moist sand. Keep cuttings moist and in light shade and transplant to the garden in fall.

Cultivation Work generous amounts of humus into soil. Thrives in moist to wet soil and full sun to light shade. Mulch generously in fall.

3-8 ⬚ 5-7

Mimulus ringens
ALLEGHENY MONKEY FLOWER

Snapdragon Family

Description Perennial. Bluish purple flowers rise on long stalks from the axils of opposite leaves on the square stem of this 12 to 36-inch plant. Bilaterally symmetrical and tubular, each flower is about 1 inch long with an erect, two-lobed upper lip and a three-lobed lower lip. Leaves are 2 to 4 inches long, narrowly egg-shaped, coarsely toothed, and unstalked.

Blooming June to September.

Soil Moist, rich.

Range Saskatchewan to Nova Scotia, south to Georgia and eastern Texas.

Propagation Divide clumps in spring and replant 12 inches apart with the tips of new shoots at the soil surface. Collect seeds in late summer or early fall and sow immediately by scattering on top of outdoor flats. Keep soil moist and transplant the seedlings to the garden after their first growing season. Take stem cuttings in July, dip in rooting hormone, insert in a moist sand-vermiculite mixture, and keep in a rooting chamber for five weeks before transplanting.

Cultivation Constant moisture is a must. Separate clumps annually to promote vigorous blooming. Mulch in fall.

Uses Wet meadows and stream banks.

3-8 ⬚ 6-7

Drosera rotundifolia
ROUND-LEAVED SUNDEW

Sundew Family

Description Perennial. White flowers, $1/4$ inch wide with five petals, grow in a one-sided cluster on a leafless stem 4 to 9 inches tall. Spoon-shaped leaves about 2 inches long grow in a basal rosette and are covered with reddish, glandular hairs that exude fluid.

Blooming June to August.

Soil Wet, poor.

Range Washington to Nova Scotia, south to Florida and California.

Propagation In fall, sow seeds thinly on the surface of peat pots filled with equal parts peat moss and vermiculite. Place the pots in a shallow tray, fill with water to a depth of $1/3$ of the pot height, and place outdoors in full sun. Carefully transplant the seedlings to a bog garden 12 weeks after germination. Take leaf cuttings from mature plants in June and place them in glass jars that have been sterilized by boiling. Fill the jars with sterilized water, seal the lids, and place in indirect sun. Roots and buds should develop in about 30 days. Remove from the jars and gently press into the surface of a peat moss-vermiculite mixture, in peat pots, and set in a tray of water in light shade.

Cultivation Create a bog garden (see p. 85).

4-9 ⬚ 4-5

JEWELWEED

Impatiens capensis

Touch-Me-Not Family

Description Annual. Golden orange flowers mottled with reddish brown dangle from arching stalks, originating in the leaf axils of succulent, translucent stems. The bilaterally symmetrical flowers are shaped like a cornucopia with a sharply bent, saclike spur at the rear. Leaves are 1 to 3 inches long, alternate, and egg-shaped, with coarse, blunt teeth. Ripe seedpods burst at the slightest touch. Height varies from 24 to 60 inches.

Blooming July to September.

Soil Wet, rich.

Range Saskatchewan to Newfoundland, south to Georgia and Oklahoma.

Propagation Collect seeds as soon as they mature. You can tell that they are mature when the seedpods burst on touching. Immediately sow the seeds thickly in seedbeds. Cover thinly with sifted soil and mulch lightly. Self-sows readily.

Cultivation Thrives in light shade to full sun, but needs constant moisture. Plant in dense colonies in sheltered areas.

Similar species Pale touch-me-not (*Impatiens pallida*).

3-7

FRAGRANT WATER LILY

Nymphaea odorata

Water Lily Family

Description Perennial. Many-petaled white or pink flowers, 3 to 5 inches wide with a multitude of yellow stamens, float on the water's surface along with round, flat, shiny green leaves measuring 4 to 12 inches in diameter. Flowers open in the morning and close in the afternoon.

Blooming June to September.

Soil Submerged, rich.

Range Manitoba to Newfoundland, south to Florida and Texas.

Propagation Divide rhizomes in fall and replant in submerged pots at the rate of one every 12 to 24 square feet of pond surface.

Cultivation Partially fill dark pots with clay topsoil low in humus, plant rhizomes 3 to 4 inches deep, and cover the soil surface with 2 inches of fine gravel to hold in the topsoil. Pots may be submerged in water up to 4 feet deep. If planted in a small, shallow garden pond in Hardiness Zone 5 or colder, where there is a danger of the pond freezing solid, bring potted plants indoors in late fall, wrap each one in wet newspaper, seal the package in a plastic bag, and store them in a cool basement where the temperature remains a few degrees above freezing.

2-10

ARROWHEAD

Sagittaria latifolia

Water Plantain Family

Description Perennial. White flowers with yellow centers grow in whorls of three on a leafless stem 12 to 36 inches tall. Flowers are about 3/4 inch wide, with three petals and 7 to 10 stamens. The basal leaves are 4 to 16 inches long and shaped like exaggerated arrowheads, with two long, pointed lobes projecting rearward.

Blooming July to September.

Soil Submerged, rich.

Range British Columbia to Nova Scotia, south to Florida and California.

Propagation Divide rhizomes in fall and replant in dark pots partially filled with clay topsoil, which in turn is covered with 2 inches of fine gravel. Submerge pots in standing water, where the rim will be 3 to 12 inches deep. Collect seeds as they mature and sow in peat pots set outdoors in a tray of water. Transplant the seedlings to a pond in late summer following germination.

Cultivation Tolerates partial shade and wet soil as well.

Attracts Waterfowl, muskrats.

3-10

Key

5-6 zone

exposure

full shade

light shade

part sun

full sun

4-5 pH

attracts

attracts

attracts

attracts

4

DESERTS

The Deserts section includes not only true deserts but also southwestern grasslands, sagebrush, and chaparral.

Engelmann's hedgehog cactus

If you had to define a desert with one word, it would be dry. Dryness is a function not only of precipitation but of evaporation as well. Large amounts of sunshine, high temperatures, and constant wind all contribute to increased evaporation. No matter how much rainfall an area receives, if the amount of evaporation exceeds precipitation, the area will be dry, and a desert will result. Although deserts may seem barren at first glance, they harbor a great diversity of plant life, including the largest variety of annuals anywhere in North America.

In order for plants to survive in deserts, they must be able to collect water when it is available, usually via their root systems, and conserve it for use when it is not available. Plants have evolved some remarkable features for coping with dryness. Some are covered with dense or wooly hair, which greatly reduces the flow of drying air over the plant's surface. Leaves are often responsible for much

. . . .

RIGHT *and* BELOW

This phacelia and Mojave desert star are just two of many desert annuals. Annuals reach their greatest diversity in deserts, where their hard-coated seeds lie dormant during extreme heat and drought, their germination triggered only by seasonal rains.

water loss, so many desert plants have very small leaves or none at all, and the plants' stems have taken over photosynthetic duties. Many annuals simply wait out the dry periods between seasonal rains as seeds, then germinate rapidly, grow, bloom, and set seed when the rains come.

An inch of rain in the desert is not an inch of rain available to plants. Evaporation claims some of it. Precipitation that falls during the colder seasons, when plants are dormant, is largely unavailable to them. Intense rainfall quickly saturates the soil surface, causing excess precipitation to run off rather than percolate deeper to the roots. Soil porosity also determines how much moisture is available to plants. Precipitation that falls on very sandy or gravelly soil will quickly drain beyond the reach of plant roots. To combat this, desert perennials often have extensive, shallow root systems that spread like an underground net to intercept as much precipitation as possible. Fine-particled clay soils are very slow to percolate, and much precipitation that falls on them either evaporates or is lost as surface runoff before it reaches the plant roots.

All of this translates into sparseness of vegetation. Plants grow at intervals so they can gather enough moisture to sustain themselves. Generally speaking, if there is more soil exposed than covered by plants, the area is probably a desert. Because of this and the generally high rate of decomposition due to higher summer temperatures, there is usually little humus in desert soils, which diminishes their fertility. Also, in porous desert soils, a fair quantity of nutrients is leached beyond the reach of plant roots by rapidly draining moisture. All of these factors result in desert soils that are usually of poor or, at best, average fertility.

This section also includes southwestern grasslands. The characteristics of grasslands are outlined in the introduction to the chapter on prairies, and they apply to these grasslands as well. In this part of the country, however, whether an area is desert, grassland,

RIGHT *Desert sunflower, another annual, is a member of the daisy, or composite, family. Each compact flower head is composed of numerous smaller ray flowers, disc florets, or both.*

DESERTS

California grasslands

Great Basin Desert

Mohave Desert

Chihuahuan Desert

Sonoran Desert

or forest is largely determined by its elevation, which in turn determines the amount of precipitation and the rate of evaporation. Generally speaking, the lowest elevations are deserts, because this is where precipitation is least and the evaporation rates are greater. Above deserts, where precipitation is somewhat higher and evaporation rates are lower, one finds grasslands. Higher still, enough precipitation falls and remains available to plants to support woodlands.

Caution: Do not remove any cactus from the wild unless it is directly threatened with imminent destruction by human activity.

. . . .

LEFT *Unlike many other species in the evening primrose family, desert primrose blooms at sunrise rather than sunset, indicating its dependence on diurnal pollinators.*

BELOW *Following seasonal rains, annuals such as desert sand verbena carpet acres of desert with brilliant color.*

GARDENING TIPS

● Select only native, drought-tolerant perennials and native annuals for your southwestern wildflower garden.

● Allow plenty of bare soil between perennials. In deserts, this should be at least equivalent to the diameter of the larger of two adjacent plants. Intervals between plants in southwestern grasslands are smaller. Annuals may be sown more densely.

● Desert soils are generally quite sandy or gravelly, with little humus and fairly poor fertility. Most desert plants require very well drained soils to avoid root rot.

● Desert soils are usually neutral, alkaline, or only slightly acidic due to the accumulation of magnesium, potassium, calcium, and other alkaline elements. In more humid climates, more of these elements are removed from the soil by higher amounts of precipitation. Higher pH levels in soil decrease the availability of certain nutrients, adversely affecting soil fertility.

● Sow seeds of annuals just before the seasonal rains, and keep the soil slightly moist until the rains begin.

Yucca whipplei
OUR LORD'S CANDLE

Agave Family

Description Perennial. A stout stem rising 4 to 11 feet supports a huge, elongated cluster bearing thousands of white or creamy white flowers on the upper 24 to 48 inches of its length. Each flower is 1 to 1 1/2 inches long, with three petals and three petal-like sepals. At the base of the plant is a dense, starburst rosette of stiff, blue-green, spine-tipped leaves that reach 36 inches in length.

Blooming April to May.

Soil Arid, poor, well-drained.

Range Southern California.

Propagation In fall, soak seeds in water for two days, then sow them 1/4 inch deep in flats or the desired locations. Transplant from the flats to their permanent locations, 36 to 60 inches apart, after their first summer. Will not normally set seed outside of its native range due to the absence of a particular pollinating moth, but flowers may be pollinated manually.

Cultivation Does not tolerate prolonged exposure to temperatures below freezing, so where this occurs the plant should be grown in large pots and moved indoors. Dies after setting seed, so start new plants annually.

Uses Great container plants.

9-10 ▢ 5-8 🦋

Delphinium parishii
DESERT DELPHINIUM

Buttercup Family

Description Perennial. A loose, narrow cluster of sky blue flowers tops the 6 to 24-inch stem. Each flower is equipped with five reflexed petal-like sepals and a backward-projecting spur. Leaves are alternate, 2 to 3 inches wide, and palmately lobed into narrow, forked divisions.

Blooming March to June.

Soil Dry, poor.

pH Unknown.

Range Central and southern California through southern Nevada to western Arizona.

Propagation Sow seeds in fall in their permanent locations or in outdoor flats and cover with a thin scattering of sandy soil. Thin the seedlings and transplant them from the flats to their desired locations after the first summer. Divide clumps in fall.

Cultivation Also grows in moist soil.

Uses Plant in desert garden.

7-9 ▢ 🐝 🐦

Opuntia basilaris
BEAVERTAIL CACTUS

Cactus Family

Description Perennial. A stem flattened into gray-green jointed pads gives rise to rose or magenta flowers on the upper edges of the pads. The flowers are 2 to 3 inches wide, with numerous petals and stamens. Tufts of short, fine glochids replace leaves. The stems seldom exceed 12 inches in height, but can form clumps up to 72 inches in diameter.

Blooming March to June.

Soil Arid, poor.

Range Southeastern California to southwestern Utah, south through Arizona.

Propagation Wear heavy gloves when handling. Pull up peripheral pads and their roots in fall and transplant several feet away. Take stem cuttings throughout the growing season by breaking off pads at the joints, dusting the broken end with B_1 vitamin, and inserting it about 2 inches deep in permanent sites with very sandy, rocky soil or in flats containing 3 parts sand to 1 part soil. Sow seeds in outdoor flats as above, and transplant seedlings to permanent locations after their first growing season.

Cultivation Requires very well drained soil and at least partial sun. Do not overwater.

Caution Do not remove from the wild.

6-9 ▢ 5-8

Echinocereus triglochidiatus
CLARET CUP CACTUS

Cactus Family

Description Perennial. Scarlet flowers, 1 to 2 inches wide with numerous waxy petals, perch atop cylindrical stems 2 to 12 inches high and covered with clusters of curved spines. The stems of older plants may form mounds 12 to 48 inches in diameter.

Blooming April to June.

Soil Dry, average, high humus, well-drained.

Range Southern California to central Colorado, south through western Texas, New Mexico, and Arizona.

Propagation Sow the seeds in flats in fall and transplant to the desired locations, 24 to 36 inches apart, after their first summer. Divide peripheral stems from the mound and replant. Wear heavy gloves when handling.

Cultivation Amend soil with leaf mold.

Uses Plant in desert garden, chaparral, oak woodlands, or pinyon-juniper woodlands.

Caution Do not remove from the wild.

5-9 ☐ 5-8

Echinocereus engelmannii
ENGLEMANN'S HEDGEHOG CACTUS

Cactus Family

Description Perennial. Mounds up to 36 inches in diameter of cylindrical stems 4 to 12 inches tall give rise to many-petaled rose, red, or magenta flowers. Each cluster of spines includes two to six long, flat spines encircled by 6 to 12 shorter ones.

Blooming April to May.

Soil Arid, poor, well-drained.

Range Southern California to western Texas, south to Mexico.

Propagation Sow seeds in outdoor flats in fall and transplant to the desired locations, 24 to 36 inches apart, after their first summer. Divide peripheral stems from the mound and replant. Wear heavy gloves when handling.

Cultivation Amend soil with plenty of sand and gravel.

Uses Plant in a desert garden among other succulents.

Caution Do not remove from the wild.

5-10 ☐ 5-8

Cleome lutea
YELLOW BEE PLANT

Caper Family

Description Annual. Dense clusters of yellow flowers grace the ends of branched stems on this 12 to 36-inch plant. The long-stalked flowers are $1/2$ inch wide and have four petals and six long, threadlike stamens. Leaves are alternate and palmately compound with three to seven canoe-shaped leaflets, each 1 to 3 inches long with smooth margins.

Blooming May to September.

Soil Dry, poor, well-drained.

Range Eastern Washington to Montana, south through western Nebraska to New Mexico and eastern California.

Propagation Collect seeds as they mature and sow immediately $1/4$ inch deep in desired locations or in outdoor flats filled with sandy soil. Keep soil moist until several weeks after germination, when seedlings may be transplanted from the flats to their permanent locations. Self-sows readily.

Cultivation No care required.

Uses Grow in desert or sagebrush gardens, meadows, or grasslands.

3-9 ☐ 5-8

Key

5-6 zone

exposure

full shade

light shade

part sun

full sun

4-5 pH

attracts

attracts

attracts

attracts

Baileya multiradiata
DESERT MARIGOLD

Daisy Family

Description Annual. A stem covered with wooly gray hair rises 12 to 24 inches to a single, brilliant yellow flower head composed of numerous ray flowers, toothed at the tips, surrounding disc florets. The long-stalked leaves are $1^1/_2$ to 3 inches long, pinnately divided into deep lobes, and wooly like the stem.

Blooming April to November.

Soil Arid, poor, well-drained.

Range Southeastern California to southern Utah, south to western Texas and Mexico.

Propagation In early spring, after the danger of frost has passed, sow seeds $1/_4$ inch deep in seedbeds or in outdoor flats of sandy soil and moisten regularly until germination. Transplant from flats to the garden after four to six weeks.

Cultivation Periodic watering will greatly extend the blooming period during drought. Soil surface should dry completely between waterings.

Uses Plant in rock gardens or in fields of other desert annuals.

3-10 ▢ 5-8

Eriophyllum confertiflorum
GOLDEN YARROW

Daisy Family

Description Perennial. Clusters of yellow flower heads, 3 to 4 inches in diameter, gather at the ends of wooly, branched stems standing 12 to 24 inches tall. Each flower head is $1/_2$ inch wide and composed of four to six rounded ray flowers and several disc florets. The leaves are also covered with dense gray hair, and their edges curl toward the undersides.

Blooming May to August.

Soil Dry, average, well-drained.

Range Central and southern California.

Propagation Sow freshly collected seeds in fall, $1/_4$ inch deep in desired locations, and keep moist until several weeks after germination. Difficult to transplant successfully.

Cultivation Needs a heavy winter mulch in Hardiness Zone 8. In colder regions, it can only be grown as an annual or as a potted plant and brought inside in winter. Add sand or gravel to improve soil drainage, if necessary.

Uses Plant in desert gardens or meadows.

8-10 ▢ 5-8

Lasthenia chrysostoma
GOLDFIELDS

Daisy Family

Description Annual. Brilliant yellow flower heads mark the ends of 4 to 10-inch branching stems. The flower heads, which may be up to 1 inch wide, are composed of 10 to 14 short, oval ray florets surrounding a conical disc of slightly darker disc florets. Leaves are about $1/_2$ to 3 inches long, opposite, and grasslike, with stiff hairs about their clasping bases.

Blooming March to May.

Soil Moist, average.

Range Southwestern Oregon south to southern California and central Arizona.

Propagation In Hardiness Zones 9 and 10, sow in fall $1/_4$ inch deep in the desired locations, and keep moist until two weeks after germination. In Hardiness Zones 8 or colder, sow outdoors in spring or indoors in late winter and transplant to the garden several weeks after germination. Self-sows readily in native range.

Cultivation Arnend soil with compost for more vigorous growth.

Uses Plant in meadows or open woodlands.

3-10 ▢ 5-8

Layia platyglossa
TIDY TIPS

Daisy Family

Description Annual. White and yellow flower heads about 1 inch wide adorn the tops of 4 to 12-inch stems. The ray florets are white-tipped and three-toothed with deep yellow bases, and they surround tubular yellow disc florets with protruding black anthers. Leaves are alternate, $^1/_2$ to 3 inches long, and narrow with a few coarse teeth. Both they and the stem are densely covered with hair.

Blooming March to June.

Soil Moist, average, well-drained.

Range Western half of California.

Propagation In Hardiness Zones 9 and 10, sow in fall $^1/_4$ inch deep in the desired locations, and keep moist until two weeks after germination. In Hardiness Zones 8 or colder, sow outdoors in spring or indoors in late winter and transplant to garden several weeks after germination. Self-sows readily in native range.

Cultivation Soil must be well-drained.

Uses Plant in meadows with other annuals or in colonies by itself.

3-10 [☼] [5-8]

Eriophyllum lanatum
WOOLY SUNFLOWER

Daisy Family

Description Perennial. Branched stems terminate in golden yellow flower heads that are $1^1/_2$ to $2^1/_2$ inches wide with 8 to 12 ray florets surrounding a central disc. The leaves are up to 3 inches long and irregularly lobed with narrow segments. Both the leaves and the 6 to 24-inch stems are densely covered with wooly gray hair.

Blooming May to August.

Soil Dry, average, well-drained.

Range Southern British Columbia to western Montana, south to western Utah and southern California.

Propagation In fall, sow freshly collected seeds $^1/_4$ inch deep in outdoor flats of sandy soil or in their desired locations, and keep moist until several weeks after germination. Transplant from flats to individual pots after second true leaf has appeared, and move into the garden in the following fall.

Cultivation Remove withered flower heads before they set seed to prolong blooming period. Add sand or gravel to improve soil drainage, if necessary.

Uses Plant in desert gardens or meadows.

5-9 [☼] [5-8]

Oenothera deltoides
DESERT EVENING PRIMROSE

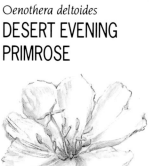

Evening Primrose Family

Description Perennial. Large white flowers grow from the leaf axils on 2 to 12-inch branches rising from a creeping stem 4 to 40 inches long. The four broad petals of this 2 to 3-inch-wide flower have a tissuelike texture. Leaves are 1 to 3 inches long, somewhat spoon-shaped, and covered with wooly gray hair, as is the stem.

Blooming March to June.

Soil Arid, poor, well-drained.

Range Eastern Oregon to Utah, south to Arizona and southern California.

Propagation Collect the seeds as they mature and sow in the desired locations or in outdoor flats of very sandy soil in fall and cover with a sprinkling of sand. Transplant from the flats to the desired locations at least 12 inches apart in the following fall, and thin those in permanent locations to similar intervals. Take stem cuttings after flowering and insert cut ends in moist sand until well-rooted.

Cultivation Will grow on sand dunes.

Uses Plant in sandy desert garden at low elevations.

5-10 [☼] [5-8] 🦋

Key

5-6
zone

exposure

[▨] full shade

[▨] light shade

[▨] part sun

[☼] full sun

[4-5] pH

🐝 attracts

🦋 attracts

🐦 attracts

🐦 attracts

Zauschneria californica
CALIFORNIA FUCHSIA

Evening Primrose Family

Description Perennial. Scarlet flowers, often oriented in the same direction, grow from the leaf axils on a many-branched stem that is 12 to 36 inches tall. Four petals and four petal-like sepals compose the tubular, trumpet-shaped flower, and eight red stamens protrude from its mouth. The leaves, ¹/₂ to 1¹/₂ inches long, are either egg-shaped and green or narrow, gray, and hairy.

Blooming August to October.

Soil Dry, poor, well-drained.

Range Southwestern Oregon to southern California.

Propagation Divide roots in early spring and replant 24 inches apart, with the crowns at the soil surface. Sow seeds in spring in desired locations or in flats, and thin seedlings or transplant from flats to the garden at intervals of at least 24 inches. Take stem cuttings in fall and insert cut ends in moist sand until well-rooted.

Cultivation Evergreen in Zones 9 and 10. Mulch for winter protection in zones colder than 9. Favors a pH between 7 and 8. Pinch back leggy plants. Drought-tolerant.

Uses Plant as a groundcover. Useful for erosion control on dry, sunny slopes.

7-10 ☐ 5-8

Clarkia amoena
FAREWELL-TO-SPRING

Evening Primrose Family

Description Annual. Pink or lavender flowers grow in loose clusters atop a 12 to 36-inch stem. The cup-shaped flowers are 2 to 4 inches wide with four broad, fan-shaped petals, each of which is marked by a central red or reddish purple spot. Leaves are alternate, narrow, smooth-edged, and 1 to 3 inches long.

Blooming June to August.

Soil Moist, average, well-drained.

Range Southern British Columbia to central California.

Propagation In Zones 9 and 10, sow seeds in fall; otherwise, in spring after the last frost. Sow in desired locations, cover with a thin scattering of soil, and keep moist until blooming. Thin seedlings to intervals of at least 6 inches.

Cultivation Tolerates full sun to light shade.

Uses Plant in meadows with other annuals.

3-10 ☐ 5-8

Oenothera hookeri
HOOKER'S EVENING PRIMROSE

Evening Primrose Family

Description Biennial. Large yellow flowers rise from the upper leaf axils to form a loose cluster on an unbranched 24 to 60-inch stem. The flowers, 2 to 3 inches wide, have four fan-shaped petals that quickly turn orangish with age. Leaves are alternate, 3 to 12 inches long, and slightly egg-shaped with smooth margins.

Blooming June to October.

Soil Moist, average.

Range Northern California to northern Utah and southern Colorado, south to Mexico and beyond; also north through western Idaho.

Propagation Collect seeds as they mature and sow in the desired locations or in outdoor flats in fall and cover with a sprinkling of soil. Transplant from the flats to the desired locations at least 12 inches apart in the following fall, and thin those in permanent locations to similar intervals. Sow seeds in two consecutive years to assure annual blooming.

Cultivation Tolerates dry soils.

Uses Plant in moist meadows, on stream banks, or in desert washes.

4-10 ☐ 5-8

Mirabilis multiflora
DESERT FOUR O'CLOCK

Four O'Clock Family

Description Perennial. Magenta flowers arise from cup-forming bracts in the outer leaf axils of this bushy plant that may reach 36 inches in height and 48 inches in diameter. Tubular flowers with a flared mouth 1 inch wide, five lobes, and five protruding stamens close during midday. The opposite leaves are up to 6 inches wide, and broadly heart-shaped or egg-shaped with smooth margins.

Blooming April to September.

Soil Arid, poor, well-drained.

Range Central California to southern Colorado, south to western Texas and Mexico.

Propagation Collect the seeds as they mature, scarify, and sow in late fall in the desired locations or in outdoor flats kept moist for the first month. Cold-moist stratification in a refrigerator for one month prior to sowing in spring may enhance germination. Divide tuberous roots in late fall. Take stem cuttings in summer, dip cut ends in rooting hormone, insert in moist sand, and mist regularly until well-rooted.

Cultivation Mow in fall after the stems die back. Drought-tolerant, but supplemental watering prolongs the blooming period.

Uses Excellent for erosion control.

5-10

Abronia villosa
DESERT SAND VERBENA

Four O'Clock Family

Description Annual. Bright pink flowers in starburst heads, 2 to 3 inches wide and rising 1 to 10 inches from leaf axils, grace a creeping stem up to 36 inches long. Many stems form a thick mat. The trumpet-shaped flowers have five curly, deeply notched lobes. Leaves are opposite, up to $1\frac{1}{2}$ inches long, and oval or egg-shaped with wavy margins.

Blooming February to August.

Soil Arid, poor, well-drained.

Range Southern California, southern Nevada, and western Arizona.

Propagation Sow freshly collected seeds $\frac{1}{4}$ inch deep in desired locations or in flats filled with sandy soil in fall or early spring, and keep moist until germination. Transplant seedlings from flats to the desired locations about four weeks after germination. Self-sows readily in its native range.

Cultivation Drought-tolerant, but supplemental watering prolongs the blooming period.

Uses Plant in desert gardens amid other annuals or as a groundcover on banks or borders.

3-10

Sisyrinchium bellum
CALIFORNIA BLUE-EYED GRASS

Iris Family

Description Perennial. Blue to violet-blue flowers with yellow centers form a loose cluster on top of 6 to 8-inch flattened stems. Flowers are $\frac{1}{2}$ inch wide with three petals and three petal-like sepals, each with a fine point. The basal leaves are 4 to 20 inches long, very narrow, and grasslike.

Blooming May to July.

Soil Moist, average, well-drained.

Range Washington south to California.

Propagation Divide clumps in spring or fall and replant 6 inches apart with crowns $\frac{1}{2}$ inch deep. Collect seeds when mature and sow promptly $\frac{1}{4}$ inch deep in outdoor flats. Keep seedlings in light shade until they are transplanted to the garden after their first growing season. Self-sows readily.

Cultivation Divide clumps every other year to promote vigorous blooming.

Uses Plant in a meadow.

8-10

Dichelostemma pulchellum
BLUE-DICKS

Lily Family

Description Perennial. Crowning a leafless 6 to 24-inch stem is a dense cluster of blue flowers, each of which has three petals and three petal-like sepals fused near the base to form a broad tube $1/2$ to $3/4$ inches long with six flared lobes. The basal leaves are 6 to 18 inches long, narrow, and grasslike.

Blooming January to May.

Soil Dry, poor, well-drained.

Range Central California to southern Utah, south to Mexico; also north through California to southern Oregon.

Propagation Divide offsets from corms in fall and replant divisions 3 inches deep and 4 inches apart. Sow fresh seeds in fall $1/4$ inch deep in the desired locations or in outdoor flats filled with a mixture of equal parts sand and loam. Transplant the corms of seedlings 2 inches deep and at 4-inch intervals in fall after their first growing season.

Cultivation Drought-tolerant. Mulch heavily in fall in zones colder than 9.

Uses Plant in dry meadows, grasslands, or chaparral.

6-10 ⬚ 5-8

Fritillaria biflora
CHOCOLATE LILY

Lily Family

Description Perennial. One to several dark brown, nodding flowers dangle from the downturned top of a 6 to 18-inch stem. The bell-shaped flowers are 1 inch wide, with three petals, three petal-like sepals, six stamens, and a three-part stigma. Narrow basal leaves, 3 to 5 inches long with smooth margins, clasp the stem.

Blooming February to June.

Soil Dry, average, well-drained.

Range Coastal California.

Propagation Separate scales from corms in early fall and replant 3 inches deep and 4 inches apart. In fall, sow freshly collected seeds $1/4$ inch deep in the desired locations or in outdoor flats and keep moist until early summer. Transplant from the flats to the garden in fall after their second growing season.

Cultivation Needs midday shade. Allow corms to dry over summer, covering them with plastic or digging them up if necessary. May be grown in Hardiness Zones 7 and 8 with a heavy winter mulch.

Uses Plant in meadows, grasslands, or rock gardens.

9-10 ◩ 5-8

Sphaeralcea ambigua
DESERT MALLOW

Mallow Family

Description Perennial. Bright orange-red flowers gather toward the ends of branches on a shrubby plant 18 to 36 inches tall. Five petals form a cup-shaped flower with many stamens united into a central column. Alternate leaves measuring 1 to $2^{1}/_{2}$ inches long are three-lobed with scalloped margins.

Blooming March to June.

Soil Dry, poor, well-drained.

Range Central California to southwestern Utah, south to Mexico.

Propagation Collect the seeds when they mature and sow in fall, $1/4$ inch deep in the desired locations or in outdoor flats of sandy soil. Transplant from the flats to the garden four to six weeks after germination. Self-sows readily. Divide rootstock in fall. Take stem cuttings in June or July, dip cut ends in rooting hormone, and insert in moist sand until well-rooted.

Cultivation Soil must be well-drained.

Uses Plant in a desert garden.

6-10 ⬚ 5-8

Sidalcea malviflora
CHECKERBLOOM

Mallow Family

Description Perennial. A loose, elongated cluster of pink or lavender flowers appears on the upper portion of a 6 to 24-inch stem. The flowers have five petals with raised white veins, and the stamens are fused into a central column. Leaves are 1 to 2 inches wide, and those at the base are rather round with scalloped margins, while the alternate stem leaves are deeply lobed.

Blooming March to June.

Soil Moist, average, well-drained.

Range Coastal California.

Propagation Divide rootstock in late fall or winter into two or three lengthwise sections, each with several buds, and replant 12 inches apart, with the buds at the soil surface. In fall, after soaking seeds in hot water overnight, sow them $^1/_4$ inch deep in the desired locations or in flats and keep moist until germination. Transplant seedlings from the flats to the garden in fall. Self-sows readily.

Cultivation Needs winter moisture. Prune dead stems to ground level in late summer.

Uses Plant in meadows, grasslands, or rock gardens.

9-10 ☐ 5-8

Stanleya pinnata
DESERT PRINCE'S PLUME

Mustard Family

Description Perennial. The 24 to 60-inch stems are topped by graceful wands of yellow flowers, each with four slender, flared petals about $^1/_4$ inch long. The leaves are 2 to 6 inches long and deeply, pinnately lobed, egg-shaped, or elliptical with smooth margins.

Blooming May to July.

Soil Arid, poor, well-drained.

pH Unknown.

Range Southeastern Oregon to western North Dakota, south to western Texas and southeastern California.

Propagation Collect the seeds in fall and sow $^1/_4$ inch deep in the desired locations or in outdoor flats of sandy soil. Transplant the seedlings from the flats to the garden six weeks after germination.

Cultivation Likes rocky soil.

Uses Plant in desert gardens among succulents, sagebrush, or chaparral, or toward the rear of a border.

4-10 ☐

Erysimum capitatum
COAST WALLFLOWER

Mustard Family

Description Perennial. Crowning a 12 to 36-inch stem is a cluster of flowers, usually burnt orange in color but sometimes bright orange, yellow, maroon, or red. Each flower is about $^3/_4$ inch wide and has four petals. The leaves are 1 to 5 inches long, in a basal rosette, and alternate along the stem. They are narrow with a few small teeth along the margin.

Blooming March to July.

Soil Moist, poor, well-drained.

Range Southern British Columbia south through eastern Washington, eastern Oregon, and western Idaho to southern California, then east to New Mexico.

Propagation Sow the seeds in fall $^1/_4$ inch deep in the desired locations or in outdoor flats; in Hardiness Zone 8 or colder, mulch well. Transplant the seedlings from the flats to the garden at 6-inch intervals after six to eight weeks. Provide supplemental water to the seedlings in spring if necessary.

Cultivation Grows as a perennial only with sufficient water; otherwise grows as a biennial.

Uses Grow in borders, rock gardens, or dry meadows.

5-10 ☐ 5-8

Key

5-6
zone

exposure

◼ full shade

◼ light shade

◼ part sun

☐ full sun

4-5
pH

🐝 attracts

🦋 attracts

🐦 attracts

🐦 attracts

Lupinus nanus
SKY LUPINE

Pea Family

Description Annual. Rich blue flowers are arranged in whorls that form a terminal cluster on a 4 to 20-inch stem. Each flower is $1/2$ inch long and bilaterally symmetrical, with two "wing" petals, two petals fused to form a keel, and a rounded banner with a central white spot with a yellow base and dark spots. Leaves are alternate and palmately compound with five to seven narrow leaflets, each 1 inch long and covered with long hairs.

Blooming April to June.

Soil Dry, average.

Range Central and coastal California.

Propagation Collect the seeds when the pods turn brown. Scarify the seeds either by soaking them in hot water overnight or by rubbing between sheets of medium sandpaper, then sow immediately $1/4$ inch deep in the desired locations in fall or spring. Thin the seedlings to intervals of 3 inches. Readily self-sows in its native range. Seeds may be started indoors in early spring but should be transplanted when young.

Cultivation Requires nitrogen-fixing bacteria in the soil. If these are not present, commercial soil inoculants are available. Needs moisture in early spring.

Lupinus succulentus
ARROYO LUPINE

Pea Family

Description Annual. Whorls of deep purple flowers form a terminal cluster on a 6 to 24-inch stem. Flowers are bilaterally symmetrical and typically pealike, with a keel, banner, and two wings. In the center of the banner is a rusty vertical zone with a yellow base. The leaves are alternate and palmately compound with seven to nine dark green, round-tipped leaflets, each 2 to 3 inches long.

Blooming February to May.

Soil Dry, average, well-drained.

Range Western California south to Mexico and east through central and southern Arizona.

Propagation Collect the seeds when the pods turn brown. Before sowing, scarify the seeds either by soaking in hot water overnight or by rubbing between sheets of medium sandpaper, then sow immediately $1/4$ inch deep in the desired locations in fall or spring. Keep the soil moist until several weeks after germination, then thin to intervals of 6 inches. Seeds may be started indoors in early spring but should be transplanted when young.

Cultivation Requires nitrogen-fixing bacteria in the soil. If these are not present, commercial soil inoculants are available.

Ipomopsis aggregata
SKYROCKET

Phlox Family

Description Perennial. Bright red flowers are clustered at the tops of 12 to 84-inch stems. Each tubular flower is 1 to $1^{1}/2$ inches long and has five narrow, pointed lobes that are spreading or reflexed. The leaves are basal or alternate, 1 to 2 inches long, and pinnately divided into narrow segments.

Blooming May to September.

Soil Dry, average, well-drained.

Range Southern British Columbia to western North Dakota, south to western Texas, northern Arizona, and central California.

Propagation Sow the seeds $1/4$ inch deep in the desired locations as soon as they mature, or start indoors in late winter. Transplant from the flats to the garden in fall. Plant dies after flowering, which may take several years, so seeds should be sown over several consecutive years to achieve annual blooming. Self-sows readily.

Cultivation Spring pruning stimulates the production of more flowering stems.

Uses Plant in dry meadows or open woodlands.

Linanthus grandiflorus
MOUNTAIN PHLOX

Phlox Family

Description Annual. White flowers, sometimes tinted pink or lavender, grow near the ends of branches on a stem 4 to 20 inches tall. Five rounded, flared lobes of the 1-inch, funnel-shaped flowers encircle an opening that reveals five golden yellow stamens. The leaves are opposite and divided into long, narrow segments, like the tines of a fork.

Blooming April to July.

Soil Moist, poor, well-drained.

Range Central coastal California.

Propagation Collect seeds as they mature. In Hardiness Zones 9 and 10, sow in fall, 1/4 inch deep in the desired locations. In colder zones, sow in spring after the last frost. Keep the soil moist until the seedlings are well-established.

Cultivation Supplemental watering prolongs the blooming period in dry regions.

Uses Plant in meadows with other annuals.

3-10 5-8

Argemone munita
PRICKLY POPPY

Poppy Family

Description Annual. Prickly stems 12 to 60 inches tall and covered with yellow spines support large white flowers, each 2 to 5 inches wide and composed of six broad, papery petals surrounding a dense cluster of yellow stamens. The leaves are pinnately lobed with spines along their margins.

Blooming March to August.

Soil Dry, poor, well-drained.

Range Central California to northern Utah, south to Mexico.

Propagation Enhance germination through heat treatment by scattering the seeds on sand in a nonflammable container, covering with a thin layer of pine needles, and igniting the needles. Recover the seeds after the flames burn out and sow them 1/8 inch deep in the desired locations in late fall or, in colder regions, in indoor pots in early spring. Transplant the seedlings to the garden when well-established, taking care not to disturb the roots. Sometimes self-sows.

Cultivation May survive as a perennial under optimum conditions. Grows in a variety of well-drained soils.

Uses Plant in dry meadows, grasslands, and open woodlands.

3-10 5-8

Stylomecon heterophylla
WIND POPPY

Poppy Family

Description Annual. Deep reddish orange flowers rise above the soil on 12 to 36-inch stems. The four broad petals each have a purple spot at the base and surround numerous bright yellow anthers to compose a flower 1 to 2 inches wide. Leaves are alternate, 1 to 6 inches long, and deeply divided twice into pinnate lobes.

Blooming April to May.

Soil Moist, average, well-drained.

Range Coastal California.

Propagation In Hardiness Zones 9 and 10, sow the seeds in the desired locations in fall; otherwise, sow in spring or start in pots in late winter. Cover the seeds with a scattering of soil and keep moist. Transplant from the pots to the garden after the last frost without disturbing roots. Self-sows in its native range.

Cultivation Tolerates full sun to light shade.

Uses Plant in woodland borders or in meadows or grasslands with other annuals.

3-10 5-8

Eschscholzia californica
CALIFORNIA POPPY

Poppy Family

Description Annual. Solitary, flaming orange or yellow flowers crown slender 8 to 24-inch stems. The flowers are 1 to 2 inches wide and have four broad, fan-shaped petals, many stamens, and a four-part stigma. Leaves are 1 to 2 1/2 inches long, alternate, bluish green, and finely divided into fernlike segments.

Blooming February to September.

Soil Moist, average, well-drained.

Range Washington south to southern California.

Propagation In Hardiness Zones 8 to 10, sow the seeds in fall 1/4 inch deep in the desired locations; otherwise, sow in spring. Keep moist. Self-sows readily. Difficult to transplant.

Cultivation Grows in a variety of well-drained soils. Supplemental watering will prolong the blooming period during drought. May survive as a perennial in Hardiness Zones 7 to 10.

Uses Plant in meadows or grasslands with other annuals.

3-10 5-8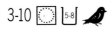

Dodecatheon clevelandii
WESTERN SHOOTING STAR

Primrose Family

Description Perennial. Pink, rose, or lavender flowers with strongly reflexed petals nod on arching stalks in a terminal cluster on a 12 to 24-inch stem. Flowers are 1 inch long, with five petals and five stamens that protrude and unite to form a cone. Pale green leaves, 1 1/2 to 3 inches long and spoon-shaped with smooth margins, form a basal rosette.

Blooming April to May.

Soil Moist, rich, well-drained.

Range Coastal California.

Propagation Divide crowns of mature plants in fall into segments, each having one or more buds and at least 3 inches of roots. Replant in the garden, spacing plants 12 inches apart with the buds 1/2 inch below the soil surface and the roots well-spread, and mulch. Sow seeds 1/4 inch deep in desired locations, flats, or individual peat pots outdoors as soon as they mature, and wait until the seedlings are two years old before transplanting to the garden.

Cultivation Mulch in fall. Tolerates full and partial sun. Needs moisture while blooming but is otherwise drought-tolerant.

Uses Plant in meadows, grasslands, and woodland borders.

8-10 6-8

Heuchera sanguinea
CORAL BELLS

Saxifrage Family

Description Perennial. Nodding, coral-colored flowers hang in a narrow terminal cluster from a stem standing 12 to 24 inches tall. Five petals make a bell-shaped flower up to 1/2 inch long. The round or heart-shaped, leathery leaves, 1 to 3 inches wide with scalloped margins, are long-stalked and mostly basal.

Blooming March to October.

Soil Moist, poor.

Range Southeastern Arizona and southwestern New Mexico, south into Mexico.

Propagation In late fall or early spring, divide the roots into sections having several buds apiece and replant them 12 inches apart, with the buds at the soil surface. Sow freshly collected seeds on the surface of flats filled with sandy soil in late summer or early fall, cover with a scattering of soil, keep moist, and transplant them to the garden in fall. Take cut leaves in late fall, insert in flats of moist sand in light shade until well-rooted, and transplant to the garden.

Cultivation Tolerates partial sun, but soil must remain moist through summer. Divide the plants every third year.

Uses Moist, shady borders or rock gardens.

4-8 6-7

Penstemon eatonii
SCARLET BUGLER

Snapdragon Family

Description Perennial. Nodding scarlet flowers grow in whorls about the top of a 12 to 36-inch purplish stem. The slender tubular flowers have five non-spreading lobes and five stamens, one of which is sterile and projects from the mouth of the flower. At the base of the stem is a rosette of 3 to 6-inch long-stalked leaves, while the leaves on the stem are shorter, opposite, and triangular with wavy margins.

Blooming March to July.

Soil Arid, poor, well-drained.

Range Central Nevada to southeastern California, east to southwestern Colorado.

Propagation Gather the seeds as they mature and sow $^1/_4$ inch deep in the desired locations or in outdoor flats of sandy soil in fall. Transplant the seedlings from the flats to the garden in the following fall. Divide the rootstock into sections with at least one bud apiece and replant 12 inches apart, with the buds at the soil surface.

Cultivation Drought-tolerant, but supplemental watering extends the blooming period.

Uses Plant in desert garden or on dry banks.

5-9

Penstemon spectabilis
SHOWY PENSTEMON

Snapdragon Family

Description Perennial. Bright rose-colored flowers, which may range from violet to pink, grow in whorls about the upper half of a 24 to 48-inch stem. The inflated tubular flowers are bilaterally symmetrical, with a two-lobed upper lip and a three-lobed lower lip. Fused together at their bases, the opposite, triangular stem leaves appear to be a single, toothed leaf pierced by the stem.

Blooming April to June.

Soil Dry, poor, well-drained.

Range Southwestern California.

Propagation Sow seeds in the desired locations in spring or in indoor flats in late winter, cover with a sprinkling of soil, and keep moist until several weeks after germination. Transplant the seedlings from the flats to the garden eight weeks after germination or after the last frost. Divide the rootstock into sections with at least one bud each and replant 12 inches apart, with the buds at the soil surface. Take stem cuttings in summer and insert in moist sand until well-rooted, then transplant to the garden.

Cultivation Tolerates partial sun or light shade.

Uses Desert garden or dry, gravelly banks.

9-10

Collinsia heterophylla
CHINESE-HOUSES

Snapdragon Family

Description Annual. Purple, blue, or lavender and white flowers are tightly packed in widely spaced whorls on the upper portion of a 12 to 24-inch stem. Measuring about $^3/_4$ inch long, the bilaterally symmetrical flowers have a two-lobed upper lip, with the lobes bent upward, and a three-lobed lower lip, with the outer lobes projecting forward and the middle lobe folded between them and encasing the stamens and pistil. The leaves are 1 to $2^1/_2$ inches long, opposite, and narrowly triangular with toothed margins.

Blooming March to June.

Soil Moist, rich, well-drained.

Range Western half of California.

Propagation Sow seeds $^1/_4$ inch deep in the desired locations in fall and spring and keep moist. Self-sows readily.

Cultivation Tolerates full sun to light shade, as well as soil of average fertility. Stagger the planting dates and pinch off expired blooms before they set seed to prolong the blooming period.

Uses Plant in meadows, rock gardens, or woodland clearings and borders.

3-10

Key

5-6 zone

exposure

full shade

light shade

part sun

full sun

4-5 pH

attracts

attracts

attracts

attracts

Orthocarpus purpurascens
OWL'S CLOVER

Snapdragon Family

Description Annual. Rose-pink and yellow or white flower clusters top 4 to 16-inch stems. Deeply divided into narrow segments, the velvety, pink-tipped floral bracts partially conceal the whorls of upward-tilted, bilaterally symmetrical flowers, each with a yellow-tipped, three-lobed lower lip and a hooked upper lip. The leaves are $1/2$ to 2 inches long and pinnately divided into narrow segments.

Blooming March to May.

Soil Moist, average, well-drained.

Range Southern two-thirds of California, east across the southern half of Arizona.

Propagation Sow freshly collected seeds in the desired locations in early fall, cover with a sprinkling of soil, and keep moist.

Cultivation Partially parasitic, so must be grown with other wildflowers or grasses. Needs moist soils in spring.

Uses Plant in meadows or grasslands with a mixture of other annuals and grasses.

3-10 ☐ 5-8

Mentzelia lindleyi
LINDLEY'S BLAZING STAR

Stick-Leaf Family

Description Annual. Solitary golden yellow flowers terminate branches of a 6 to 48-inch stem. Five rounded petals with pointed tips surround a burst of golden stamens on the 2 to 3-inch flowers. The alternate leaves are 2 to 4 inches long and pinnately lobed with clasping bases.

Blooming March to June.

Soil Moist, average, well-drained.

Range Central California.

Propagation Sow $1/8$ inch deep in the desired locations in late fall in Hardiness Zones 9 and 10; otherwise, sow in spring after the last frost. Keep moist, and thin to intervals of 6 inches after germination. Self-sows readily in its native range.

Cultivation Tolerates almost any well-drained soil. Keep moist until the plants begin blooming.

Uses Plant in meadows, grasslands, and woodland borders or clearings with other annuals.

3-10 ☐ 5-8

Verbena gooddingii
SOUTHWESTERN VERBENA

Verbena Family

Description Perennial. Small clusters of lavender flowers appear at the ends of hairy, sticky, sprawling stems that form mats of vegetation. The inch-long tubular flowers have five spreading lobes, and the opposite leaves are 2 to 4 inches long, hairy, and deeply divided into three major lobes.

Blooming February to October.

Soil Dry, poor, well-drained.

Range Central California to southern Utah and western Texas, south to Mexico.

Propagation Sow seeds in the desired locations in spring and cover with a sprinkling of soil, or sow in indoor flats in late winter and transplant to the garden after the last frost. Thin the seedlings in the garden to 12-inch intervals. Readily self-sows in its native range.

Cultivation Mulch heavily in fall and remove in spring. Drought-tolerant. Precise blooming period depends upon moisture and temperature.

Uses Makes an excellent desert groundcover.

7-10 ☐ 5-8 🐝 🦋 🐦

Nemophila menziesii
BABY-BLUE-EYES

Waterleaf Family

Description Annual. Sky blue flowers with white or cream-colored centers top branched stems 4 to 12 inches tall. Bowl-shaped in appearance, the flowers are $1/2$ to $1 1/2$ inches wide and have five round petals and five stamens with dark anthers. The leaves are 1 to 2 inches long, opposite, and pinnately lobed.

Blooming March to June.

Soil Moist, average, well-drained.

Range Central Oregon to southern California.

Propagation Sow $1/8$ inch deep in desired locations in late fall in Hardiness Zones 9 and 10; otherwise, sow in spring after the last frost. Keep moist, and thin to intervals of 6 inches after germination. Self-sows readily in its native range.

Cultivation Tolerates most well-drained soils. The blooming period can be prolonged with supplemental watering during drought.

Uses Plant in meadows or woodland clearings or borders with other annuals.

3-10 5-8

Phacelia campanularia
DESERT BLUEBELL

Waterleaf Family

Description Annual. Light to deep blue flowers on coiled branch tips form loose clusters on top of 6 to 36-inch stems. The bell-shaped flowers are up to $1 1/2$ inches long and have five rounded petals and five protruding stamens with yellow anthers. Leaves are 1 to 3 inches long, alternate, and heart- or egg-shaped with coarsely toothed margins.

Blooming February to May.

Soil Dry, poor, well-drained.

Range Southern California.

Propagation Sow the seeds $1/8$ inch deep in the desired locations in late fall in Hardiness Zones 9 and 10; otherwise, sow in spring after the last frost. Keep moist, and thin to intervals of 6 inches after germination. Self-sows readily in its native range.

Cultivation Stagger sowing dates to extend the blooming period.

Uses Plant in desert gardens or grasslands with other annuals.

3-10 5-8

Phacelia tanacetifolia
TANSY PHACELIA

Waterleaf Family

Description Annual. Tight coils of pale blue to lavender flowers unfurl on the ends of the branches of 12 to 36-inch stems. Long stamens and a forked style protrude beyond the $1/2$-inch-wide, five-lobed, bell-shaped flowers. Stiff hairs cover the fernlike leaves as well as the stem.

Blooming March to May.

Soil Moist, average, well-drained.

Range Southern two-thirds of California.

Propagation In fall, scarify the seeds by rubbing between sheets of medium sandpaper, soak in water overnight, then sow $1/8$ inch deep in the desired locations and keep moist. Follow the same procedure in midspring for planting outside of its native range.

Cultivation Keep soil moist until plants are full-grown.

Uses Plant in desert gardens or grasslands with other annuals.

1-10 5-8

Key

5-6
zone

exposure

full shade

light shade

part sun

full sun

4-5
pH

attracts

attracts

attracts

attracts

5
PRAIRIES

Prairies includes the three major grasslands of the Great Plains: tallgrass prairie, shortgrass prairie, and mixed-grass prairie.

Black-eyed Susan

South of the Arctic tundra, forests grow where there is abundant rainfall, and deserts occur where moisture is generally sparse. In between the two, where there is not enough precipitation to support a forest but too much for a desert, lie grasslands, millions of acres of land where grasses and wildflowers are the major forms of native plant life.

The largest and best known grasslands in North America are the prairies, which extend roughly from the Mississippi River westward to the foothills of the Rocky Mountains and eastward into Illinois and Indiana. However, other sizable grasslands exist, such as the desert grasslands of the Southwest, the intermountain grasslands between the Rocky Mountains to the east and Cascade Range and Sierra Nevada Mountains to the west, and the California grasslands. Most grasslands west of the Rocky Mountains do not grow on great, flat expanses like the prairies but rather occur on the slopes of mountain ranges, within a particular range of elevations that receives the proper amount of precipitation. Travel higher and you will encounter forest; lower, and the grasses yield to desert.

The prairies themselves may be divided into three distinct belts running north and south through the Midwest. Bordering the Rocky Mountain foothills to the extreme west lies the

ABOVE *Common in eastern wet meadows as well as in the prairies, New England aster is popular with bees and butterflies.*

BELOW LEFT *Virtually synonymous with prairies, common sunflower grows throughout the United States and southern Canada.*

BELOW *Grasses and wildflowers are the dominant plants in prairies. Trees become scarcer as dryness increases.*

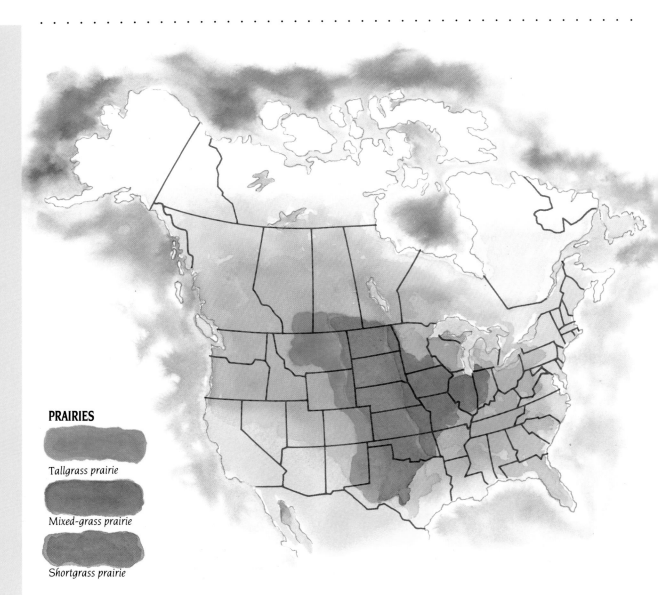

PRAIRIES

Tallgrass prairie

Mixed-grass prairie

Shortgrass prairie

shortgrass prairie, which receives the least precipitation of the three, accounting for the sparse vegetation there. In the middle, where the short bunch grasses mingle with the taller sod-forming grasses, we have the mixed prairie. To the east is the tallgrass prairie, which actually receives enough precipitation to support a forest but was historically maintained as a grassland by natural fires during the dry season. Sadly, most of the original tallgrass prairie is gone, lost to agriculture or overtaken by forest when the white man moved in and suppressed grassland fires. Most of the remaining tallgrass prairie occurs as isolated patches that have been left undisturbed, such as along railroad beds. Thankfully, though, there

RIGHT A *member of the daisy family, purple coneflower is a prairie native but also thrives in other parts of the United States. It is often sold as part of a meadow mixture.*

is currently a strong movement to preserve prairie remnants and to restore tallgrass prairie wherever possible using native species of grasses and wildflowers.

Most grassland wildflowers need full sunlight in order to grow best. They generally bloom throughout the late spring, summer, and into fall, although the tallgrass prairie flowers tend to bloom earlier, before the grasses reach their full height of 8 feet or taller.

Competition for water is keen in most grasslands. Although they receive more precipitation than deserts, much can be lost to evaporation by the drying winds and warming sunshine. Wildflowers native to this habitat have evolved many mechanisms for obtaining and conserving enough water to survive. Some are covered with dense whitish or silvery hairs, which both reflect some of the sun's rays and cut down evaporation losses by reducing the flow of drying air over plant surfaces. Many employ large taproots that reach deep into the soil to obtain water.

GARDENING TIPS

● Locate the prairie garden in full sun.
● Work the soil well to a depth of at least 18 inches. Add topsoil, if feasible, to increase the topsoil depth to 18 inches or more.
● Amend the soil with plenty of organic matter, such as composted grass clippings, leaves, vegetable scraps, or manure.
● Incorporate plenty of native grasses with your wildflowers. Their roots will reach deep into the soil to aerate it, to improve its drainage, and, after they die, to contribute substantial amounts of humus. Native grasses also help support the stems of wildflowers and generally make a prairie garden look more natural.
● Burn your prairie garden every year or two, preferably in early spring, while plants are still dormant. (Check local fire regulations first, and get the proper permits.) Fire is a natural part of a prairie, repelling invading trees, shrubs, and alien plants while converting dead plant matter into a nutrient-rich seedbed. The roots of native plants and wildflowers are unharmed by periodic burning. Burn on a day with no more than a light breeze. Do not burn during a drought. Create a fire line by rototilling the perimeter of the prairie garden. Start the fire on the downwind side so that it progresses slowly into the wind. Keep a hose, rake, and shovel handy, and do not leave the fire unattended.

ABOVE Birdfoot violet thrives in dry, sunny habitats and so is perfectly suited to prairie life as well as to dry meadows and forest clearings.

BELOW Grasses and herbaceous wildflowers epitomize the plant life found in prairies.

Hypoxis hirsuta
YELLOW STAR GRASS

Amaryllis Family

Description Perennial. Several yellow flowers, each forming a six-pointed star, appear at the top of a hairy stem 3 to 7 inches tall. Three petals, three petal-like sepals, and six stamens compose each flower. The grasslike basal leaves are 4 to 12 inches tall.

Blooming May to August.

Soil Moist, rich.

Range Manitoba to Newfoundland, south to Florida and Texas.

Propagation Separate corms in fall and replant 1 1/2 inches deep and 6 inches apart. Collect seeds as soon as they mature, sow them on the soil surface of outdoor flats, and cover thinly with a sprinkling of soil. Keep flats moist and transplant seedlings to the garden after their first growing season.

Cultivation Mulch with grass clippings in fall for winter protection.

3-9 ☐ 5-6

Campanula americana
TALL BELLFLOWER

Bluebell Family

Description Annual. Light blue flowers growing in the axils of alternate leaves form an elongated cluster atop a 24 to 72-inch stem. The flowers are flat and 1 inch wide, with five deep lobes united at the base and a long, recurved style. Leaves are 3 to 6 inches long, egg-shaped, and toothed.

Blooming June to August.

Soil Moist, average.

Range Minnesota to New York, south to Florida and Oklahoma.

Propagation Collect seeds when they mature and sow on the surface of a seedbed, so that they are exposed to light. Keep soil moist for several weeks after germination.

Cultivation No care required.

Uses Plant by themselves in marginal areas.

4-8 ☐ 6-7

Lithospermum canescens
HOARY PUCCOON

Borage Family

Description Perennial. A dense, terminal cluster of yellowish orange flowers crowns a 4 to 18-inch stem. The tubular flowers are 1/2 inch wide across the five flared lobes. The alternate leaves are narrow, stalkless, and about 1 inch long, and both they and the stem are covered with fine, soft hair.

Blooming April to June.

Soil Dry, poor, well-drained.

Range Saskatchewan to southern Ontario, south to Georgia and Texas.

Propagation Take root cuttings in spring. Make 2-inch sections, dip the lower end in rooting hormone, and insert the cuttings halfway in moist, sandy loam. Cuttings may be transplanted to permanent locations, 12 inches apart with the buds 2 inches deep, after about one year.

Cultivation Good drainage is important and can be improved with the addition of sand or gravel to the soil. Tolerates soil of rich to poor fertility.

Uses Plant in dry marginal areas with native grasses.

3-8 ☐ 6-7

Anemone patens
PASQUE FLOWER

Buttercup Family
Description Perennial. A solitary lavender, blue, or white flower rises above a cluster of basal leaves on a stem 6 to 16 inches tall. The flower measures about 2¹/₂ inches wide and includes five to seven petal-like sepals. Basal leaves are 2 to 3 inches long, and a whorl of smaller unstalked leaves circles the stem, just below the flower. The leaves are divided into long, narrow segments, and the entire plant is covered with silky hair.
Blooming March to June.
Soil Dry, rich, well-drained.
Range Alaska to Northwest Territories, south to Wisconsin, northern Illinois, and northeastern New Mexico.
Propagation Collect seeds as they mature, sow in fall in outdoor flats containing sandy loam, cover with a thin sprinkling of soil, mulch, and keep moist. Remove mulch in early spring and transplant the seedlings to the garden early in the following spring. In fall, take root cuttings several inches in length and replant 12 inches apart, with the crowns 1 inch deep. Divide large plants in early spring.
Cultivation Thrives in full sun to light shade. Needs moisture while flowering, but otherwise drought-tolerant.

1-6

Anemone canadensis
CANADA ANEMONE

Buttercup Family
Description Perennial. Long-stalked white flowers with numerous golden stamens crown a 12 to 24-inch stem. The showy flowers measure up to 1¹/₂ inches wide and have five broad, petal-like sepals. Upper stem leaves are opposite and stalkless, lower stem leaves are stalkless and occur in a whorl of three, and basal leaves are long-stalked. Leaves are deeply divided into three to seven lobes with toothed margins.
Blooming May to July.
Soil Moist, average.
Range Alberta to Maine, south to New Jersey and Colorado.
Propagation In fall, divide rhizomes into segments several inches long with buds and roots, and replant 12 inches apart and ¹/₂ inch deep, with buds at the soil surface. Sow seeds as soon as they mature in outdoor flats or directly in the garden. Move seedlings from the flats to the garden after their first growing season. Divide clumps of plants in fall.
Cultivation Tolerates partial shade and a variety of soils. Aggressive in gardens, and may need to be confined by edging strips buried in the soil. Divide crowded plants to encourage vigorous blooming.

2-6

Opuntia polyacantha
PLAINS PRICKLY PEAR

Cactus Family
Description Perennial. Jointed stems are flattened into fleshy, prickly pads that function as leaves. The waxy, luminous yellow flowers are stalkless and have many sepals, petals, and stamens. Attains a height of up to 24 inches.
Blooming May to June.
Soil Dry, average, well-drained.
Range Southern British Columbia to Manitoba and Minnesota, south to western Texas and northern Arizona.
Propagation Sow seeds as soon as they mature in seedbeds or outdoor flats with a mixture of 3 parts sand to 1 part soil. Transplant the seedlings to their permanent locations in fall. Take cuttings by breaking off pads at the joints and inserting them in a 3 parts sand/1 part soil mixture. Moisten the soil when dry, and transplant the cuttings to the garden after four weeks. Divide large clumps in fall, taking roots with each division.
Cultivation Mix generous amounts of sand into the soil when planting. Requires at least ¹/₂ day of direct sunlight regularly.
Uses Good for rock gardens, accents, borders of living areas, or dry, sunny embankments.

3-7 5-8

Key

5-6 zone

exposure

full shade

light shade

part sun

full sun

4-5 pH

attracts

attracts

attracts

attracts

Cleome serrulata
ROCKY MOUNTAIN BEE PLANT

Caper Family

Description Annual. Dense, elongated clusters of pink, lavender, or white flowers grace the ends of branched stems on this 24 to 60-inch-tall plant. The long-stalked flowers are $1/2$ inch long and have four petals and six long, threadlike stamens. Leaves are alternate and palmately compound with three canoe-shaped leaflets, each 1 to 3 inches long with smooth or slightly toothed margins.

Blooming June to September.

Soil Dry, poor, well-drained.

Range Central Saskatchewan to southwestern Ontario, south to Missouri, New Mexico, and northeastern California.

Propagation Collect seeds as they mature and sow immediately $1/4$ inch deep in the desired locations or in outdoor flats filled with sandy soil. Keep soil moist until several weeks after germination, when the seedlings may be transplanted to their permanent locations. Self-sows readily.

Cultivation No care required.

Uses Plant in meadows, prairie gardens, or marginal sites.

2-9 ⬚ 5-8 🐝

Eryngium yuccifolium
RATTLESNAKE MASTER

Carrot Family

Description Perennial. Clusters of small, greenish white flowers are packed tightly among pointed bracts to form globular flower heads about $3/4$ inch wide, which themselves grow in a branched cluster atop a 24 to 72-inch stem. Leaves are up to 36 inches long and narrow, with large, pointed teeth and clasping bases.

Blooming July to August.

Soil Moist, poor, well-drained.

Range Minnesota to Connecticut, south to Florida and Texas.

Propagation Collect seeds in fall and immediately sow $1/4$ inch deep in permanent locations or in outdoor flats filled with moist, sandy soil. Transplant seedlings from flats to individual pots six to eight weeks after germination in spring, and move to the garden after another year. In fall, divide clumps into individual rosettes and replant immediately.

Cultivation Tolerates dry to temporarily wet soils. Add sand or gravel to improve soil drainage if necessary.

Uses Plant in sunny borders or in meadows or prairies.

4-9 ⬚ 5-7

Gaillardia pulchella
INDIAN BLANKET

Daisy Family

Description Annual. Branched stems 12 to 24 inches tall terminate with showy yellow and red flowers. The composite flowers are 2 to 3 inches wide and have red disc florets and three-toothed ray flowers that are red at the base and yellow-tipped. Alternate leaves are 1 to 3 inches long, downy, stalkless. The upper leaves are narrowly egg-shaped with smooth margins, while the lower ones are usually lobed.

Blooming May to July.

Soil Dry, poor, well-drained.

Range Colorado to southern Minnesota and southern Virginia, south to Florida and Arizona.

Propagation Collect seeds when they mature in fall and store them dry in the refrigerator. Sow seeds $1/4$ inch deep in outdoor flats, pots, or the desired locations in spring. Transplant seedlings from the flats in June. Take cuttings in June, insert in moist sand and vermiculite, mist regularly, and transplant to the garden after three weeks.

Cultivation Add generous amounts of sand to clay soils. Remove old flower heads early in the season, before they set seed, to prolong blooming period.

4-9 ⬚ 5-8 🐝 🦋

Gaillardia aristata
BLANKET FLOWER

Daisy Family
Description Perennial. Multiple stems 8 to 30 inches tall bear showy yellow flowers with red centers. Flower heads are 2 to 4 inches wide with red disc florets and three-toothed yellow ray flowers that may or may not have red bases. Leaves are hairy, alternate, up to 6 inches long, and either lobed or narrowly egg-shaped.
Blooming June to August.
Soil Dry, poor.
Range British Columbia to Saskatchewan, south to South Dakota, Colorado, northern Utah, and northern Oregon.
Propagation Collect seeds when they mature in fall and store them dry in the refrigerator. Sow seeds $1/4$ inch deep in outdoor flats, pots, or the desired locations in spring. Transplant seedlings from the flats in June. Divide the taproot vertically in early spring with at least one bud and many lateral roots per section, and replant 12 inches apart, with buds at the soil surface.
Cultivation Add generous amounts of sand to clay soils. Remove old flower heads early in the season, before they set seed, to prolong blooming period. Divide clumps every other year.

3-8

Echinacea purpurea
PURPLE CONEFLOWER

Daisy Family
Description Perennial. Single reddish purple flower heads, $2^{1}/_{2}$ to 4 inches wide, are situated on top of a 24 to 60-inch hairy, rigid stem. Drooping ray flowers are 1 to 2 inches long, while the purplish brown disc florets form a bristling central cone. Leaves are alternate, egg-shaped, 3 to 6 inches long, and have toothed margins.
Blooming June to October.
Soil Moist, rich, well-drained, high humus.
Range Iowa to Michigan and Virginia, south to Georgia and northeastern Texas.
Propagation Collect seeds when they are mature and sow immediately, $1/4$ inch deep, in seedbeds or outdoor flats. Transplant seedlings to their permanent locations after the first growing season. Divide plants in fall by separating the multiple crowns from the parent plant, making sure each division has at least one bud and well-developed roots, and replant 12 inches apart, with the buds just under the soil surface.
Cultivation Tolerates full sun to light shade, dry to moist soil, and various soil types as long as they are well-drained. Drainage can be improved by working sand or fine gravel into the soil. Divide plants every third year.

5-8

Liatris pycnostachya
PRAIRIE BLAZING STAR

Daisy Family
Description Perennial. Lavender flower heads, each $1/2$ inch wide and composed of disc florets, crowd the upper portion of a hairy 24 to 48-inch stem, forming a terminal cylindrical cluster. Alternate leaves, 2 to 12 inches long and grasslike, crowd the stem, increasing in size from top to bottom.
Blooming July to October.
Soil Moist, fertile, well-drained.
Range Eastern South Dakota to Wisconsin and Indiana, south to Louisiana and eastern Texas.
Propagation In spring, divide the corms vertically, with at least one bud per section, and replant 12 inches apart, with buds 1 inch below the soil surface. Collect seeds as they mature in fall, scarify by rubbing them between two sheets of medium sandpaper, and sow $1/4$ inch deep in outdoor flats containing equal parts sand, loam, and compost. Transfer seedlings to their permanent locations after the first growing season.
Cultivation Mulch in fall for winter protection, and remove mulch in spring. Plant with native grasses to support the stems.
Uses Plant in borders or meadows.

3-9

Key

5-6
zone

exposure

full shade

light shade

part sun

full sun

4-5
pH

attracts

attracts

attracts

attracts

Solidago speciosa
SHOWY GOLDENROD

Daisy Family

Description Perennial. Small, yellow flower heads, each $1/4$ inch long, are crowded into dense, pyramid-shaped, terminal clusters on top of 24 to 72-inch stems. The alternate leaves, measuring 2 to 10 inches, are canoe-shaped and have irregular or vaguely toothed margins.

Blooming August to October.

Soil Moist, average, well-drained.

Range Southern Minnesota to southern New Hampshire, south to North Carolina and Louisiana.

Propagation Divide clumps in late fall, saving only the outer parts of the clumps. Trim roots to 4 inches, and replant 24 inches apart, with the crowns at the soil surface. Collect seeds in fall after they've turned gray, sow thickly in an outdoor flat, transfer to peat pots four weeks after germination, and move to the garden after six more weeks.

Cultivation Divide clumps every third year to promote vigorous growth.

Uses Plant in borders or meadows.

4-8

Aster novae-angliae
NEW ENGLAND ASTER

Daisy Family

Description Perennial. Violet or lavender ray flowers surround yellow disc florets on heads 1 to 2 inches wide, clustered at the ends of branches on 36 to 84-inch stems. The alternate leaves are very narrowly egg-shaped and 2 to 5 inches long, with smooth margins and clasping bases.

Blooming August to October.

Soil Moist, average.

Range Alberta to southwestern Quebec, south to Delaware, western North Carolina, Arkansas, and Colorado.

Propagation Divide clumps in late fall, creating sections with one or more stems, and replant 18 inches apart, with the roots 1 inch deep and the tips of the rhizomes just below the soil surface. Collect seeds as they mature in fall and sow thickly, $1/4$ inch deep, in seedbeds or outdoor flats, and move to desired locations about 10 weeks after germination.

Cultivation Tolerates partial shade, but prefers constant moisture. Prune in late spring to create bushy plants. Divide clumps every third year to promote vigorous growth.

Uses Plant in meadows or along roadsides.

3-7

Aster sericeus
WESTERN SILVERY ASTER

Daisy Family

Description Perennial. Lavender or pale blue ray flowers surround yellow disc florets to form $1/2$ to $1 1/2$-inch flower heads, found in loose clusters on many-branched 12 to 24-inch stems. The silvery, silky leaves are alternate, 1 inch in length, and oblong with smooth margins.

Blooming August to September.

Soil Dry, average, high humus.

Range Manitoba to southwestern Ontario, south through Illinois to Arkansas and Texas.

Propagation Divide clumps in fall and replant 12 inches apart. Collect mature seeds in fall, sow in seedbeds or outdoor flats containing a mixture of equal parts sand, peat moss, and compost, cover with a light sprinkling of sand, and moisten. Transplant seedlings to the desired locations about eight weeks after germination in the following spring. Self-sows readily.

Cultivation Tolerates light shade and may be planted in dry woodlands. Divide clumps every third year to promote vigorous growth.

Uses Plant in meadow or prairie garden.

3-8

Ratibida columnifera
MEXICAN HAT

Daisy Family

Description Perennial. A 1 to 2-inch conical disc of purplish brown flowers stands above three to seven drooping yellow or yellow and purplish brown ray flowers. Each flower head rests atop a branch of the 12 to 48-inch stem, which also bears alternate leaves 1 to 6 inches long and deeply divided into pinnate lobes.

Blooming July to September.

Soil Dry, average, well-drained.

Range Southeastern British Columbia to Manitoba, south through Illinois to Texas and Arizona.

Propagation Collect seeds in fall and promptly sow $1/4$ inch deep in seedbeds or in outdoor flats containing sandy loam. Keep the flats moist, and transplant the seedlings to their permanent locations, 12 inches apart, after the first growing season.

Cultivation Mulch in fall for winter protection, and remove mulch in spring. Drought-tolerant.

Uses Plant in a meadow or prairie garden.

3-9 6-8

Silphium laciniatum
COMPASS PLANT

Daisy Family

Description Perennial. Flower heads measuring 2 to 3 inches wide are composed of long, lemon yellow ray flowers and yellow disc florets, with large, hairy, green bracts lying beneath them. Flower heads occur at the ends of branched, hairy, sticky stems that stand 36 to 120 inches tall and also bear alternate, deeply lobed leaves. The blades of the leaves, which are typically 12 to 18 inches long, are mostly oriented in a north-south direction to avoid the intense rays of the midday sun.

Blooming July to September.

Soil Moist, average.

Range North Dakota to Michigan, south to Alabama and Texas.

Propagation Collect seeds in fall and scarify the seed coats by nicking each one with a sharp knife before sowing them $1/2$ inch deep in an outdoor flat, seedbed, or their permanent locations. Seedlings may be transplanted after they have attained a height of several inches.

Cultivation Tolerates a wide range of soil, moisture, and pH conditions, but must have full sun.

Uses Plant in a tallgrass prairie garden.

3-8 5-7

Helianthus annuus
COMMON SUNFLOWER

Daisy Family

Description Annual. One or more terminal yellow flower heads top a rough stem 36 to 120 inches tall. Overlapping yellow ray flowers surround brownish disc florets on the heads, which are 3 to 6 inches wide. Leaves are alternate, 3 to 12 inches long, and egg-shaped, heart-shaped, or triangular with toothed margins and coarse hairs.

Blooming July to October.

Soil Moist, average, well-drained.

Range Southern Canada south through most of the United States.

Propagation Cover young seed heads with nylon hose or cheesecloth to prevent birds from stealing seeds. Collect seeds as they mature, dry thoroughly, and sow in desired locations or in peat pots kept outdoors. Seedlings may be transplanted after attaining a height of several inches in spring.

Cultivation Tolerates a wide variety of growing conditions, but must have full sun. Moister, more fertile soils produce larger plants and flower heads, but stems may be weaker. Subject to rust in very wet conditions. Decaying roots inhibit the growth of other plants, so remove the entire plant, including roots, after it has set seed.

3-9 5-7

Key

5-6 zone

exposure

full shade

light shade

part sun

full sun

4-5 pH

attracts

attracts

attracts

attracts

Rudbeckia hirta
BLACK-EYED SUSAN

Daisy Family

Description Biennial. Golden yellow ray flowers surround a conical cluster of rich brown disc florets in 2 to 3-inch flower heads that crown a 12 to 36-inch rough stem. The leaves are alternate and basal, 2 to 6 inches long, canoe- or egg-shaped, covered with rough hairs, and distinguished by three prominent veins.

Blooming June to October.

Soil Moist, average, well-drained.

Range Manitoba to Nova Scotia, south to Florida and Oklahoma.

Propagation Collect seeds as they mature in fall and immediately sow 1/4 inch deep in seedbeds or outdoor flats containing loam. Water regularly, but allow the soil surface to dry out between waterings. Transplant seedlings after they have developed four leaves. Self-sows readily.

Cultivation Sow seeds two years in a row for yearly blooming. Mow meadows in late fall to scatter seeds. Tolerates many different soil, moisture, and pH conditions, but rich soils tend to produce weak-stemmed plants.

Uses Plant in a meadow or prairie garden.

3-9 ☐ 5-7

Coreopsis lanceolata
LANCE-LEAVED COREOPSIS

Daisy Family

Description Perennial. Solitary yellow flower heads, 2 inches wide with eight four-lobed ray flowers surrounding central disc florets, crown 12 to 24-inch stems. The stalkless, grasslike leaves are 3 to 6 inches long and opposite or basal.

Blooming May to August.

Soil Moist, average, well-drained.

Range Iowa to Michigan and western New York, south to Florida and Louisiana.

Propagation Collect seeds as they mature in late summer and promptly sow on the soil surface of outdoor flats, covering with just a sprinkling of soil. Transfer seedlings to individual pots three to four weeks after germination, and to the garden in the midsummer of their first growing season. Divide clumps in fall, remove a few leaves from each rosette to minimize water loss, replant 12 inches apart, and water immediately.

Cultivation Divide clumps every third year. Tolerates a wide range of conditions as long as it receives full sun. Drought-tolerant.

Uses Plant in meadows and prairies.

Attracts Goldfinches.

4-9 ☐ 5-7 🐦

Oenothera missourensis
MISSOURI EVENING PRIMROSE

Evening Primrose Family

Description Perennial. Large, lemon yellow flowers rise from the leaf axils of hairy, 8 to 10-inch stems. The flowers are 2 to 4 inches wide, with four broad, overlapping petals. Leaves are alternate, 3 to 5 inches long, and narrowly canoe- or egg-shaped with smooth margins.

Blooming May to August.

Soil Dry, average, well-drained.

Range Nebraska to Missouri, south to Texas.

Propagation Collect seeds in late summer and sow in the desired locations or peat pots. Seedlings may be transferred in their pots to the garden after one growing season. Take stem cuttings in July, dip cut ends in rooting hormone, insert in a moist sand-vermiculite mixture, and mist often. Transplant the cuttings to their permanent locations in fall.

Cultivation Soil must be very well drained. Work in extra amounts of sand or gravel if needed.

Uses A good choice as a groundcover or in a rock garden, or plant in a meadow.

4-8 ☐ 5-7

Linum perenne subsp. *lewisii*
PRAIRIE FLAX

Flax Family
Description Perennial. A branching cluster of sky blue, saucer-shaped flowers adorns the top of a 12 to 30-inch stem. The flowers have five petals and are 1 to 1$^1/_2$ inches wide. The alternate leaves are about 1 inch long, stalkless, and grow densely on the stem.
Blooming May to August.
Soil Dry, average, well-drained.
Range Alaska to Ontario, south to Texas and California.
Propagation Difficult to transplant. Collect seeds as they mature and sow in fall in desired locations on the soil surface and cover with a light sprinkling of soil.
Cultivation Soil should be very well drained, so work in extra sand or gravel if necessary.
Uses Plant in meadows or prairies.

1-10 ▢ |5-7|

Trillium recurvatum
PRAIRIE TRILLIUM

Lily Family
Description Perennial. A solitary maroon flower with three erect petals and three drooping sepals rests directly above a whorl of three mottled, egg-shaped leaves on a 6 to 16-inch stem.
Blooming April to May.
Soil Moist, rich, high humus.
Range Iowa to Ohio, south to Alabama and Arkansas.
Propagation Divide rhizomes in midsummer, replant horizontally 3 inches deep and 12 inches apart, and mulch with deciduous leaves. Collect seeds as they mature in July or August and immediately sow $^1/_4$ inch deep in a mixture of sand, loam, and compost in outdoor flats or seedbeds. Mulch with deciduous leaves and keep moist. Transplant seedlings to the garden after their first growing season.
Cultivation Ideally planted in sandy loam with lots of humus, where it remains consistently moist and receives spring sun. Mulch with deciduous leaves for winter protection.
Uses Plant in midwestern woodland gardens.

5-7 ▨ |6-7|

Callirhoe involucrata
POPPY MALLOW

Mallow Family
Description Trailing stems arch upward 12 to 24 inches, terminating with magenta or wine-colored, cup-shaped flowers about 2 inches wide with five petals. Leaves are deeply and intricately lobed, alternate, and 2 to 4 inches wide.
Blooming March to July.
Soil Dry, average, well-drained.
Range Wyoming to North Dakota, south to Missouri, Texas, and New Mexico.
Propagation Collect seeds in late summer, scarify with a knife or sandpaper, and sow $^1/_4$ inch deep in outdoor flats. Transplant seedlings to permanent locations, 24 inches apart with crowns at the soil surface, in the spring following their first growing season.
Cultivation Mulch in fall. Extend blooming period by removing expired flowers before they set seed. Remove and destroy leaves that may be infected with rust during wet seasons.
Uses Plant as a groundcover or in a rock garden.

4-8 ▢ |5-7| 🐝

Asclepias tuberosa
BUTTERFLY WEED

Milkweed Family

Description Perennial. Clusters of bright orange flowers up to 3 inches wide adorn the tops of 12 to 36-inch hairy stems. Each flower is roughly $1/2$ inch wide and has five strongly reflexed petals and a central five-part crown. The alternate leaves are 2 to 5 inches in length and oblong with smooth margins.

Blooming May to September.

Soil Dry, average, well-drained.

Range Utah to Minnesota and Maine, south to Florida and Arizona.

Propagation In fall, cut the rhizome into 2-inch pieces with one or more buds apiece and replant sections vertically in sandy soil, 24 inches apart with the buds 2 inches deep. Collect seeds as they mature and sow immediately, $1/2$ inch deep, in seedbeds or deep outdoor flats containing sandy loam. If deep flats are not available, transplant seedlings into deep pots four weeks after germination; otherwise, move them to the garden in late fall.

Cultivation Good drainage is critical, so add sand or fine gravel to soil if required. Plants are subject to rot in rich or damp soil. Tolerates light shade. Mulch in late fall for winter protection in colder regions.

3-10 [ ] 5-7

Monarda fistulosa
WILD BERGAMOT

Mint Family

Description Perennial. A dense, round, terminal cluster of lavender flowers crowns a square stem 24 to 48 inches tall. The asymmetrical flowers are tubular, two-lipped, and about $1^1/2$ inches. The dark green, opposite leaves are egg-shaped, coarsely toothed, and 3 to 6 inches long.

Blooming June to August.

Soil Dry, average, well-drained.

Range Minnesota to Quebec, south to Georgia and eastern Texas.

Propagation Divide clumps in early spring, before they send up stems, and replant 12 inches apart with rhizomes 1 inch deep and their tips at the soil surface. Immediately after collection, sow seeds $1/4$ inch deep in their permanent locations or in outdoor flats. Transfer from the flats to individual pots seven weeks after germination in spring, and move to the garden in early fall.

Cultivation Tolerates varying soil fertility from rich to poor, as long as it is well-drained, but the stems of plants grown in rich soil are weaker. Work generous amounts of sand into the soil. Also tolerates full sun to light shade. Divide this plant annually to keep it vigorous.

Uses Plant in meadows and prairies.

3-8 [ ] 5-7

Salvia azurea
BLUE SAGE

Mint Family

Description Perennial. Blue, two-lipped flowers grow in a terminal cluster and in whorls around the 24 to 60-inch stem. The flowers are up to 1 inch long and bilaterally symmetrical. The lower lip is much larger than the upper one, and two stamens protrude from between them. Leaves are opposite and 2 to 4 inches long, and the lower ones are somewhat egg-shaped and toothed.

Blooming July to September.

Soil Dry, average.

Range Nebraska to North Carolina, south to Florida and Texas.

Propagation Collect mature seeds in fall. Sow them promptly $1/4$ inch deep in their permanent locations or in outdoor flats containing sandy loam, and keep moist. Divide clumps in fall and replant 12 inches apart, with crowns just below the soil surface. Take 6-inch stem cuttings in July, dip ends in rooting hormone, and insert halfway into moist sand and vermiculite. Keep cuttings lightly shaded and transfer to the garden after about four weeks.

Cultivation Mulch in fall for winter protection, and remove in spring. Tolerates light shade.

4-9 [ ] 5-7

LEAD PLANT

Amorpha canescens

Pea Family

Description Perennial. Numerous spiked clusters of small purple flowers occur at the ends of branches on 18 to 40-inch stems. A single petal and ten bright orange or yellow stamens constitute the flower. The leaves are pinnately compound and divided into many 1/2-inch leaflets. Both the leaves and stem are covered with dense, wooly gray hair.

Blooming June to August.

Soil Dry, average, well-drained.

Range Saskatchewan to Michigan, south to Arkansas and New Mexico.

Propagation Collect seeds as they mature, scarify, and immediately sow 1/4 inch deep in seedbeds or outdoor flats containing equal parts sand, loam, and compost. Transplant seedlings to desired locations in fall after their first growing season. Take stem cuttings in July, dip ends in rooting hormone, and insert in moist sand and vermiculite. Transplant rooted cuttings after about eight weeks.

Cultivation Requires nitrogen-fixing bacteria in the soil. If these are not present, commercial soil inoculants are available.

Uses Plant in a prairie garden.

PURPLE PRAIRIE CLOVER

Petalostemon purpureum

Pea Family

Description Perennial. Small rose-purple flowers grow in cylindrical clusters on top of branched, rigid stems standing 12 to 36 inches tall. Flower parts include one heart-shaped petal, four petal-like modified stamens, and five true stamens. The leaves are pinnately compound with three to seven very slender leaflets, each about 3/4 inch long.

Blooming June to September.

Soil Dry, average, well-drained.

Range Southern Saskatchewan to Manitoba, southeast to Indiana, and south to Arkansas and New Mexico.

Propagation Collect seeds as they mature, when the heads turn dry and gray. Scarify the seeds by rubbing them between two sheets of medium sandpaper, and sow immediately, 1/4 inch deep, in outdoor flats containing sandy soil. Thin the seedlings in the flats to 6 inches apart, or transfer them to individual pots four to six weeks after germination. Move to permanent locations in fall.

Cultivation Needs nitrogen-fixing bacteria in soil. If these are not present, commercial soil inoculants are available.

Uses Plant in prairie garden.

TEXAS BLUEBONNET

Lupinus texensis

Pea Family

Description Annual. Deep blue flowers grow in a dense, terminal cluster on 6 to 18-inch stems. The bilaterally symmetrical flowers are each 1/2 inch long, with a central reddish or yellowish spot. Leaves are alternate and palmately compound, with four to seven leaflets measuring 1 inch apiece.

Blooming April to May.

Soil Dry, poor, well-drained.

Range Texas.

Propagation Collect seeds as they mature. Sow in fall in seedbeds after scarifying seeds or soaking in warm water for three days.

Cultivation Tolerates a wide range of soil types. Requires moisture in fall to germinate and in spring to flower. Needs nitrogen-fixing bacteria in soil. If these are not present, commercial soil inoculants are available.

Uses Plant in a prairie garden.

Similar species Texas bluebonnet (*Lupinus subcarnosus*).

Key

5-6 zone

exposure

full shade

light shade

part sun

full sun

4-5 pH

attracts

attracts

attracts

attracts

Desmodium canadense
SHOWY TICK TREFOIL

Pea Family

Description Perennial. Elongated terminal clusters of pink, rose-purple, or blue flowers grow on this branched, bushy plant. Flowers are about 1/2 inch long and bilaterally symmetrical. Stems and leaves are hairy, and leaves are pinnately compound with three oblong leaflets, each 1 to 3 inches long with smooth margins.

Blooming July to August.

Soil Moist, average.

Range Saskatchewan to Nova Scotia, south to Maryland and Kansas.

Propagation Gather seeds in fall, scarify the seed coat with a sharp knife or by rubbing between two sheets of medium sandpaper, then sow 1/2 inch deep in outdoor flats containing loam or in permanent locations. Transplant seedlings from flats to individual pots in midsummer, then to the garden in fall.

Cultivation Tolerates sun to light shade and various types of soil fertility. Should this species prove difficult to establish, commercial soil inoculants will provide root nodules with the necessary nitrogen-fixing bacteria.

Uses Plant in a prairie or meadow garden.

3-6  5-7

Phlox pilosa
DOWNY PHLOX

Phlox Family

Description Perennial. Clusters of lavender or pink flowers occur at the top of a downy 12 to 30-inch stem. Five rounded, flaring petals unite at their bases to form the long, tubular corolla of each flower. The opposite leaves are 2 to 3 inches long, narrow, pointed, and covered with downy hair.

Blooming May to June.

Soil Dry, average.

Range Wisconsin to Connecticut, south to Florida and Texas.

Propagation Because seedpods open abruptly, seeds are best collected by fashioning a mesh sack around the developing fruit. In fall, sow seeds 1/4 inch deep in seedbeds or in outdoor flats, and transfer seedlings to the garden after their first growing season. Divide roots in fall and replant sections 12 inches apart, with the crowns at the soil surface. Take 6-inch stem cuttings in June, dip cut ends in rooting hormone, and insert in a mixture of moist sand and vermiculite. Transplant rooted cuttings to the garden in fall.

Cultivation Blooming may be renewed by cutting back mature plants after the first flowering.

3-9 5-6

Filipendula rubra
QUEEN-OF-THE-PRAIRIE

Rose Family

Description Perennial. A feathery, branching cluster of pink flowers tops a 36 to 72-inch stem. The flowers are up to 1/2 inch wide, each with five petals and numerous protruding stamens. Leaves are alternate and pinnately compound, with deeply lobed and toothed leaflets 2 to 8 inches in length.

Blooming June to August.

Soil Moist, rich, high humus.

Range Iowa to Michigan and New England, south to Georgia and Tennessee.

Propagation In fall, divide rhizomes connecting rosettes and replant sections horizontally 2 inches deep and 12 inches apart, with the crowns at the soil surface. Collect seeds in late summer, promptly sow them heavily in lightly shaded seedbeds or outdoor flats, and keep moist. In spring, transplant to pots after seedlings have developed several leaves, keep moist and shaded, and move to garden in fall. Take stem cuttings in May, dip in rooting hormone, and insert in wet sand and vermiculite. Move rooted cuttings midsummer.

Cultivation Needs constant moisture and high humus. Mulch in spring. Tolerates full sun to light shade. Divide clumps every third year.

4-7 5-7

Geum triflorum
PRAIRIE SMOKE

Rose Family

Description Perennial. Several pink or rose-colored, nodding flowers occur on top of a hairy 6 to 16-inch stem. The flowers are $1/2$ to $3/4$ inch long with five petals and later give rise to mauve plumes of fruiting structures resembling feather dusters. Leaves are up to 9 inches long and pinnately compound, with oblong leaflets that are irregularly toothed or lobed.

Blooming April to August.

Soil Dry, average, well-drained.

Range British Columbia to Ontario, south to Illinois and Utah.

Propagation Divide rhizomes in late summer to early fall and replant 18 inches apart, with crowns at the soil surface. Collect seeds when mature, sow heavily $1/4$ inch deep in outdoor flats, and keep moist. Transplant seedlings to the desired locations in fall and mulch lightly.

Cultivation Divide rhizomes every third or fourth year to alleviate overcrowding.

Attracts Goldfinches.

3-5

Euphorbia marginata
SNOW-ON-THE-MOUNTAIN

Spurge Family

Description Annual. Five white, petal-like bracts surround minute, greenish flower clusters on top of 12 to 36-inch stems. Leaves are 1 to 3 inches long, alternate, and oblong with smooth margins. The upper leaves are variegated, ranging from mostly white at the top to all green on the lower stem.

Blooming June to October.

Soil Dry, poor.

Range Montana to Minnesota, south to Texas and New Mexico.

Propagation Collect seeds when mature and sow $1/4$ inch deep in seedbeds or desired locations. Clear competing plants within a radius of 6 inches before sowing.

Cultivation Tolerates a wide range of soil conditions, but does not compete well with sod-forming grasses.

Uses Plant in a prairie garden.

3-10

Viola pedata
BIRDFOOT VIOLET

Violet Family

Description Perennial. Bluish purple flowers rise directly from the rootstock on 4 to 10-inch stalks. The large flowers are up to $1^{1}/_{2}$ inches wide and bilaterally symmetrical with five petals, the lower one spurred and veined with deep purple, and five stamens with conspicuous orange anthers. Leaves are basal and deeply, palmately lobed into toothed sections.

Blooming April to May.

Soil Dry, poor, well-drained.

Range Minnesota to New Hampshire, south to Florida and Texas.

Propagation Collect seeds as they mature, indicated by the brown color of seedpods, and sow immediately $1/4$ inch deep in seedbeds or outdoor flats filled with sandy soil. Transfer the seedlings from the flats to individual pots four to six weeks after germination, and move to the garden in fall. Self-sows readily in sandy sites. Divide rhizomes in fall and replant segments 6 inches apart and 1 inch deep.

Cultivation Tolerates partial sun. Mulch in fall. Good drainage is critical.

Uses Great groundcover for banks or marginal areas.

3-8 5-6

6
FIELDS AND ROADSIDES

Fields and Roadsides
encompasses any
habitat with recently
disturbed soil or scant
topsoil, such as railroad
beds and landslides.

Many roadside inhabitants are aliens.

Roadsides, abandoned farm fields, meadows, pastures, railroad beds, construction sites, landslides, lawns, gardens, and similar places may all be classified as "altered habitats," a vague classification referring to areas where the soil has been disturbed, usually, but not always, by human activity. Undisturbed sites with only a thin layer of soil, such as rock ledges, often support wildflower species common to disturbed areas.

Not surprisingly, many of the plants inhabiting such areas are aliens, species not native to North America. Aliens have been transported here, accidentally or on purpose, from other continents, mostly from Europe and Asia, where they have lived in close proximity to humans for thousands of years and have evolved to cope with harsh conditions because they faced less competition from other plants in

RIGHT *Goldenrod is quite adept at colonizing disturbed areas. Contrary to belief, it does not cause hay fever.*

BELOW *Here growing in an unused railroad bed, butterfly weed is also a common prairie resident.*

GARDENING TIPS

● Soils should be well-drained, poor to average, and dry or moist. These plants usually tolerate a wide range of pH levels, but usually do not do well in rich or wet soil or in shade.

● Add sand or gravel to existing soil if it is too rich or does not drain well.

● Choose a location that receives full sun.

● Mow meadows in fall to distribute seeds.

● Don't fuss too much – these plants do best with little or no care.

• • • • • • • •

ABOVE *Another opportunist, lance-leaved coreopsis readily colonizes disturbed areas but here was planted by the highway department on Cape Cod, Massachusetts.*

these areas. Nearly all of them require direct sunlight to thrive, however, and do not do well in constant shade.

Most altered habitats have in common a lack of, or a reduced amount of, topsoil, the upper nutrient-rich soil layer. It may take as long as 10,000 years to form 1 inch of topsoil when starting from bare rock, and once this is gone, it is not easily replaced. Wildflowers that grow where topsoil has been removed or reduced are able to get along with fewer nutrients, and they also often grow where topsoil is just beginning to form, such as in cracks and crevices on cliffs and rocky outcrops. Altered habitats may also have had topsoil buried by sand, gravel,

LEFT The ancestor of our modern garden carrot, Queen-Anne's-lace is reported to have a taproot that is edible when cooked.

· · · · · · · · ·

BELOW Aliens do particularly well in roadsides and other disturbed areas because they spent thousands of years adapting to such habitats in Europe and Asia.

mining waste, or other such material, to a depth where it is unavailable to plant life.

Agricultural areas, by contrast, usually have a plentiful amount of topsoil, but the native vegetation has been cleared away. Wildflowers that take advantage of such sites are often those with short life cycles, usually annuals or biennials, that are able to invade, put down roots, grow, flower, and set seed quickly. Many such plants have evolved to produce large numbers of seeds, which disperse over great distances. The idea is that a few of their offspring will chance to land on a suitable spot at the right time. Meadows, which are maintained by mowing, must be reseeded periodically, and this is when many invaders get their chance. Pastures, maintained by grazing, may not be completely cleared of vegetation, but the livestock's hooves create openings for pioneering plants. Abandoned fields, in transition between agriculture and forest, will host alien species until the forest encroaches and shades them out.

Campanula rotundifolia
HAREBELL

Bluebell Family

Description Perennial. Violet-blue, bell-shaped flowers nod on slender stalks at the ends of branched stems. Flowers are ³/₄ to 1 inch long with five slightly flared, pointed lobes, a three-part stigma, and five stamens. Stem leaves are very narrow, grasslike, and up to 3 inches long. Basal leaves, if present, are broadly heart-shaped with scalloped margins. Height is 6 to 18 inches.

Blooming June to September.

Soil Moist, average, good drainage.

Range Alaska to Labrador, south to New Jersey, Missouri, New Mexico, and northern California.

Propagation Divide clumps in late spring or late summer and replant 12 inches apart with basal leaves just above the soil surface. Remove offsets from rhizomes and plant 1 inch deep and 12 inches apart. Collect the seeds as they mature and sow in fall, either on the surface of outdoor flats containing sandy loam or randomly in well-drained garden sites. Transplant the seedlings after their first growing season, but clear a 6-inch radius around each one.

Cultivation Add sand to soil to improve drainage, if needed.

2-6 | 5-6

Lobelia spicata
SPIKED LOBELIA

Bluebell Family

Description Biennial. Pale blue flowers grow in a slender, elongated cluster on top of a 24 to 48-inch leafy stem. The two-lipped, bilaterally symmetrical flowers reach ¹/₂ inch in length. Leaves are 1 to 4 inches long, pale green, and egg-shaped or oval.

Blooming June to August.

Soil Dry, poor.

Range Minnesota to New Brunswick, south to Georgia and Texas.

Propagation Sow the seeds in their permanent locations or in outdoor flats containing sandy soil. Transplant the seedlings from the flats after their first growing season. Sow for at least two consecutive years to assure annual blooming. Self-sows readily in open soil.

Cultivation No care required.

Uses Plant in marginal areas.

3-8 | 5-8

Opuntia humifusa
PRICKLY PEAR

Cactus Family

Description Perennial. Large yellow flowers with or without reddish centers grow on stems that have been modified into flattened, fleshy pads covered with clusters of short bristles. Flowers are 2 to 3 inches wide with many petals and stamens.

Blooming June to August.

Soil Dry, poor.

Range Minnesota to southern Ontario and Massachusetts, south to Florida and Oklahoma.

Propagation Caution – wear heavy gloves when handling cacti! Divide clumps in fall by pulling up peripheral pads and their roots and transplanting them several feet away. Take stem cuttings throughout the growing season by breaking off pads at the joints and inserting the broken end about 2 inches deep in permanent sites with very sandy soil or in flats containing 3 parts sand to 1 part soil. Sow seeds in very sandy seedbeds or in outdoor flats containing the same ratio of sand to soil as above. Transplant the seedlings to permanent locations after their first growing season.

Cultivation Requires very well drained soil and at least partial sun.

4-9 | 4-6

QUEEN-ANNE'S-LACE
Daucus carota **var.** *carota*

Carrot Family

Description Biennial. Lacy, flat-topped clusters of creamy white flowers crown 24 to 36-inch stems. Floral clusters, which progress from slightly umbrella-shaped to bowl-shaped with age, have one brownish purple flower at the center. The alternate leaves are compound, fernlike, and 2 to 8 inches long.

Blooming May to October.

Soil Moist, poor.

Range Southern Canada south throughout the United States.

Propagation Collect the seeds as they mature and sow immediately in their permanent locations, seedbeds, or outdoor flats filled with sandy soil. Transplant the seedlings from flats to pots four weeks after germination, and move to permanent sites after the first growing season. Mow in fall to distribute seeds. Also self-sows in disturbed soil. Sow seeds for at least two consecutive years to ensure annual blooming.

Cultivation Soil with high fertility will produce weak, leggy stems that need support.

Uses Sow as part of a meadow mixture.

2-9

PEARLY EVERLASTING
Anaphalis margaritacea

Daisy Family

Description Perennial. Spherical flower heads are arranged in a flat-topped cluster atop a 12 to 36-inch stem covered with white, wooly hair. Each flower head is about $1/4$ inch wide and composed of white disc florets surrounded by pearly bracts. Male flowers have yellow centers. The alternate leaves are 3 to 5 inches long, narrow, grasslike, grayish green above, and wooly white underneath.

Blooming July to September.

Soil Dry, poor.

Range British Columbia to Labrador, south to Virginia and North Dakota, south in the Rocky Mountains to New Mexico, and south in the Cascades and Sierra Nevada to southern California.

Propagation Collect the seeds as they mature and sow in fall in their permanent locations or in outdoor flats, and cover with a very thin layer of sandy soil. Transplant from flats to the desired locations in late spring. Divide rhizomes in early spring and replant segments $1/2$ inch deep and 12 inches apart.

Cultivation Add sand to increase soil drainage if necessary.

Uses Plant in marginal areas or in a meadow or woodland border.

2-10

OXEYE DAISY
Chrysanthemum leucanthemum

Daisy Family

Description Perennial. Solitary, yellow and white flower heads rest at the summit of 12 to 36-inch stems. The central disc of yellow florets is depressed in the center and surrounded by white ray flowers. Leaves are 3 to 6 inches long, alternate, and irregularly toothed.

Blooming June to August.

Soil Dry, average, well-drained.

Range Throughout temperate North America.

Propagation Collect the seeds as they mature, and sow immediately and heavily in their desired locations or in outdoor flats filled with sandy loam. Transplant the seedlings from the flats to the garden in fall, after germination. Self-sows readily. Divide clumps of basal rosettes in late summer or fall, and replant 12 inches apart, with the crowns at the soil surface and roots spread evenly. Take stem cuttings in midsummer and insert cut ends in a moist sand-vermiculite mixture. Keep in a humid rooting chamber and mist often until well-rooted.

Cultivation Divide clumps every third year to avoid overcrowding. Soil that is too rich will produce plants with weak stems that cannot stand on their own. Tolerates partial shade.

3-10

Achillea millefolium
COMMON YARROW

Daisy Family

Description Perennial. Flat-topped clusters of white flower heads top grayish green, 12 to 36 -inch stems. Individual flower heads are about $1/4$ inch wide. The alternate leaves are 2 to 6 inches long and very finely divided into fernlike structures.

Blooming June to September.

Soil Moist, average, well-drained.

Range Throughout temperate North America.

Propagation Divide clumps in fall and replant 12 inches apart, with the rhizomes $1/2$ inch deep. Collect mature seeds, sow immediately in permanent locations or in outdoor flats, and keep moist until germination. Transfer from the flats to individual pots eight weeks after germination and move to the garden in late summer.

Cultivation Mulch in spring to conserve soil moisture and inhibit competitors. Tolerates partial shade. Divide clumps every other year.

Uses Plant on banks for erosion control or in meadow mixtures.

3-10 ☐ 5-8

Solidago canadensis
CANADA GOLDENROD

Daisy Family

Description Perennial. Very small, yellow flower heads line short, arching branches near the top of a leafy 12 to 60-inch stem. Each flower head is about $1/8$ inch long. The alternate leaves are 2 to 5 inches long, canoe-shaped, and coarsely toothed.

Blooming May to September.

Soil Moist, poor.

Range Throughout most of temperate North America.

Propagation Divide clumps in fall and replant 24 inches apart, with the rhizome 1 inch deep and its tip at the soil surface. Collect the seeds as they mature, indicated by a grayish color, and sow heavily in seedbeds or in outdoor flats. Transplant to their permanent locations in fall after their first growing season. Self-sows readily in open soil.

Cultivation Tolerates partial shade and a variety of soil types. Divide clumps every third year to avoid overcrowding.

Uses Plant as a border along woodlands, old fences, or stone walls, or in a meadow.

3-9 ☐ 5-7

Centaurea cyanus
BACHELOR'S-BUTTON

Daisy Family

Description Annual. Bright blue flowers (sometimes pink or white) terminate a 12 to 24-inch hairy stem. Flower heads are 1 to 2 inches wide, composed of all disc florets, with coarsely toothed peripheral flowers in each head. Leaves are alternate, narrow, and grasslike.

Blooming June to September.

Soil Dry, poor, well-drained.

Range Throughout temperate North America.

Propagation Collect mature seeds and sow in fall in desired locations.

Cultivation Tolerates full sun to light shade. This species may become aggressive and may need to be controlled by removing flower heads before they set seed.

Uses Plant in marginal areas or in meadows.

3-9 ☐ 5-8

Cichorium intybus
COMMON CHICORY

Daisy Family

Description Perennial. Blue flower heads occur along an erect, rigid, branched stem standing 12 to 48 inches tall. Flower heads are about 1½ inches wide and composed of square-tipped, toothed ray flowers. Leaves are alternate, 3 to 8 inches long, and usually strongly lobed, with toothed margins and clasping bases.

Blooming June to October.

Soil Dry, poor, well-drained.

Range British Columbia to Newfoundland, south throughout the United States.

Propagation Collect the seeds as they mature and sow in the desired locations or in deep pots of sandy or gravelly soil. Transplant the seedlings in fall after their first growing season, spacing them 24 inches apart, with the crowns at the soil surface. Self-sows readily.

Cultivation Flowers open for only a few hours one morning, then close to set seed. Remove expired flower heads to curtail the self-sowing of this invasive species.

Uses Sow in colonies on gravelly waste areas, or incorporate into a meadow mixture.

3-10 [5-8]

Tanacetum vulgare
COMMON TANSY

Daisy Family

Description Perennial. Flat-topped clusters of golden flower heads are found at the pinnacle of 12 to 36-inch stems. The buttonlike flower heads are ½ inch wide and depressed in the center to resemble that of an oxeye daisy (*Chrysanthemum leucanthemum*) without the white ray flowers. Leaves are alternate, 4 to 8 inches long, and pinnately divided into narrow, toothed segments.

Blooming July to September.

Soil Dry, poor.

Range British Columbia to Newfoundland, south throughout the United States.

Propagation Collect the mature seeds and sow in the desired locations or in outdoor flats of sandy soil. Transplant the seedlings from the flats in fall, spacing them 24 inches apart, with the rhizome 1 inch deep.

Cultivation Tolerates a wide range of soil conditions, but grows out of control in fertile soil, where the spreading rhizome should be controlled with an underground barrier.

Uses Plant in waste areas.

3-10 [5-8]

Tragopogon pratensis
YELLOW GOATSBEARD

Daisy Family

Description Biennial. A solitary yellow flower head caps the 12 to 36-inch stem. Flower heads are 1 to 2½ inches wide and composed of square-tipped, toothed ray flowers underlain by long green bracts that are no longer than the outer rays. Grasslike leaves up to 12 inches long clasp the stem alternately.

Blooming June to August.

Soil Dry, poor.

Range Manitoba to Nova Scotia, south to Georgia and Kansas.

Propagation Sow the mature seeds in the desired locations or in outdoor pots. Transplant the potted seedlings after their first growing season, spacing them at least 12 inches apart. Sow seeds for two consecutive years to assure annual blooming.

Cultivation No special care required.

Uses Plant along roadsides or in meadows.

2-7 [5-8]

Key

5-6 zone

exposure

full shade

light shade

part sun

full sun

4-5 pH

 attracts

attracts

 attracts

attracts

Antennaria plantaginifolia
PLANTAIN-LEAVED PUSSY-TOES

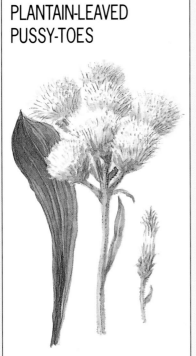

Daisy Family

Description Perennial. A dome-shaped cluster of fuzzy white flower heads sits atop a 4 to 16-inch wooly stem. Flower heads are $1/2$ inch wide and composed of disc florets. The stem rises from a basal rosette of spoon-shaped, grayish green, wooly leaves that are 3 inches long with prominent veins. Stem leaves are short, narrow, and pointed.

Blooming April to June.

Soil Dry, poor, well-drained.

Range Minnesota to Maine, south to Georgia and Missouri.

Propagation Cut stolons and transplant individual plants from a colony in late summer or fall, replanting them at intervals of 6 inches, with the crowns at the soil surface. Collect the seeds as they mature and sow in outdoor flats of sandy soil in fall. Transplant from the flats after one full growing season.

Cultivation No care required.

Uses Plant in colonies as a groundcover in open, sandy areas or on banks to control erosion.

3-7 ☐ 5-8

Cosmos bipinnatus
COSMOS

Daisy Family

Description Annual. Solitary pink, white, or red flower heads crown 36 to 60-inch stems. Flower heads are about 3 inches wide with broad ray flowers and a central disc. Fernlike leaves are twice pinnately divided into narrow segments.

Blooming June to September.

Soil Dry, average, well-drained.

Range Mexico, introduced to the United States.

Propagation Sow in their permanent locations in spring after all danger of frost has passed. In northern latitudes, start the plants indoors in late winter and transplant them to a meadow after the last frost.

Cultivation Drought-tolerant.

Uses Plant in a meadow mixture.

9-10 ☐ 5-8

Coreopsis tinctoria
ANNUAL COREOPSIS

Daisy Family

Description Annual. Yellow flower heads with dark red centers adorn the ends of branches on the 24 to 48-inch stem. Flower heads are 1 to 2 inches wide and composed of a reddish brown central disc and yellow, three-lobed rays with reddish brown bases. Sometimes flower heads are all yellow or all red. The opposite leaves are 2 to 4 inches long and divided into long, narrow segments.

Blooming June to September.

Soil Moist, average, well-drained.

Range British Columbia to Manitoba, south to Louisiana and California.

Propagation Sow seeds in desired locations after the last frost in spring. Mow in fall to distribute seeds.

Cultivation Tolerates partial shade but needs regular watering.

Uses Plant in a meadow mixture.

3-9 ☐ 5-7

Epilobium angustifolium
FIREWEED

Evening Primrose Family

Description Perennial. A spiked cluster of magenta flowers, which blooms from the bottom up, tops a 36 to 72-inch stem. Each flower is about 1 inch wide and consists of four rounded petals, eight stamens, and a four-part stigma on a long style. The alternate leaves are 3 to 8 inches long and canoe-shaped.

Blooming July to September.

Soil Moist, average.

Range Alaska to Labrador, south to western North Carolina, eastern Tennessee, northern Ohio, South Dakota, New Mexico, and California.

Propagation Divide rhizomes in early spring and replant segments 24 inches apart and $^1/_2$ inch deep. Sow seeds in fall in desired locations on bare mineral soil or in individual pots. Transplant seedlings from pots to garden about six weeks after germination.

Cultivation Tolerates dry soil but not shade. Thrives in burned areas.

Uses Plant in colonies for erosion control.

2-9

Oenothera fruticosa
SUNDROPS

Evening Primrose Family

Description Perennial. A loose cluster of yellow flowers decorates the upper portion of the 12 to 36-inch stem. The flowers are 1 to 2 inches wide with four round petals, eight stamens with orange anthers, and a pistil with a four-part stigma. Leaves are 1 to 4 inches long, alternate, and canoe-shaped.

Blooming June to August.

Soil Moist, average, well-drained.

Range Minnesota to Nova Scotia, south to Georgia and Texas.

Propagation Divide clumps in fall and replant 18 inches apart, with the basal leaves just above the soil surface. Collect the seeds as they mature and immediately sow them thinly in outdoor flats. Transplant the seedlings from the flats to pots about six weeks after germination in spring, and move to the desired locations at summer's end. Take stem cuttings in late summer, lay them horizontally on a moist sand-vermiculite mixture, and cover lightly. Small rosettes of leaves and roots will arise from the leaf nodes and can be separated and transplanted when roots reach about 1 inch in length.

Cultivation Tolerates partial shade. Stems will be weak if soil is too fertile.

3-8

Corydalis sempervirens
PALE CORYDALIS

Fumitory Family

Description Biennial. Pink and yellow flowers droop in clusters at the ends of branches on a 6 to 24-inch stem. The flowers are $^1/_2$ inch long with four petals, the upper of which has a round spur projecting upward. Leaves are 1 to 4 inches long, bluish green, alternate, and pinnately divided into three-lobed leaflets.

Blooming May to September.

Soil Moist, poor.

Range British Columbia to Newfoundland, south to northern Georgia, Illinois, Minnesota, and Montana.

Propagation Collect the seeds as they mature and sow promptly in the desired locations. Sow for two consecutive seasons to ensure annual blooming.

Cultivation No special care required.

3-7

Belamcanda chinensis
BLACKBERRY LILY

Iris Family

Description Perennial. Several orange flowers grow at the ends of a branched 24 to 48-inch stem. The flowers are about 2 inches wide and resemble those of lilies, with three red-speckled petals and three similar petal-like sepals. Its leaves are narrow, flat, and swordlike, growing up to 18 inches.

Blooming June to July.

Soil Moist, rich.

Range Nebraska to Connecticut, south to Georgia and eastern Texas.

Propagation As soon as the seeds mature, sow them in the desired locations or in outdoor flats. Maintain the flats for two years if germination is slow. Transplant the seedlings from the flats to the garden in fall after their first growing season. Divide clumps in fall and replant 12 inches apart, with the rhizomes $1^{1}/_{2}$ inches deep.

Cultivation Will look after itself.

Uses Plant in meadow mixture.

5-8 ▢ 5-7 🐦

Sisyrinchium angustifolium
BLUE-EYED GRASS

Iris Family

Description Perennial. Blue to violet-blue flowers with yellow centers form a loose cluster on top of 6 to 18-inch flattened stems. Flowers are $^{1}/_{2}$ inch wide with three petals and three petal-like sepals, each with a fine point. The basal leaves are 4 to 20 inches long, very narrow, and grasslike.

Blooming May to July.

Soil Moist, average, well-drained.

Range Throughout most of North America.

Propagation Divide clumps in spring or fall and replant 6 inches apart, with crowns $^{1}/_{2}$ inch deep. Collect the seeds when mature and sow promptly $^{1}/_{4}$ inch deep in outdoor flats. Keep the seedlings in light shade until they are transplanted to the garden after their first growing season. Self-sows readily.

Cultivation Divide clumps every other year to promote vigorous blooming.

Uses Plant in meadow mixture.

3-10 ▢ 5-6

Lilium tigrinum
TIGER LILY

Lily Family

Description Perennial. One to several nodding, orangish red flowers are found at the apex of a 24 to 48-inch stem. Each flower has three petals and three petal-like sepals, all strongly recurved with dark spots, and six conspicuously protruding stamens. The alternate leaves are narrowly egg-shaped with small black bulblets in the axils.

Blooming July to August.

Soil Moist, average.

Range North Dakota to New England, south to Virginia and Oklahoma.

Propagation Collect bulblets as they fall from the leaf axils and plant them 12 inches apart and $^{1}/_{2}$ inch deep in permanent locations.

Cultivation Tolerates full sun to light shade. Can also be grown in humus-rich soil in a woodland garden.

Uses Plant as a border along fences and drives.

3-7 ▢ 5-7 🐦

Ornithogalum umbellatum
STAR-OF-BETHLEHEM

Lily Family

Description Perennial. White flowers form a
loose cluster 4 to 12 inches above the
ground. Shaped like a six-pointed star, the
flowers have waxy white petals and petal-like
sepals with a green stripe on the underside of
each. The basal leaves are long and grasslike
with a whitish midrib.

Blooming April to June.

Soil Moist, average.

Range Nebraska to Ontario and
Newfoundland, south to North Carolina,
Mississippi, and Kansas.

Propagation Divide clumps of bulbs in fall
and replant 6 inches apart and 1 inch deep.

Cultivation Tolerates full sun to light shade.
May also be grown in a woodland garden.

4-7 [⧅] [5-8]

Muscari botryoides
COMMON GRAPE HYACINTH

Lily Family

Description Perennial. Grapelike clusters of
spherical blue flowers cling to the top of a 4
to 10-inch stem. The flowers are about $1/8$
inch in diameter and nodding. Leaves are
basal, grasslike, and grooved.

Blooming April to May.

Soil Moist, average.

Range Minnesota to New England, south to
Virginia and Kansas.

Propagation Divide clumps in fall and
replant bulbs 6 inches apart and 2 inches
deep.

Cultivation May also be grown in rich
woodland soils. Tolerates partial shade.

4-7 [○] [6-7] 🐝

Hedyotis caerulea
BLUETS

Madder Family

Description Perennial. Slender stems, each
2 to 8 inches tall with a terminal, pastel blue,
yellow-centered flower, grow in clumps to
form tufts of bloom in grassy areas. Each
tubular flower is $1/2$ inch wide with four
spreading petals. Stem leaves are narrow,
opposite, and less than $1/4$ inch long, while
basal leaves are $1/2$ inch long and egg-shaped
with the terminal end widest.

Blooming April to June.

Soil Moist, average.

Range Wisconsin to Nova Scotia, south to
northern Georgia and Arkansas.

Propagation Divide clumps in fall or early
spring and replant 24 inches apart, with the
basal leaves just above the soil surface.
Collect the seeds as they mature, sow them
in individual pots outdoors, cover with a
sprinkling of potting mix, and keep moist.
Transplant the potted seedlings after their
first growing season. Self-sows readily.

Cultivation Do not mow early in spring, or if
you must, set the lawn mower at its highest
level to avoid clipping the flowers before they
set seed.

Uses Great addition to a lawn or meadow.
Can also be planted alone in dry stone walls.

4-7 [○] [5-6]

Key

5-6
zone

exposure

⧅ full shade

⧄ light shade

⬚ part sun

○ full sun

[4-5] pH

🐝 attracts

🦋 attracts

🐦 attracts

🐦 attracts

Asclepias syriaca
COMMON MILKWEED

Milkweed Family

Description Perennial. Somewhat drooping clusters of mauve-pink flowers crown a 24 to 60-inch downy stem. Clusters are 2 inches wide, and each flower is $1/2$ inch wide with five strongly reflexed petals and a five-part central crown. The opposite leaves are 4 to 10 inches long and oblong in shape with smooth margins. Their undersides are covered with wooly gray hair.

Blooming June to August.

Soil Moist, average, well-drained.

Range Saskatchewan to New Brunswick, south to Georgia and Kansas.

Propagation In fall, cut the rhizome into 2-inch pieces with one or more buds apiece and replant sections 12 inches apart with the buds 2 inches deep. Gather the seeds in early fall, sow $1/2$ inch deep in outdoor flats, and mulch lightly. Transplant the seedlings to their permanent locations in fall.

Cultivation Thrives in most soils, but needs full sun.

Uses Plant at the rear of a border or in meadows.

Salvia coccinea
SCARLET SAGE

Mint Family

Description Perennial. Whorls of bilaterally symmetrical, scarlet flowers form a spiked cluster at the pinnacle of a 12 to 24-inch square stem. The tubular flowers are 1 inch long with a three-lobed lower lip and a two-lobed upper lip. Leaves are 1 to 2 inches long, opposite, and heart-shaped with a scalloped margin.

Blooming May to November.

Soil Dry, poor.

Range South Carolina to Texas on the coastal plain.

Propagation Can be grown as an annual in hardiness zones colder than 7. Sow the seeds indoors in late winter, $1/4$ inch deep in flats of sandy soil, and keep moist. Transplant the seedlings to the desired locations after the last frost. Self-sows readily in its native range. Take stem cuttings from mature plants in late spring and insert in a moist sand-vermiculite mixture in light shade. Transplant rooted cuttings to the garden after about six to eight weeks.

Cultivation Mature plants may survive winter if heavily mulched.

Uses Plant in sandy areas.

Ajuga reptans
BUGLEWEED

Mint Family

Description Perennial. Whorls of powder blue flowers intermingled with bracts form short leafy spikes on top of 4 to 12-inch stems. The tubular, bilaterally symmetrical flowers are $1/2$ inch long, with a short, two-lobed upper lip, a spreading three-lobed lower lip, and protruding stamens. Leaves are about 1 inch long, opposite, egg-shaped or oval, and bluntly toothed.

Blooming May to July.

Soil Dry, rich, well-drained.

Range Wisconsin to Newfoundland, south to Pennsylvania and Ohio.

Propagation Divide clumps in fall or early spring and replant 6 inches apart, with crowns at the soil surface. Seeds are difficult to collect, but established plants self-sow readily.

Cultivation Mulch in fall for winter protection. Thrives in rich to poor soil and full sun to light shade.

Uses Plant as a groundcover or use for erosion control on steep banks.

4-5 | 5-8

Lobularia maritima
SWEET ALYSSUM

Mustard Family

Description Annual. Small white flowers appear in a compact cluster on a 2 to 12-inch stem, many of which branch from the base to form a low cushion. Each flower has four round petals and a dark center. Leaves are about 2 inches long, opposite, narrow, and somewhat canoe-shaped with smooth margins.

Blooming April to August.

Soil Dry, average.

Range Throughout most of the United States.

Propagation Sow the seeds in spring in the desired locations after the last frost, or sow in flats indoors in late winter and transplant to the garden in four to six weeks. Blooms all year as a perennial in mild regions, and may be propagated there by dividing clumps.

Cultivation Prefers soil with a high lime content. Also tolerates partial sun or light shade. Drought-tolerant.

Hesperis matronalis
DAME'S ROCKET

Mustard Family

Description Perennial. Long-stalked purple, pink, or white flowers form a loose cluster at the top of a 24 to 36-inch stem. The flowers are up to 1 inch wide and have four spreading petals. The alternate leaves are 3 to 6 inches long and egg-shaped with toothed margins.

Blooming May to July.

Soil Moist, average, well-drained.

Range Southern Canada and northern United States.

Propagation Collect the seeds as they mature and sow immediately in the desired locations or in outdoor flats. Transplant to the garden six to eight weeks after germination.

Cultivation Tolerates partial shade.

Uses Plant in meadow mixtures.

Ipomopsis rubra
STANDING CYPRESS

Phlox Family

Description Biennial. Tubular scarlet flowers form an elongated cluster on a 24 to 72-inch stem. Each flower is about 1 inch long with five spreading lobes and protruding stamens with yellow anthers. Leaves are alternate and pinnately divided into many narrow segments.

Blooming May to September.

Soil Dry, poor.

Range Oklahoma to North Carolina, south to Florida and Texas.

Propagation Sow seeds $^{1}/_{4}$ inch deep in desired locations as soon as they mature, or start indoors in late winter. Transplant the seedlings from pots to the garden six to eight weeks after germination. Sow seeds for at least two consecutive years to achieve annual blooming. Self-sows readily. Survives as a perennial in warmer climates. Can be grown in cooler climates as an annual.

Cultivation Tolerates drought and partial shade.

Uses Plant in the rear of a border.

Key

5-6
zone

exposure

full shade

light shade

part sun

full sun

4-5
pH

attracts

attracts

attracts

attracts

Anagallis arvensis
SCARLET PIMPERNEL

Primrose Family

Description Annual. Long-stalked, reddish orange flowers grow in the leaf axils on a 4 to 12-inch stem. Each flower is ¼ inch wide with five petals. Leaves are up to 1 inch long and egg-shaped with smooth margins.

Blooming June to August.

Soil Dry, poor, well-drained.

Range Southern Canada and south throughout most of the United States.

Propagation Sow the seeds in the desired locations in sandy soil after the last spring frost.

Cultivation Tolerates partial shade and a variety of soils, but prefers sandy areas.

Uses Plant in meadow mixtures.

3-9 ▢ 5-8

Lysimachia nummularia
MONEYWORT

Primrose Family

Description Perennial. Yellow flowers rise on long stalks from leaf axils on a trailing stem up to 24 inches long. The bowl-shaped flowers are 1 inch wide and have five petals. Leaves are up to 1 inch long, opposite, and nearly round with smooth margins.

Blooming June to August.

Soil Moist, average.

Range Ontario to Newfoundland, south to Georgia and Kansas.

Propagation Divide clumps in fall and replant 12 inches apart, with the crowns at the soil surface. Take stem cuttings during June or July, lay them where new plants are desired, and cover both ends with moist soil. Sow the seeds in pots outdoors in fall, and transplant to the garden when the stems grow long enough to begin trailing.

Cultivation Tolerates poor to rich soil and light shade to full sun. Divide the clumps every other year or so to prevent overcrowding.

Uses Makes an excellent groundcover. Plant in the front of a border, at the edge of a pond or on a stream bank, or around trees and rocks.

3-7 ▢ 5-6

Potentilla canadensis
COMMON CINQUEFOIL

Rose Family

Description Perennial. Yellow flowers rise on long stalks from axils on a somewhat trailing stem covered with silvery hair. Flowers are about ½ inch wide with five petals and numerous stamens and pistils. The leaves are alternate and divided into five leaflets, each up to 1½ inches long and toothed on the rounded end.

Blooming March to June.

Soil Dry, average.

Range Minnesota to Nova Scotia, south to Georgia and Missouri.

Propagation Divide rooted runners in fall and replant 12 inches apart, with rhizomes ½ inch deep. Collect seeds as they mature and sow immediately in outdoor flats filled with equal parts sand and soil. Keep seedlings in light shade, transfer to pots six weeks after germination, and move them to the garden in fall. Take stem cuttings in June or July, dip cut ends in rooting hormone, and insert in a moist sand-vermiculite mixture until roots are about 1 inch long, at which time they can be potted and kept outdoors until they can be transplanted to the garden in spring.

Cultivation Tolerates full sun to light shade. Divide plants every two or three years.

3-7 ▢ 5-7

Rosa carolina
PASTURE ROSE

Rose Family

Description Perennial. Pink flowers with yellow centers are found on this 12 to 36-inch shrub. Each flower is about 2 inches wide and has five almost heart-shaped petals and a multitude of yellow stamens. The alternate leaves are pinnately divided into oval, coarsely toothed leaflets about 1 inch long. Stems are armed with straight thorns.

Blooming June to July.

Soil Moist, average, well-drained.

Range Minnesota to Nova Scotia, south to Florida and Texas.

Propagation In fall, separate stems by cutting the underground stolons connecting them and replant with the crown at the soil surface. Collect the seeds as soon as the hips turn red and sow immediately 1/4 inch deep in outdoor flats containing a moist mixture of equal parts peat moss and sand. Maintain the flats for two years if germination is slow. Transplant the seedlings to the desired locations after they have reached 6 inches in height.

Cultivation Tolerates partial shade.

Uses Plant in meadow mixtures.

4-9   5-6

Linaria vulgaris
BUTTER-AND-EGGS

Snapdragon Family

Description Annual. Yellow and orange flowers form a terminal cluster on a 12 to 36-inch stem. Each bilaterally symmetrical, inch-long flower has a two-lobed upper lip and a three-lobed lower lip with a prominent downward spur. Leaves are 1 to 3 inches long, alternate, narrow, and grasslike.

Blooming June to October.

Soil Dry, poor, well-drained.

Range Throughout most of North America.

Propagation Collect the mature seeds in fall and sow in the desired locations or in outdoor flats of sandy soil. Transplant from the flats to the desired locations four to six weeks after germination.

Cultivation No care required.

Uses Plant in meadows or marginal areas.

2-10   5-8

Tradescantia virginiana
SPIDERWORT

Spiderwort Family

Description Perennial. Bluish violet flowers grow in a terminal cluster on a 12 to 24-inch stem. Flowers are 1 to 2 inches wide with three roundish petals and six stamens with yellow anthers. The alternate leaves are 6 to 18 inches long, grasslike, and grooved.

Blooming April to July.

Soil Moist, average, well-drained.

Range Wisconsin to Connecticut, south to northwestern Georgia and Missouri.

Propagation Divide the clumps in late fall and replant 12 inches apart. Collect the seeds as they mature and sow immediately in outdoor flats. Transplant to the garden after one full growing season. Take stem cuttings in June or July, dip ends in rooting hormone, and insert in a moist sand-vermiculite mixture. Transfer rooted cuttings to pots after three weeks and move to garden in fall.

Cultivation Tolerates partial sun and light shade. Divide the clumps every third year to promote vigorous growth. Plants will bloom again if flowering stems are removed after the first blossoms fade.

Uses Plant in moist meadows.

4-7   5-6

Identification Charts

To use these tables first locate the habitat below in which the flower was found. (Remember that wildflowers may grow in more than one habitat). Next determine whether the unknown flower is regular, irregular, composite, or has petal-like parts that are very small or absent. If the parts seem to be fused into a funnel, bell, cup, pouch, or other shape check this sub-heading first. Other sub-headings list species by the number of petal-like parts (usually 3, 4, 5, or 6), or unusual shape or features (pealike, spathe and spadix, etc.). Next decide which color best describes it. (Remember that wildflower colors can vary and are subject to interpretation). Although this book includes many of the more common wildflowers, it can only list a small percentage of North American species. However, even if you cannot find a match, similar species may give you a clue as to where to look in a more comprehensive field guide.

pink	red	yellow	white	blue	purple lavender	greenish	brownish	orange

EASTERN WOODLANDS

REGULAR: PETAL-LIKE PARTS FUSED INTO FUNNEL, TRUMPET, OR BELL

pink	red	yellow	white	blue	purple lavender	greenish	brownish	orange
trailing arbutus	trumpet honeysuckle / trumpet creeper	large-flowered bellwort / downy false foxglove / small Solomon's seal	wintergreen / trailing arbutus / partridgeberry	wild blue phlox	small Solomon's seal			

3 PETAL-LIKE PARTS

pink	red	yellow	white	blue	purple lavender	greenish	brownish	orange
large-flowered trillium	purple trillium	yellow trillium	nodding trillium / large-flowered trillium / painted trillium					

4 PETAL-LIKE PARTS

pink	red	yellow	white	blue	purple lavender	greenish	brownish	orange
cut-leaved toothwort		celandine poppy	partridgeberry / Canada mayflower / wood anemone / toothwort / cut-leaved toothwort					celandine poppy

5 PETAL-LIKE PARTS

pink	red	yellow	white	blue	purple lavender	greenish	brownish	orange
round-lobed hepatica / trailing arbutus / herb Robert / shooting star	trumpet honeysuckle / wild columbine / fire pink / trumpet creeper	downy false foxglove / wild columbine	round-lobed hepatica / wintergreen / trailing arbutus / wood anemone / rue anemone / spring beauty / foamflower / wild sarsaparilla / starry campion / shinleaf / shooting star	round-lobed hepatica / wild blue phlox / Venus's looking glass / Virginia bluebells / fern-leafed phacelia	round-lobed hepatica / Venus's looking glass / wild geranium	wild sarsaparilla		

6 OR MORE PETAL-LIKE PARTS

pink	red	yellow	white	blue	purple lavender	greenish	brownish	orange
round-lobed hepatica	wood lily	bluebead lily / small Solomon's seal / large-flowered bellwort	wood anemone / rue anemone / atamasco lily / fly poison	round-lobed hepatica / wild hyacinth	round-lobed hepatica / wild hyacinth	bluebead lily / fly poison / small Solomon's seal		wood lily

pink	red	yellow	white	blue	purple lavender	greenish	brownish	orange
		wild oats Indian cucumber root trout lily	starflower bloodroot twinleaf round-lobed hepatica wild leek nodding mandarin mayapple					

IRREGULAR: PETAL-LIKE PARTS FUSED INTO TUBE, POUCH, OR LIPS

pink	red	yellow	white	blue	purple lavender	greenish	brownish	orange
fringed polygala pink lady's slipper fringed bleeding heart		yellow lady's slipper	Dutchman's-breeches hoary mountain mint squirrel corn	great lobelia downy skullcap	hyssop skullcap			

PETAL-LIKE PARTS: OTHER – PEALIKE/SPATHE AND SPADIX, ETC.

pink	red	yellow	white	blue	purple lavender	greenish	brownish	orange
		smooth yellow violet	sweet white violet	wild lupine common blue violet	common blue violet		Jack-in-the-pulpit	

COMPOSITE

pink	red	yellow	white	blue	purple lavender	greenish	brownish	orange
				bigleaf aster	bigleaf aster			

PETAL-LIKE PARTS VERY SMALL, OR ABSENT

pink	red	yellow	white	blue	purple lavender	greenish	brownish	orange
			black cohosh				Jack-in-the-pulpit	

WESTERN WOODLANDS

REGULAR: PETAL-LIKE PARTS FUSED INTO FUNNEL, TRUMPET, OR BELL

pink	red	yellow	white	blue	purple lavender	greenish	brownish	orange
rosy twisted-stalk bearberry twinflower			creeping snowberry bearberry twinflower				rosy twisted-stalk	

3 PETAL-LIKE PARTS

pink	red	yellow	white	blue	purple lavender	greenish	brownish	orange
Douglas's iris	giant trillium		Douglas's iris giant trillium					

4 PETAL-LIKE PARTS

pink	red	yellow	white	blue	purple lavender	greenish	brownish	orange
			tufted evening primrose red baneberry bunchberry					

5 PETAL-LIKE PARTS

pink	red	yellow	white	blue	purple lavender	greenish	brownish	orange
twinflower sticky cranesbill redwood sorrel fringe cups common pipsissewa	California Indian pink		twinflower blue columbine red baneberry redwood sorrel fringe cups common pipsissewa	blue columbine sky pilot	sticky cranesbill			

6 OR MORE PETAL-LIKE PARTS

pink	red	yellow	white	blue	purple lavender	greenish	brownish	orange
rosy twisted-stalk bitter root nodding wild onion	leopard lily	yellow fawn lily creeping Oregon grape sulfur flower	bear grass queen's cup sulfur flower starry false Solomon's seal				rosy twisted-stalk	leopard lily

(continued)

pink	red	yellow	white	blue	purple lavender	greenish	brownish	orange
			red baneberry / false Solomon's seal / nodding wild onion					

IRREGULAR: PETALS FUSED INTO TUBE, POUCH, OR LIPS

pink	red	yellow	white	blue	purple lavender	greenish	brownish	orange
western bleeding heart			mountain lady's slipper	gill-over-the-ground / Rocky Mountain penstemon				

PETAL-LIKE PARTS: OTHER – PEALIKE/SPATHE AND SPADIX, ETC.

pink	red	yellow	white	blue	purple lavender	greenish	brownish	orange
			Canada violet	blue-pod lupine / western monkshood				

COMPOSITE

pink	red	yellow	white	blue	purple lavender	greenish	brownish	orange
Oregon fleabane		heart-leaved arnica / mule's ears	Oregon fleabane		Oregon fleabane			

WETLANDS

REGULAR: PETAL-LIKE PARTS FUSED INTO FUNNEL, TRUMPET, OR BELL

pink	red	yellow	white	blue	purple lavender	greenish	brownish	orange
			Culver's root	soapwort gentian / closed gentian / mountain bluebells	soapwort gentian			

3 PETAL-LIKE PARTS

pink	red	yellow	white	blue	purple lavender	greenish	brownish	orange
			arrowhead					

4 PETAL-LIKE PARTS

pink	red	yellow	white	blue	purple lavender	greenish	brownish	orange
Virginia meadow beauty	Virginia meadow beauty		Culver's root					

5 PETAL-LIKE PARTS

pink	red	yellow	white	blue	purple lavender	greenish	brownish	orange
New York ironweed / swamp milkweed	pitcher plant	marsh marigold / swamp candles / silverweed / spreading globeflower	goldthread / swamp rose mallow / grass-of-Parnassus / round-leaved sundew / spreading globeflower	forget-me-not	New York ironweed / pitcher plant			

6 OR MORE PETAL-LIKE PARTS

pink	red	yellow	white	blue	purple lavender	greenish	brownish	orange
fragrant water lily / purple loosestrife		marsh marigold / Canada lily / spreading globeflower	goldthread / fragrant water lily / tall meadow rue / spreading globeflower					Turk's cap lily / Canada lily / Michigan lily

IRREGULAR: PETAL-LIKE PARTS FUSED INTO TUBE, POUCH, OR LIPS

pink	red	yellow	white	blue	purple lavender	greenish	brownish	orange
elephant heads / obedient plant	elephant heads / bee balm		white turtlehead	Allegheny monkey flower	pickerel weed / Allegheny monkey flower			jewelweed

pink	red	yellow	white	blue	purple lavender	greenish	brownish	orange
	cardinal flower							

PETAL-LIKE PARTS: OTHER – PEALIKE/SPATHE AND SPADIX, ETC.

pink	red	yellow	white	blue	purple lavender	greenish	brownish	orange
		water arum	water arum	crested iris	crested iris	skunk cabbage	skunk cabbage	
		green dragon		blue flag	blue flag	green dragon		

COMPOSITE

pink	red	yellow	white	blue	purple lavender	greenish	brownish	orange
spotted Joe-Pye weed		tickseed sunflower	flat-topped aster		spotted Joe-Pye weed			
New York ironweed		flat-topped aster	boneset		New York ironweed			

PETAL-LIKE PARTS VERY SMALL, OR ABSENT

pink	red	yellow	white	blue	purple lavender	greenish	brownish	orange
spotted Joe-Pye weed		common cattail	tall meadow rue		spotted Joe-Pye weed			
			boneset					

DESERTS

REGULAR: PETAL-LIKE PARTS FUSED INTO FUNNEL, TRUMPET, OR BELL

pink	red	yellow	white	blue	purple lavender	greenish	brownish	orange
desert four o'clock			mountain phlox	desert bluebell	mountain phlox		chocolate lily	desert mallow
desert sand verbena				tansy phacelia	southwestern verbena			
					tansy phacelia			

4 PETAL-LIKE PARTS

pink	red	yellow	white	blue	purple lavender	greenish	brownish	orange
farewell-to-spring	California fuchsia	yellow bee plant	desert evening primrose	California poppy	farewell-to-spring			Hooker's evening primrose
		Hooker's evening primrose						coast wallflower
		desert prince's plume						California poppy
								wind poppy

5 PETAL-LIKE PARTS

pink	red	yellow	white	blue	purple lavender	greenish	brownish	orange
coral bells	skyrocket	Lindley's blazing star	mountain phlox	desert bluebell	mountain phlox			coral bells
desert four o'clock				tansy phacelia	tansy phacelia			desert mallow
checker bloom				desert delphinium	western shooting star			
western shooting star				baby-blue-eyes				
desert sand verbena								

6 OR MORE PETAL-LIKE PARTS

pink	red	yellow	white	blue	purple lavender	greenish	brownish	orange
beavertail cactus	California fuchsia		our Lord's candle	California blue-eyed grass			chocolate lily	
	claret cup cactus		prickly poppy	blue-dicks				
	beavertail cactus							
	Englemann's hedgehog cactus							

IRREGULAR: PETAL-LIKE PARTS FUSED INTO TUBE, POUCH, OR LIPS

pink	red	yellow	white	blue	purple lavender	greenish	brownish	orange
showy penstemon	scarlet bugler	owl's clover	owl's clover	showy penstemon	southwestern verbena			
owl's clover				Chinese-houses	showy penstemon			
					Chinese-houses			

(continued)

pink	red	yellow	white	blue	purple lavender	greenish	brownish	orange

PETAL-LIKE PARTS: OTHER – PEALIKE/SPATHE AND SPADIX, ETC.

pink	red	yellow	white	blue	purple lavender	greenish	brownish	orange
		arroyo lupine		sky lupine arroyo lupine	arroyo lupine			

COMPOSITE

pink	red	yellow	white	blue	purple lavender	greenish	brownish	orange
		desert marigold tidy tips wooly sunflower golden yarrow gold fields	tidy tips					

PRAIRIES

REGULAR: PETAL-LIKE PARTS FUSED INTO FUNNEL, TRUMPET, OR BELL

pink	red	yellow	white	blue	purple lavender	greenish	brownish	orange
downy phlox		hoary puccoon		tall bellflower	downy phlox			hoary puccoon

3 PETAL-LIKE PARTS

pink	red	yellow	white	blue	purple lavender	greenish	brownish	orange
	prairie trillium							

4 PETAL-LIKE PARTS

pink	red	yellow	white	blue	purple lavender	greenish	brownish	orange
Rocky Mountain bee plant		Missouri evening primrose	Rocky Mountain bee plant		Rocky Mountain bee plant			

5 PETAL-LIKE PARTS

pink	red	yellow	white	blue	purple lavender	greenish	brownish	orange
poppy mallow queen-of-the-prairie downy phlox prairie smoke		hoary puccoon	pasque flower Canada anemone snow-on-the-mountain	tall bellflower pasque flower prairie flax	pasque flower downy phlox			hoary puccoon butterfly weed

6 OR MORE PETAL-LIKE PARTS

pink	red	yellow	white	blue	purple lavender	greenish	brownish	orange
		yellow star grass plains prickly pear	pasque flower	pasque flower	pasque flower			

IRREGULAR: PETAL-LIKE PARTS FUSED INTO TUBE, POUCH, OR LIPS

pink	red	yellow	white	blue	purple lavender	greenish	brownish	orange
wild bergamot					wild bergamot			

PETAL-LIKE PARTS: OTHER – PEALIKE/SPATHE AND SPADIX, ETC.

pink	red	yellow	white	blue	purple lavender	greenish	brownish	orange
showy tick trefoil				blue sage Texas bluebonnet showy tick trefoil	lead plant birdfoot violet showy tick trefoil purple prairie clover			

COMPOSITE

pink	red	yellow	white	blue	purple lavender	greenish	brownish	orange
New England aster	Indian blanket blanket flower	lance-leaved coreopsis Indian blanket blanket flower Mexican hat compass plant common sunflower black-eyed Susan		western silvery aster	purple coneflower New England aster western silvery aster		Mexican hat black-eyed Susan	

pink	red	yellow	white	blue	purple lavender	greenish	brownish	orange

PETAL-LIKE PARTS VERY SMALL, OR ABSENT

pink	red	yellow	white	blue	purple lavender	greenish	brownish	orange
		showy goldenrod	rattlesnake master		prairie blazing star	rattlesnake master		

FIELDS AND ROADSIDES

REGULAR: PETAL-LIKE PARTS FUSED INTO FUNNEL, TRUMPET, OR BELL

pink	red	yellow	white	blue	purple lavender	greenish	brownish	orange
	standing cypress			common grape hyacinth bluets harebell				

3 PETAL-LIKE PARTS

pink	red	yellow	white	blue	purple lavender	greenish	brownish	orange
				spiderwort				

4 PETAL-LIKE PARTS

pink	red	yellow	white	blue	purple lavender	greenish	brownish	orange
fireweed dame's rocket		sundrops	bluets sweet alyssum dame's rocket	bluets	dame's rocket			

5 PETAL-LIKE PARTS

pink	red	yellow	white	blue	purple lavender	greenish	brownish	orange
common milkweed scarlet pimpernel pasture rose	scarlet pimpernel standing cypress	moneywort common cinquefoil		harebell	common milkweed			scarlet pimpernel

6 OR MORE PETAL-LIKE PARTS

pink	red	yellow	white	blue	purple lavender	greenish	brownish	orange
	tiger lily	prickly pear	star-of-Bethlehem	blue-eyed grass				blackberry lily tiger lily

IRREGULAR: PETAL-LIKE PARTS FUSED INTO TUBE, POUCH, OR LIPS

pink	red	yellow	white	blue	purple lavender	greenish	brownish	orange
pale corydalis	scarlet sage	pale corydalis butter-and-eggs		spiked lobelia bugleweed				butter-and-eggs

COMPOSITE

pink	red	yellow	white	blue	purple lavender	greenish	brownish	orange
bachelor's-button cosmos	cosmos	common tansy oxeye daisy annual coreopsis yellow goatsbeard	plantain-leaved pussy-toes bachelor's-button oxeye daisy cosmos common yarrow pearly everlasting	bachelor's-button common chicory				

PETAL-LIKE PARTS VERY SMALL, OR ABSENT

pink	red	yellow	white	blue	purple lavender	greenish	brownish	orange
		common tansy Canada goldenrod	Queen-Anne's-lace plantain-leaved pussy-toes					

Contacts

NOTE: The following list is offered as a convenience to readers and in no way implies endorsement by either the author or the publisher. Most of those listed reportedly do not collect wild plants, but potential customers should take great care to ascertain that any plants they buy are nursery-propagated (see page 30).

Holland Wildflower Farm
290 O'Neal Lane
Elkins, AR 72727

Southwestern Native Seeds
Box 50503
Tuscon, AZ 85703

C. H. Baccus
900 Boynton Ave.
San Jose, CA 95117

Clyde Robin Seed Co.
3670 Enterprise Ave.
Hayward, CA 94545

Larner Seeds
P.O. Box 407
Bolinas, CA 94924

Las Pilitas Nursery
Las Pilitas Rd.
Santa Margarita, CA 93453

Moon Mountain Wildflowers
P.O. Box 34
Morro Bay, CA 93443

Midwest Wildflowers
P.O. Box 64
Rockton, IL 61072

Country Road Greenhouses, Inc.
R.R. 1, Box 62
Malta, IL 60150

The Natural Garden
38W443 Hwy. 64
St. Charles, IL 60175

The Wildflower Source
Box 312
Fox Lake, IL 60020

Sharp Bros. Seed Co.
P.O. Box 140
Healy, KS 67850

Louisiana Nature & Science Center
P.O. Box 870610
New Orleans, LA 70187-0610

Conley's Garden Center
145 Townsend Ave.
Boothbay Harbor, ME 04538

Environmental Concern, Inc.
210 West Chew Ave.
P.O. Box P
St. Michaels, MD 21663

New England Wildflower Society
Garden in the Woods
Hemenway Rd.
Framingham, MA 01701

Far North Gardens
16785 Harrison
Livonia, MI 48154

Orchid Gardens
2232 139th Ave. NW
Andover, MN 55304

Prairie Moon Nursery
Rt. 3, Box 163
Winona, MN 55987

Prairie Restorations, Inc.
P.O. Box 327
Princeton, MN 55371

Missouri Wildflowers Nursery
9814 Pleasant Hill Rd.
Jefferson City, MO 65109

Stock Seed Farms, Inc.
R.R. 1, Box 112
Murdock, NE 68407

Plants of the Southwest
930 Baca St.
Santa Fe, NM 87501

Bernardo Beach Native Plant Farm
1 Sanchez Rd.
Veguita, NM 87062

Wildginger Woodlands
P.O. Box 1091
Webster, NY 14580

Niche Gardens
1111 Dawson Rd.
Chapel Hill, NC 27516

We-Du Nurseries
Rt. 5, Box 724
Marion, NC 28752

Russell Graham
4030 Eagle Crest Rd. NW
Salem, OR 97304

Siskiyou Rare Plant Nursery
2825 Cummings Rd.
Medford, OR 97501

Appalachian Wildflower Nursery
Rt. 1, Box 275A
Reedsville, PA 17084

The Primrose Path
R.D. 2, Box 110
Scottsdale, PA 15683

Wildflower Patch
442RC Brookside
Walnutport, PA 18088

Oak Hill Farm
204 Pressly St.
Clover, SC 29710

Woodlanders, Inc.
1128 Colleton Ave.
Aiken, SC 29801

Native Gardens
Rt. 1, Box 494, Fisher Lane
Greenback, TN 37742

Natural Gardens
113 Jasper Lane
Oak Ridge, TN 37830

Sunlight Gardens, Inc.
Rt. 1, Box 600A, Hillvale Rd.
Andersonville, TN 37705

Green Horizons
218 Quinlan, Suite 571
Kerrville, TX 78028

J'Don Seeds International
P.O. Box 10998-533
Austin, TX 78766

The Lowrey Nursery
2323 Sleepy Hollow Rd.
Conroe, TX 77385

Putney Nursery, Inc.
Rt. 5, Box 265
Putney, VT 05346

The Vermont Wildflower Farm
Rt. 7, Box 5
Charlotte, VT 05445

Frosty Hollow
Box 53
Langley, WA 98260

McLaughlin's Seeds
Buttercup's Acre
Mead, WA 99021-0550

Plants of the Wild
P.O. Box 866
Tekoa, WA 99033

Country Wetlands Nursery and Consulting
S. 75 W. 20755 Field Dr.
Muskego, WI 53150

Boehlke's Woodland Gardens
W. 140 N. 10829 Country Aire Rd.
Germantown, WI 53022

Little Valley Farm
RR. 3, Box 544
Spring Green, WI 53588

Prairie Nursery
P.O. Box 365
Westfield, WI 53964

Prairie Ridge Nursery
CRM Ecosystems, Inc.
R.R. 2, 9738 Overland Rd.
Mount Horeb, WI 53572

Prairie Seed Source
P.O. Box 83
North Lake, WI 53064

. . . .

For further information, contact:

National Wildflower Research Center
2600 FM 973 North
Austin, TX 78725
(512) 929-3600

Their *Wildflower Handbook* is very reasonably priced and packed with information covering all 50 states, including botanical gardens and organizations, sources of seeds and plants, regional bibliographies, wildflower conservation, seed collection, propagation from seed, and other topics.

Also quite useful to the wildflower gardener would be Hal Morgan's *The Mail Order Gardener*, listed in the bibliography. In addition to suppliers of wildflower seeds and plants, it also lists many sources of garden tools, furniture, books, and other items of interest to gardeners.

Index

Bibliography

The following books were valuable references used in researching *Wildflowers* and are highly recommended for anyone wishing additional information.

Art, Henry W. *A Garden of Wildflowers*. Pownal, Vt: Storey Communications, Garden Way Publishing, 1986.

.... *The Wildflower Gardener's Guide: Northeast, Mid-Atlantic, Great Lakes and Eastern Canada Edition*. Pownal, Vt: Storey Communications, Garden Way Publishing, 1987.

...............*The Wildflower Gardener's Guide: Pacific Northwest, Rocky Mountain and Western Canada Edition*. Pownal, Vt: Storey Communications, Garden Way Publishing, 1990.

...............*The Wildflower Gardener's Guide: California, Desert Southwest, and Northern Mexico Edition*. Pownal, Vt: Storey, Garden Way Publishing, 1990.

...............*The Wildflower Gardener's Guide: Midwest, Great Plains, and Canadian Prairies Edition*. Pownal, Vt: Storey Communications, Garden Way Publishing, 1991.

Austin, Richard L. *Wild Gardening: Strategies and Procedures Using Native Plantings*. New York: Simon & Schuster, 1986.

Birdseye, Clarence, and Eleanor G. *Growing Woodland Plants*. New York: Dover Publications, 1972.

Cox, Jeff. *Landscaping with Nature*. Emmaus, Pa: Rodale Press, 1991.

Craighead, John J., Frank C. Craighead, Jr., and Ray J. Davis. *A Field Guide to Rocky Mountain Wildflowers*. Boston: Houghton Mifflin Co., 1963.

Dennis, John V. *The Wildlife Gardener*. New York: Alfred A. Knopf, 1985.

Ernst, Ruth Shaw. *The Naturalist's Garden*. Emmaus, Pa: Rodale Press, 1987.

Henderson, Carrol L. *Landscaping for Wildlife*. St. Paul: Minnesota Department of Natural Resources, 1987.

Keator, G. *Complete Garden Guide to the Native Perennials of California*. San Francisco: 1990.

Kruckeberg, Arthur R. *Gardening with Native Plants of the Pacific Northwest*. Seattle: University of Washington Press, 1982.

Kress, Stephen W. *The Audubon Society Guide to Attracting Birds*. New York: Macmillan Publishing Co., Charles Scribner's Sons, 1985.

Leighton, Phebe, and Calvin Simonds. *The New American Landscape Gardener*. Emmaus, Pa: Rodale Press, 1987.

Martin, Alexander C., Herbert S. Zim, and Arnold L. Nelson. *American Wildlife and Wild Plants: A Guide to Wildlife Food Habits*. New York: Dover Publications, 1961.

Martin, Laura C. *The Wildflower Meadow Book: A Gardener's Guide*. 2nd ed. Chester, Conn: The Globe Pequot Press, 1990.

Merilees, Bill. *Attracting Backyard Wildlife*. Stillwater, Minn: Voyageur Press, 1989.

Morgan, Hal. *The Mail Order Gardener*. New York: Harper & Row, 1988.

National Wildflower Research Center. *Wildflower Handbook*. Austin: Texas Monthly Press, 1989.

National Wildlife Federation. *Planting an Oasis for Wildlife*. Washington D.C.: National Wildlife Federation, 1986.

Newcomb, Lawrence. *Newcomb's Wildflower Guide*. Boston: Little, Brown and Co., 1977.

Niehaus, Theodore F. *A Field Guide to Pacific States Wildflowers*. Boston: Houghton Mifflin Co., 1976.

Niering, William A., and Nancy C. Olmstead. *The Audubon Society Field Guide to North American Wildflowers: Eastern Region*. New York: Alfred A. Knopf, 1979.

Odum, Eugene P. *Fundamentals of Ecology*. Philadelphia: Saunders College Publishing, 1971.

Peterson, Roger Tory, and Margaret McKenny. *A Field Guide to Wildflowers of Northeastern and North-central America*. Boston: Houghton Mifflin Co., 1968.

Phillips, Harry R. *Growing and Propagating Wildflowers*. Chapel Hill: The University of North Carolina Press, 1985.

Phillips, Judith. *Southwestern Landscaping with Native Plants*. Santa Fe: Museum of New Mexico Press, 1980.

Schmidt, Marjorie G. *Growing Californian Native Plants*. Berkley: University of California Press, 1980.

Schneck, Marcus. *Butterflies*. Emmaus, Pa: Rodale Press, 1990.

Smith, Robert Leo. *Ecology and Field Biology*. New York: Harper & Row, 1980.

Smyster, Carol A., and the editors of Rodale Press Books. *Nature's Design: A Practical Guide to Natural Landscaping*. Emmaus, Pa: Rodale Press, 1982.

Spellenberg, Richard. *The Audubon Society Field Guide to North American Wildflowers: Western Region*. New York: Alfred A. Knopf, 1979.

Sperka, Maria. *Growing Wildflowers: A Gardener's Guide*. New York: Charles Scribner's Sons, 1973.

Stern, Kingsley R. *Introductory Plant Biology*. Dubuque, Iowa: William C. Brown Publishers, 1988.

Tufts, Craig. *The Backyard Naturalist*. Washington, D.C.: National Wildlife Federation, 1988.

Venning, Frank D. *Wildflowers of North America*. New York: Western Publishing Co., Golden Press, 1984.

Wilson, William H. W. *Landscaping with Wildflowers and Native Plants*. San Francisco: Ortho Books, 1984.

· ·

Acknowledgments

Quarto would like to thank the following for providing photographs and for permission to reproduce copyright material. While every effort has been made to trace and acknowledge all copyright holders, we would like to apologize should any omissions have been made.

Key: a = above, b = below, l = left, r = right, c = center

page 1 A Peter Margosian (Photo/Nats); 2-3 background Carl Hanninen (Photo/Nats), inset Hal Horwitz (Photo/Nats); 4-5 Ted Levin; 8 background Wildlife Matters, inset Hal Horwitz (Photo/Nats); 9 Herbert B. Parsons (Photo/Nats); 12 a Greg Crisci (Photo/Nats), b Morgan Hebard (Photo/Nats); 13 Rick Imes; 14 John A. Lynch (Photo/Nats); 15 David M. Stone (Photo/Nats); 21 David M. Stone (Photo/Nats); 23 Bruce Matheson (Photo/Nats); 24 John J. Smith (Photo/Nats); 25 Rick Imes; 26 a Jerry Pavia, b Wildlife Matters; 27 a&b Wildlife Matters, c Jerry Pavia; 28 Scott Weidensaul; 29 a Rick Imes, b John F. O'Connor (Photo/Nats); 30 a Paul M. Brown (Photo/Nats), b Hal Horwitz (Photo/Nats); 31 Scott Weidensaul; 37 Wildlife Matters; 40 background Louis Borie (Photo/Nats), inset Don Johnston (Photo/Nats); 41 a David M. Stone (Photo/Nats), b Hal Horwitz (Photo/Nats); 42 Greg Crisci (Photo/Nats); 43 a Hal Horwitz (Photo/Nats), b Ann Reilly (Photo/Nats); 66 Scott Weidensaul; 67 a Jeff March (Photo/Nats), b Sydney Karp (Photo/Nats); 68 Scott Weidensaul; 69 a Scott Weidensaul, b Rick Imes; 82 background Dorothy S. Long (Photo/Nats), inset Rick Imes; 83 Rick Imes; 84 al Rick Imes, ar Hal Horwitz (Photo/Nats), b Priscilla Connell (Photo/Nats); 85 Rick Imes; 118 background Kim Todd (Photo/Nats), inset Ann Reilly (Photo/Nats); 119 a Rick Imes, bl Robert E. Lyons (Photo/Nats), br Priscilla Connell (Photo/Nats); 120 Robert E. Lyons (Photo/Nats); 121 a Scott Weidensaul, b Priscilla Connell (Photo/Nats); 134 background Liz Ball (Photo/Nats), inset Kim Todd (Photo/Nats); 135 a Wildlife Matters, b David M. Stone (Photo/Nats); 136 David M. Stone (Photo/Nats); 137 a Greg Crisci (Photo/Nats), b Wildlife Matters; 100 Ted Levin; 101 Ted Levin; 102 Ted Levin; 103 Ted Levin.

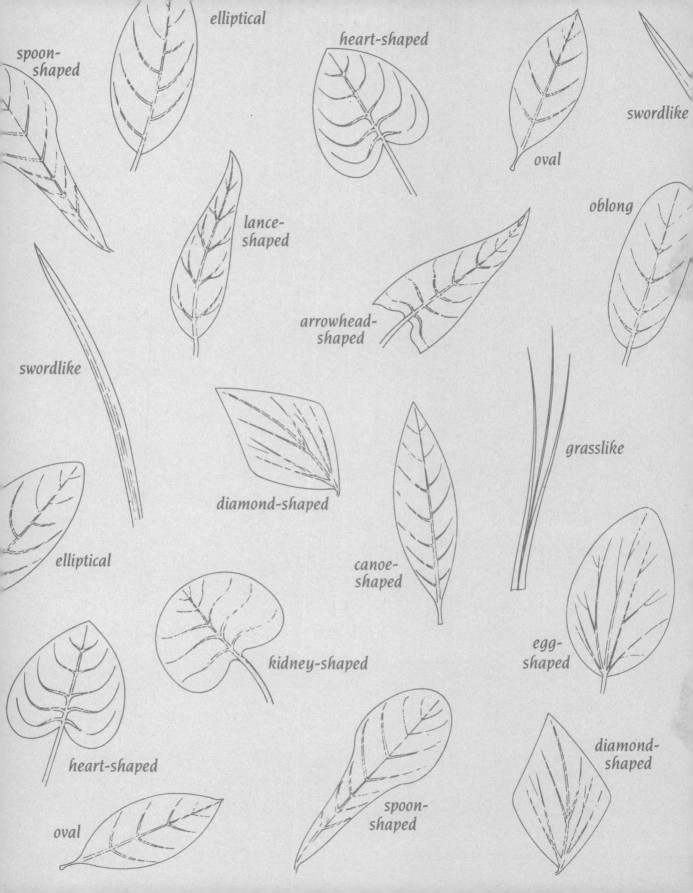